Introducing Java EE 7

A Look at What's New

Josh Juneau

Apress®

Introducing Java EE 7: A Look at What's New

ISBN-13 (pbk): 978-1-4302-5848-3

ISBN-13 (electronic): 978-1-4302-5849-0

Distributed to the book trade worldwide by Springer Science+Business Media New York, 233 Spring Street, 6th Floor, New York, NY 10013. Phone 1-800-SPRINGER, fax (201) 348-4505, e-mail `orders-ny@springer-sbm.com`, or visit `www.springeronline.com`.

For information on translations, please e-mail `rights@apress.com`, or visit `www.apress.com`.

Apress and friends of ED books may be purchased in bulk for academic, corporate, or promotional use. eBook versions and licenses are also available for most titles. For more information, reference our Special Bulk Sales–eBook Licensing web page at `www.apress.com/bulk-sales`.

Any source code or other supplementary materials referenced by the author in this text is available to readers at `www.apress.com`. For detailed information about how to locate your book's source code, go to `www.apress.com/source-code`.

This book is dedicated to my wife, Angela, and my four children, Kaitlyn, Jacob, Matthew, and Zachary. You are my joy and inspiration. It is also dedicated to the many Java developers worldwide. I hope that this book can lead you to develop the sophisticated solutions of tomorrow.

—Josh Juneau

Contents at a Glance

Contents

About the Author

Josh Juneau has been developing software and enterprise since the early days of Java EE (at the time, J2EE). Enterprise application programming and database development has been his focus since the start of his career. He became an Oracle database administrator and adopted the PL/SQL language for performing administrative tasks and developing applications for Oracle database. In an effort to build more complex solutions, he began to incorporate Java into his PL/SQL applications, and later developed stand-alone and web applications with Java. Josh wrote his early Java web applications utilizing JDBC to work with backend databases. Later, he incorporated frameworks into his enterprise solutions, including Java EE and JBoss Seam. Today, he primarily develops enterprise web solutions utilizing Java EE and other enterprise technologies, such as the Python or Jython programming language with Django.

Since 2006, Josh has been the editor and publisher for the *Jython Monthly* newsletter. In late 2008, he began a podcast dedicated to the Jython programming language. Josh was the lead author for *The Definitive Guide to Jython, Oracle PL/SQL Recipes, Java 7 Recipes,* and solo author of *Java EE 7 Recipes*, which were all published by Apress. He works as an application developer and system analyst at Fermi National Accelerator Laboratory, and he is the lead for the *Django-Jython* project (`http://code.google.com/p/django-jython/`). Josh has a wonderful wife and four children who he loves very much. He enjoys spending time with his family fishing, swimming, playing ball, and watching his kids' sporting events. To hear more from Josh, follow his blog, which can be found at `http://jj-blogger.blogspot.com`. You can also follow him on Twitter via `@javajuneau`.

About the Technical Reviewer

David Coffin is the author of *Expert Oracle and Java Security* (Apress, 2011). Find his recent blogs at `http://oraclejavasecure.blogspot.com`. He is an IT analyst working at the Savannah River Site, a large U.S. Department of Energy facility. For more than 30 years, his expertise has been in multiplatform network integration and systems programming. Before coming to the Savannah River Site, he worked for several defense contractors and served as the technical lead for office and network computing at the National Aerospace Plane Joint Program Office at Wright-Patterson Air Force Base in Ohio. As a perpetual student, he has completed one master's degree program and has begun several others. As a family man, he has raised eight children. Coffin is an athlete and distance swimmer who competes in the middle of the pack. He is also a classical guitar player, but he's not quitting his day job.

Acknowledgments

To my wife, Angela: I am still amazed by you and always will be. Thanks for being such a great wife and mother to our children. You've helped me make it through another book, as your inspiration always keeps me moving forward. Thanks for all you do. I love the way that you do so much for our family, including Girl Scouts, Boy Scouts, being a great room Mom, preparing tasty meals, keeping track of our appointments, etc., etc., and so much more . . . you are the best, and I love you dearly.

To my children, Kaitlyn, Jacob, Matthew, and Zachary: I love you all so much and I cherish every moment we have together. I love each of your softball, baseball, and T-Ball games, and I enjoy all of the times that we spend together. Don't grow up too fast, please! I am so proud of each of you.

I want to thank my family for their continued support of my career. I also want to thank my co-workers at Fermilab, including Kent Collins, for allowing me to guide the organization's application development efforts and build successful solutions to keep us moving forward.

To the folks at Apress, I thank you for providing me with the chance to share my knowledge with others. I especially thank Jonathan Gennick for the continued support of my work and for providing the continued guidance to produce useful content for our readers. You've become a good friend over the last couple of years and I really enjoy working with you. I also thank James Markham for his hand in editing this book. I thank Kathleen Sullivan and Kevin Shea for doing a great job coordinating this project. I thank my technical reviewer, David Coffin, who has done an excellent job of solidifying the book content. Thanks again for your hard work and technical expertise. Lastly, I'd like to thank everyone else at Apress who had a hand in this book. I also thank Kevin and James for talking hockey with a Chicago Blackhawks fan, even though they are die-hard Bruins fans!

To the Java community: thanks for helping to make the Java platform such an innovative and effective realm for application development. We all have the privilege of working with a mature and robust platform, and it would not be successful today if it weren't for everyone's continued contributions to the technology. I also thank all the Oracle Java experts; the roadmap for the future is still looking great. I am looking forward to using Java technology for many years to come.

—Josh Juneau

Introduction

The Java platform is one of the most widely used platforms for application development in the world. The platform is so popular that there are several different flavors of Java that can be used for developing applications that run on different mediums. From development for desktop or mobile, to web applications and hardware operating systems, Java can be utilized for development of just about any solution. As such, Java has become a very popular platform for development of enterprise applications, offering web services, reliability, security, and much more.

Java Enterprise Edition was originally released in 1999 as Java 2 Platform, Enterprise Edition (J2EE). Although several enterprise frameworks were available for development of reliable and secure applications on the Java platform, it made sense to standardize some solutions in order to minimize customization and help to make Java Enterprise development more prevalent in the industry. The platform originally included a terse number of specifications for standardization, including Java Servlet, JavaServer Pages, RMI, Java Database Connectivity (JDBC), Java Message Service API (JMS), Java Transaction API (JTA), and Enterprise JavaBeans. Development of J2EE applications had a steep learning curve, and it was cumbersome because it required the use of XML for lots of configurations. Even with these setbacks, it became popular amongst larger organizations and companies due to the prevalence of Java and its well-known security benefits. In 2001, J2EE 1.3 was released, adding more specifications to the platform, including the JavaServer Pages Standard Tag Library (JSTL, and Java Authentication and Authorization Service (JAAS). Other specifications, such as Java Servlet, also gained enhancements under the J2EE 1.3 release, making evolutionary enhancements to the platform. The release of J2EE 1.4 in 2003 marked a major milestone for Java Enterprise, as many new specifications were added to the platform, providing standards for even more Java technologies. The release of J2EE 1.4 marked the first iteration of Web Services for J2EE 1.1, JavaServer Faces (JSF), and Java APIs for XML solutions such as JAXP, JAXR, and more. Although the release of J2EE 1.4 included many specifications, it was still deemed as "difficult to learn" and "cumbersome."

Over the next few years, J2EE was re-worked in an attempt to make it easier to learn and utilize. Although XML is an excellent means for configuration, it can be cumbersome and hard to manage, so configuration was a big item that was being addressed for the next release. Technologies such as Enterprise JavaBeans (EJB) included some redundant characteristics, making EJB coding time consuming and difficult to manage, so an overhaul of EJB was also in order. In May of 2006, Java EE 5 was released, leaving the J2EE acronym behind, changing to simply Java EE instead. The Java EE 5 platform was significantly easier to use and maintain because features such as annotations were introduced, cutting down the amount of XML configuration significantly. EJBs were made easier to develop, making EJB a marketable technology for object-relational mapping once again. Java Enterprise Edition has since become a widely adopted and mature platform for enterprise development. Java EE 6 was released in 2009, making configuration and technologies even easier, and adding more specifications to the platform. Specifications such as Contexts and Dependency Injection and Bean Validation were introduced, making usability even easier and development more productive.

This latest release, Java EE 7, enhances the platform even more by adding new specifications such as WebSockets and JSON-P. Specifications such as JSF and EJB were enhanced, adding even more features to increase productivity and functionality. This book focuses on Java Enterprise as a whole, covering most of the widely used specifications that make up Java EE. You will learn how to make use of each of the major specifications, using examples where applicable. This book will cover APIs that have been updated for Java EE 7, as well as those that have been enhanced, providing complete coverage on the latest features of the platform.

I work with Java Enterprise on a daily basis, and I have a deep passion for the technologies involved in the platform. I hope that this book increases your passion for Java EE and the Java platform in its entirety.

Who This Book Is For

This book is intended for all those who are interested in learning the latest features of Java enterprise edition (Java EE 7). Intermediate and advanced Java developers who are looking to update their arsenal with the latest features that Java EE 7 has to offer may benefit by reading the book from cover to cover, or they may choose to read chapters that discuss the latest about only their favorite APIs.

How This Book Is Structured

This book is structured so that it does not have to be read from cover to cover. In fact, it is structured so that developers can chose which topic(s) they'd like to read about and jump right to them. The book is designed to allow developers to get up and running quickly with the latest features so that they can be home in time for dinner.

Conventions

Throughout the book, I've kept a consistent style for presenting Java code, SQL, command-line text, and results. Where pieces of code, SQL, reserved words, or code fragments are presented in the text, they are presented in fixed-width Courier font, such as this (working) example:

```
public class MyExample {
    public static void main(String[] args){
        System.out.println("Java EE 7 is excellent!");
    }
}
```

Downloading the Code

The code for the examples shown in this book is available on the Apress web site, `www.apress.com`. A link can be found on the book's information page under the Source Code/Downloads tab. This tab is located underneath the Related Titles section of the page.

Note The sources for this book may change over time, to provide new implementations that incorporate the most up-to-date features in Java EE. That said, if any issues are found within the sources, please submit them via the Apress web site "Errata" form, and code will be adjusted accordingly.

Configuring a Database for the Book Sources

This book's sources have been developed using the Apache Derby database, which ships with Netbeans IDE and GlassFish. The book sources have also been optimized for use with an Oracle 11g database. Please install and configure the database for use with the book sources using either of those database choices prior to working with the sources. The database configuration involves creation of a database schema or user, as well as execution of the create_database.sql script (contained within the book sources) that goes along with the database of your choice. You must also place the appropriate database JDBC driver into the Glassfish CLASSPATH. You can do this by copying the ojdbc6.jar (Oracle) or derbyclient.jar (Apache Derby) JAR file into your Integrated Development Environment (IDE) project for the book sources, or into the <GlassFish-Home>\glassfish4\domains\domain1\lib\ext directory. If copying into the Glassfish lib directory, then once the JAR file has been copied into place the GlassFish server will need to be restarted, if it is already running.

Once the database has been installed/configured, and the SQL scripts contained within the book sources have been executed, please log into the Glassfish administrative console and set up a database connection pool to work with the database of your choice.

After a connection pool has been configured, please update the persistence.xml file that is contained within the book sources accordingly, so that the data source name aligns with the one you've assigned to the Glassfish JDBC resource.

Setting Up a NetBeans Project

**Before setting up a NetBeans project for the book sources, please install and configure Glassfish v4 accordingly.

***Before setting up NetBeans project for the book sources, please install and/or configure Apache Derby or Oracle database accordingly.

Please perform the following steps to set up the NetBeans project:

1. Open NetBeans IDE 7.3 or greater.
2. Choose the File ➤ New Project ➤ Java Web ➤ Web Application menu option.
3. Title the project "IntroToJavaEE7", and choose a desired Project Location.
4. Server and Settings:
   - If you have not yet registered your Glassfish v4 server with Netbeans, please click the "Add" button in this dialog, and add the server. To do so, you will need to know the location of the Glassfish server on your file system.
   - Java EE Version: Java EE 7 Web
5. Frameworks:
   - Select JavaServer Faces, and then accept all defaults.
6. Click "Finish"
7. Go to your file system and copy the contents from within the IntroducingJavaEE7Sources\src directory into your new NetBeans project "src" directory.

CHAPTER 1

New Servlet Features

Along with the release of Java EE 7 comes an incremental upgrade to Java servlet technology. The servlet technology has been updated to include features that help bring the technology inline for use with newer technologies, such as HTML 5. The previous release, Servlet 3.0, focused on making servlets easier to write and manage. Such upgrades as optional `web.xml` configuration, asynchronous request processing, and the addition of the FileUpload technology make writing servlets much easier than before. The Servlet 3.1 release brings forth more enhancements to help bring the technology inline with current technologies, including the following:

- Builds upon the new features of Servlet 3.0, introducing the Non-Blocking I/O API
- The ability to work with the WebSockets protocol
- Includes security enhancements
- Offers other, miscellaneous updates

Non-Blocking I/O

Servlet technology has allowed only traditional (blocking) input/output during request processing since its inception. In the Servlet 3.1 release, the new Non-Blocking I/O API makes it possible for servlets to read or write without any blocking. This means that other tasks can be performed at the same time as a read or write is occurring, without any wait. This in turn means that now you can more easily accomplish Ajax and partial-page refreshes without making separate calls to the servlet for each update. Such a solution opens up a new realm of possibilities for servlets, making them much more flexible for use along with modern technologies such as the WebSockets protocol (covered in Chapter 9).

To implement a nonblocking I/O solution, new programming interfaces have been added to `ServletInputStream` and `ServletOutputStream`, as well as two event listeners: `ReadListener` and `WriteListener`. The `ReadListener` and `WriteListener` interfaces make the servlet I/O processing occur in a nonblocking manner via callback methods that are invoked when the container is able to do so without blocking other processes. Use the `ServletInputStream.setReadListener(ServletInputStream, AsyncContext)` method to register a `ReadListener` with a `ServletInputStream`, and use the I/O read `ServletInputStream.setWriteListener(ServletOutputStream, AsyncContext)` method for registering a `WriteListener`. The following lines of code demonstrate how to register a `ReadListener` implementation with a `ServletInputStream`:

```
AsyncContext context = request.startAsync();
ServletInputStream input = request.getInputStream();
input.setReadListener(new ReadListenerImpl(input, context));
```

■ **Note** In Servlet 3.0, `AsyncContext` was introduced to represent an execution context for an asynchronous operation that is initiated on a servlet request. To use the asynchronous context, a servlet should be annotated as `@WebServlet`, and the `asyncSupported` attribute of the annotation must be set to `true`. The `@WebFilter` annotation also contains the `asyncSupported` attribute.

Let's take a look at how to perform a nonblocking read. After a listener has been registered with a `ServletInputStream`, the status of a nonblocking read can be checked by calling the methods `ServletInputStream.isReady` and `ServletInputStream.isFinished`. For instance, a read can begin once the `ServletInputStream.isReady` method returns a `true`, as shown here:

```
while (is.isReady() && (b = input.read()) != -1)) {
    len = is.read(b);
    String data = new String(b, 0, len);
}
```

To create a `ReadListener` or `WriteListener`, three methods must be overridden: `onDataAvailable`, `onAllDataRead`, and `onError`. The `onDataAvailable` method is invoked when data is available to be read or written, `onAllDataRead` is invoked once all the data has been read or written, and `onError` is invoked if an error is encountered. The following code demonstrates one way to implement the `ReadListener` interface. You can view these sources in the `org.javaee7.chapter01.ReadListenerImpl.java` file.

```
package org.javaee7.chapter01;

import java.io.IOException;
import java.util.concurrent.CountDownLatch;
import java.util.logging.Level;
import java.util.logging.Logger;
import javax.servlet.AsyncContext;
import javax.servlet.ReadListener;
import javax.servlet.ServletInputStream;
import javax.servlet.ServletOutputStream;

public class ReadListenerImpl implements ReadListener {

    private ServletInputStream is = null;
    private AsyncContext context = null;

    public ReadListenerImpl(ServletInputStream in, AsyncContext ac) {
        this.is = is;
        this.context = ac;
    }

    @Override
    public void onDataAvailable() {
        try {
            StringBuilder sb = new StringBuilder();
            int len = -1;
            byte b[] = new byte[1024];
```

```
            while (is.isReady()
                    && (len = is.read(b)) != -1) {
                String data = new String(b, 0, len);
                System.out.println(data);
            }
        } catch (IOException ex) {
            Logger.getLogger(ReadListenerImpl.class.getName()).log(Level.SEVERE, null, ex);
        }
    }

    @Override
    public void onAllDataRead() {
        context.complete();

    }

    @Override
    public void onError(Throwable thrwbl) {
        System.out.println("Error: " + thrwbl);
        // perform cleanup here
        context.complete();
    }

}
```

The AsyncContext.complete method is called in the onAllDataRead method to indicate that the read has been completed and to commit the response. This method is also called in the onError implementation so that the read will complete, so it is important to perform any cleanup within the body of the onError method to ensure that no resources are leaked.

Similarly, a WriteListener implementation can use the new ServletOutputStream.canWrite method, which determines whether data can be written in a nonblocking manner. A WriteListener implementation class must override a couple of methods: onWritePossible and onError. The onWritePossible method is invoked when a nonblocking write can occur. The write implementation should take place within the body of this method. The onError method is much the same as its ReadListener implementation counterpart, because it is invoked when an error occurs.

The following lines of code demonstrate how to register a WriteListener with a ServletOutputStream:

```
AsyncContext context = request.startAsync();
ServletOutputStream os = response.getOutputStream();
os.setWriteListener(new WriteListenerImpl(os, context));
```

As mentioned previously, the WriteListener implementation class must include overriding methods for onWritePossible and onError, as shown in the next example. The following sources are that of the org.javaee7.chapter01.WriteListenerImpl class.

```
import javax.servlet.AsyncContext;
import javax.servlet.ServletOutputStream;
import javax.servlet.WriteListener;
```

```
public class WriteListenerImpl implements WriteListener {

    ServletOutputStream os;
    AsyncContext context;

    public WriteListenerImpl(ServletOutputStream out, AsyncContext ctx){
        this.os = out;
        this.context = ctx;
        System.out.println("Write Listener Initialized");
    }

    @Override
    public void onWritePossible() {
        System.out.println("Now possible to write...");
        // Write implementation goes here...
    }

    @Override
    public void onError(Throwable thrwbl) {
        System.out.println("Error occurred");
        context.complete();
    }

}
```

■ **Note** In most cases, the `ReadListener` and `WriteListener` implementation classes can be embedded within the calling servlet. They have been broken out into separate classes for the examples in this book for demonstration purposes.

The new Non-Blocking I/O API helps bring the Servlet API into compliance with new web standards. The new API makes it possible to create web-based applications that perform in an asynchronous fashion, making it possible to handle a larger number of requests.

Upgrade Protocol

An HTTP response protocol can now be upgraded from HTTP 1.1 to some other protocol via a new protocol upgrade API. Typically this is used for upgrading to WebSocket for more advanced communication. All protocol processing takes place in a servlet named `HttpUpgradeHandler`, and although the servlet container is responsible for performing the upgrade, the servlet code needs to invoke the process. An `HttpServletResponse` can be upgraded by invoking its upgrade method, and when this occurs, the appropriate `HttpUpgradeHandler` for the requested protocol is instantiated. Upon instantiation, the `HttpUpgradeHandler.init` method is invoked, which passes a `WebConnection` to allow the protocol handler to access the data streams. If servlet filters are used before and during the upgrade process, they will continue to process normally, and after the upgrade has been completed, then all servlet filters will stop performing operations. Finally, the `HttpUpgradeHandler.destroy` method is invoked once the upgrade processing is complete.

In the following code, a decision is made to upgrade the protocol, and the upgrade method is invoked:

```
protected void processRequest(HttpServletRequest request, HttpServletResponse response)
            throws ServletException, IOException {
        boolean decideToUpgrade = true;  // Hard coded to force the upgrade...
        if (decideToUpgrade){
            request.upgrade(EchoProtocolHandler.class);

        }
        // perform processing as normal
        ...
}
```

The HttpUpgradeHandler class in the previous example is named EchoProtocolHandler. An example implementation of this class would look similar to the following:

```
public class EchoProtocolHandler implements HttpUpgradeHandler {

    @Override
    public void init(WebConnection wc) {
        try {
              ServletInputStream input = wc.getInputStream();
              ServletOutputStream output = wc.getOutputStream();
              ReadListener readListener = new ReadListenerImpl(input,output);
              input.setReadListener(readListener);
      } catch (Exception e){
            System.out.println("Exception has occurred " + e);
      }

    }

    @Override
    public void destroy() {
        throw new UnsupportedOperationException("Not supported yet.");
    }

}
```

As you can see, the HttpUpgradeHandler accepts a WebConnection in the init method, and the HttpUpgradeHandler.init passes that WebConnection automatically upon invocation. While most of the work takes place behind the scenes, it is important to note that the upgrade process must be invoked within the code itself.

Such a solution makes sense when working with APIs such as the new WebSocket. In cases where a half-duplex protocol is in use (see Chapter 9 for details), it would need to be upgraded to a full-duplex protocol for working with a WebSocket.

■ **Note** HttpUpgradeHandler can use nonblocking I/O to complete upgrade requests.

Enhanced FileUpload

The Servlet 3.0 API included a new FileUpload mechanism that allows a servlet to be specified as a file upload handler, making it unnecessary for third-party libraries to enable file uploading. As a brief review, any servlet that is marked with the `@MultipartConfig` annotation can handle file upload requests. The processing for saving the file to disk then occurs within the file upload servlet. The `@MulipartConfig` annotation can accept the following attributes, which can be used to specify details for the file upload:

- `location`: Absolute path to the directory on the file system
- `fileSizeThreshold`: File size in bytes after which the file will be temporarily stored on disk
- `maxFileSize`: Maximum file size accepted, in bytes
- `maxRequestSize`: Maximum size allowed for the multipart/form-data request, in bytes

For example, suppose that an HTML page contained a file input and the request was sent to a servlet named `FileUploadHandler`. The code for the `FileUploadHandler` servlet may look like the following:

```
@MultipartConfig
@WebServlet(name = "FileUploadHandler", urlPatterns = {"/uploadFile"})
public class FileUploadHandler extends HttpServlet {

    private final static Logger LOGGER =
            Logger.getLogger(FileUploadHandler.class.getCanonicalName());

   /**
     * Handles the HTTP
     * <code>GET</code> method.
     *
     * @param request servlet request
     * @param response servlet response
     * @throws ServletException if a servlet-specific error occurs
     * @throws IOException if an I/O error occurs
     */
    @Override
    protected void doGet(HttpServletRequest request, HttpServletResponse response)
            throws ServletException, IOException {
        processRequest(request, response);
    }

    /**
     * Handles the HTTP
     * <code>POST</code> method.
     *
     * @param request servlet request
     * @param response servlet response
     * @throws ServletException if a servlet-specific error occurs
     * @throws IOException if an I/O error occurs
     */
```

```
@Override
protected void doPost(HttpServletRequest request, HttpServletResponse response)
        throws ServletException, IOException {
    processRequest(request, response);
}

/**
 * Processes requests for both HTTP
 * <code>GET</code> and
 * <code>POST</code> methods.
 *
 * @param request servlet request
 * @param response servlet response
 * @throws ServletException if a servlet-specific error occurs
 * @throws IOException if an I/O error occurs
 */
protected void processRequest(HttpServletRequest request,
                                       HttpServletResponse response)
        throws ServletException, IOException {
    response.setContentType("text/html;charset=UTF-8");

    final String filepath = request.getParameter("destination");
    final Part filePart = request.getPart("myfile");
    final String fileName = getFileName(filePart);

    final PrintWriter writer = response.getWriter();

    try(
        OutputStream out = new FileOutputStream(new File(filepath + File.separator + fileName));
        InputStream filecontent = filePart.getInputStream()){

        int read = 0;
        final byte[] bytes = new byte[1024];

        while ((read = filecontent.read(bytes)) != -1) {
            out.write(bytes, 0, read);
        }
        writer.println("New file " + fileName + " created at " + filepath);
        LOGGER.log(Level.INFO, "File{0}being uploaded to {1}",
                new Object[]{fileName, filepath});

        out.flush();

    } catch (FileNotFoundException fne) {
        writer.println("You either did not specify a file to upload or are " +
               "trying to upload a file to a protected or nonexistent location.");
        writer.println("<br/> ERROR: " + fne.getMessage());
```

```
            LOGGER.log(Level.SEVERE, "Problems during file upload. Error: {0}",
                    new Object[]{fne.getMessage()});
        } finally {

            if (writer != null) {
                writer.close();
            }
        }
    }

    private String getFileName(final Part part) {
        final String partHeader = part.getHeader("content-disposition");
        LOGGER.log(Level.INFO, "Part Header = {0}", partHeader);
        for (String content : part.getHeader("content-disposition").split(";")) {
            if (content.trim().startsWith("filename")) {
                return content.substring(
                        content.indexOf('=') + 1).trim().replace("\"", "");
            }
        }
        return null;
    }

}
```

In the Servlet 3.1 release, the specification has been updated to include support for containers that do not provide `multipart/form-data` processing. If the container does not provide the processing, then the data will be available via `HttpServletRequest.getInputStream`. However, if the container does provide support, then the data will be made available through the following methods in `HttpServletRequest`, as shown in the previous example:

- `public Collection<Part> getParts();`
- `public Part getPart(String name);`

The following example code demonstrates how a servlet without `multipart/form-data` processing may be coded:

```
...
protected void processRequestNoMultipart(HttpServletRequest request,
                                          HttpServletResponse response)
            throws ServletException, IOException {
        response.setContentType("text/html;charset=UTF-8");

        final String filepath = request.getParameter("destination");
        final String path = request.getServletPath();
        final String fileName = getFileName(path, request);
        final PrintWriter writer = response.getWriter();

        try(

            InputStream filecontent = request.getInputStream();
            OutputStream out = new FileOutputStream(new File(filepath + File.separator +
request.getLocalName()))){
            int read = 0;
```

```
        final byte[] bytes = new byte[1024];

        while ((read = filecontent.read(bytes)) != -1) {
            out.write(bytes, 0, read);
        }
        writer.println("New file " + fileName + " created at " + filepath);
        LOGGER.log(Level.INFO, "File{0}being uploaded to {1}",
                new Object[]{fileName, filepath});
        out.flush();

    } catch (FileNotFoundException fne) {
        writer.println("You either did not specify a file to upload or are " +
                "trying to upload a file to a protected or nonexistent location.");
        writer.println("<br/> ERROR: " + fne.getMessage());

        LOGGER.log(Level.SEVERE, "Problems during file upload. Error: {0}",
                new Object[]{fne.getMessage()});
    } finally {

        if (writer != null) {
            writer.close();
        }
    }
}

private String getFileName(final String path, HttpServletRequest req){
    String name;
    if (path.length() > 0 && path.charAt(0) == '/'){
        name = path.substring(1);
    } else {
        name = path;
    }

    name.replace('/', File.pathSeparatorChar);
    return req.getServletContext().getRealPath(name);
}
...
```

Filter Life Cycle

Some minor changes have been made in the filter life cycle of a servlet in release 3.1. In an effort to better understand the changes, let's review the life cycle of a filter. After a web application is deployed but before the application can begin serving requests, the container must locate the list of filters that are to be applied to the web resource. The list of filters can be defined in the `web.xml` file or via annotations that have been applied to servlet classes. Only one instance per `<filter>` declaration is instantiated per JVM of the container. When the container receives an incoming request, it applies the first filter instance in the list of filters that need to be applied and calls its corresponding `doFilter` method.

For example, let's say that the `web.xml` file contains two filter specifications for the given servlet path: `FilterA` and `FilterB`. When a servlet in the path is requested, both of these filters must be applied to the request. Therefore, the first filter's `doFilter` method is invoked, and the filter is processed accordingly. Once complete, the next filter's `doFilter` method is invoked, and so on. It is possible that a filter's `doFilter` method will invoke the next entity in the filter chain. In this case, a small change has been made to the life cycle. As of release 3.1, the service method is required to run in the same thread as all filters that apply to the servlet. The following web.xml excerpt provides a visual overview of this update:

```
<!–Filters to be applied ->

<filter>
   <filter-name>FilterA</filter-name>
   <filter-class>FilterA</filter-class>
</filter>
<filter>
   <filter-name>FilterB</filter-name>
   <filter-class>FilterB</filter-class>
</filter>
<filter-mapping>
    <filter-name>FilterA</filter-name>
    <servlet-name>ServletOne</servlet-name>
</filter-mapping>
```

In this example, when ServletOne is processed, FilterA must be applied because it is the first filter in the chain. If FilterA contains a doFilter method that invokes FilterB, then the service method of FilterA must be executed in the same thread as the service method of FilterB. This enhancement is handled by the container, but it is important to understand for concurrency purposes.

Security Enhancements

The new Servlet 3.1 API includes security enhancements that improve the reliability and integrity of servlet-based applications by applying the following:

- Run-as security roles to init and destroy methods
- Session fixation attack defense
- Default security semantics for nonspecified HTTP methods

This section will provide a quick overview of these new security enhancements, along with some example code to help you begin implementing them.

Specifying an Identity for Executing init and destroy Methods

Security roles that are defined for a particular application can be mapped to a servlet by annotating the servlet class with @RunAs. Any calls that a servlet makes to an EJB must provide a security identity, or principal, and the @RunAs is a means to do just that. In Servlet 3.1, if a security role is bound via run-as to a servlet, then calls made from that servlet to an EJB will be executed under the permission set of the role bound by the @RunAs. As such, even if a call is made from a servlet's init or destroy method, it will be initiated under the specified permission set.

For example, suppose you want to initiate a call to an EJB from a servlet under an administrative role named "Admin." To do so, simply annotate the servlet accordingly and make the calls, as needed. In the following example, a servlet named AcmeServlet is configured for access by any user who is part of the "user" role.

```
@RunAs("user")
@WebServlet(name = "AcmeServlet", urlPatterns = {"/AcmeServlet"})
public class AcmeServlet extends HttpServlet {
```

```
    @EJB
    EmployeeSession employeeSession;

    /**
     * Processes requests for both HTTP
     * <code>GET</code> and
     * <code>POST</code> methods.
     *
     * @param request servlet request
     * @param response servlet response
     * @throws ServletException if a servlet-specific error occurs
     * @throws IOException if an I/O error occurs
     */
    protected void processRequest(HttpServletRequest request, HttpServletResponse response)
            throws ServletException, IOException {
        response.setContentType("text/html;charset=UTF-8");
        PrintWriter out = response.getWriter();
        List<Employee> empList = employeeSession.obtainActiveEmployeeCount();
        try {
            /* TODO output your page here. You may use following sample code. */
            out.println("<!DOCTYPE html>");
            out.println("<html>");
            out.println("<head>");
            out.println("<title>Servlet AcmeServlet</title>");
            out.println("</head>");
            out.println("<body>");
            out.println("<h1>Servlet AcmeServlet at " + request.getContextPath() + " is running as
Admin user</h1>");
            out.println("<h2>Employee List</h2>");
            for(Employee emp: empList){
                out.println(emp.getFirst() + " " + emp.getLast());
            }
            out.println("</body>");
            out.println("</html>");
        } finally {
            out.close();
        }
    }

    // <editor-fold defaultstate="collapsed" desc="HttpServlet methods. Click on the + sign on the
left to edit the code.">
    /**
     * Handles the HTTP
     * <code>GET</code> method.
     *
     * @param request servlet request
     * @param response servlet response
     * @throws ServletException if a servlet-specific error occurs
     * @throws IOException if an I/O error occurs
     */
```

```
    @Override
    protected void doGet(HttpServletRequest request, HttpServletResponse response)
            throws ServletException, IOException {
        processRequest(request, response);
    }

    /**
     * Handles the HTTP
     * <code>POST</code> method.
     *
     * @param request servlet request
     * @param response servlet response
     * @throws ServletException if a servlet-specific error occurs
     * @throws IOException if an I/O error occurs
     */
    @Override
    protected void doPost(HttpServletRequest request, HttpServletResponse response)
            throws ServletException, IOException {
        processRequest(request, response);
    }

    /**
     * Returns a short description of the servlet.
     *
     * @return a String containing servlet description
     */
    @Override
    public String getServletInfo() {
        return "Short description";
    }// </editor-fold>
}
```

When a user visits this servlet, the servlet will be executed under the specified role. For more information regarding the configuration of principals and roles in Glassfish, please refer to the online documentation.

Thwarting Session Fixation Attack

It is possible for a web hacker to obtain security IDs used by web sites for authentication purposes. When a malicious hacker gets ahold of such an identifier, havoc could be wreaked upon a victim's account because a security ID could possibly grant a hacker full permissions to the hacked account. Such attacks are known as *session fixation attacks*.

In Servlet 3.1, session fixation attacks can be thwarted by changing the session ID once a user has successfully authenticated to the application. The session ID can be changed by calling the new `HttpServletRequest.changeSessionId` method after the session has already been created. The new `HttpSessionIdListener` interface can be used to implement listener classes that are responsible for changing a session identifier.

The Servlet 3.1 code base has been updated to use the new `HttpSessionIdListener` as a standard listener. As such, the following APIs now accept listener classes that implement the `HttpSessionIdListener` interface:

- `addListener(String className)`
- `<T extends EventListener> void addListener(T t)`
- `void addListener(Class <? extends EventListener> listenerClass)`

- `<T extends EventListener> void createListener(Class<T> clazz)`
- `@WebListener`

The following excerpt from the servlet `org.javaee.7.chapter01.SessionIdTest` demonstrates how to change a session identifier using this new technique.

```
...
protected void processRequest(HttpServletRequest request, HttpServletResponse response)
            throws ServletException, IOException {
        response.setContentType("text/html;charset=UTF-8");
        PrintWriter out = response.getWriter();
        HttpSession session = request.getSession();

        try {
            /* TODO output your page here. You may use following sample code. */
            out.println("<!DOCTYPE html>");
            out.println("<html>");
            out.println("<head>");
            out.println("<title>Servlet SessionIdTest</title>");
            out.println("</head>");
            out.println("<body>");
            out.println("<h1>Servlet SessionIdTest at " + request.getContextPath() + "</h1>");
            out.println("<p>the current sesion id is: " + session.getId());

            request.changeSessionId();
            out.println("<p>the current session id has been changed, now it is: " +
                        session.getId());
            out.println("</body>");
            out.println("</html>");
        } finally {
            out.close();
        }
    }...
```

Denying Uncovered HTTP Methods

To specify permissions for a given servlet, one must configure security constraints in the `web.xml` to specify role `auth-constraint` for a given `web-resource-collection`. That said, in Servlet 3.0 and prior, any servlet that was not explicitly configured with a security constraint within the `web.xml` was made available for everyone. The new element `<deny-uncovered-http-methods/>` can be added to a `web.xml` in order to deny access to any of the http methods that have not been specifically addressed within the security constraint.

For example, given the following security constraint configuration, members of the users role will be allowed `GET` and `POST` access to all servlets within the url pattern. Without specifying `<deny-uncovered-http-methods/>`, all other http methods, such as `POST`, would be open to everyone. However, by specifying the new `<deny-uncovered-http-methods>` element, all other methods are not available to anyone. For instance, the following could be listed within the `web.xml` for a Servlet 3.0 application in order to secure only the `GET` method.

```
<security-constraint>
        <web-resource-collection>
            <web-resource-name>secured</web-resource-name>
            <url-pattern>/*</url-pattern>
            <http-method>GET</http-method>
        </web-resource-collection>

        <auth-constraint>
            <role-name>users</role-name>
        </auth-constraint>

</security-constraint>
```

In contrast, the following could be specified in a Servlet 3.1 application in order to deny any http method that is uncovered without explicitly listing them within the `web.xml`.

```
<deny-uncovered-http-methods/>
```

Changing the Content Length

Sometimes it is useful to manually set the content length of a servlet header by invoking the `ServletRequest setContentLength` method. Usually this is done to help facilitate the creation of certain types of documents, among other reasons. The Servlet API has always allowed you to get or set the content length in `byte` format using the Java `int` type. With the inception of Servlet 3.1, it is also possible to utilize the `long` data type for working with the content length. This can aid in the scenario where a content length greater than 2GB needs to be specified. In previous releases, setting a long value that was equal to 2GB would cause a negative header to be sent. The following methods have been added to the Servlet API for utilizing the `long` data type:

- `ServletRequest.getContentLengthLong`
- `ServletResponse.setContentLengthLong`

Summary

The Servlet 3.1 specification includes many nice enhancements. The non-blocking I/O support makes Servlets more feasible for producing modern web applications that utilize asynchronous operations. The ability to easily upgrade protocol allows Servlet processing to change and allows for full-duplex protocol usage, when needed. The other updates that have been outlined in this chapter also help to enhance the Servlet API, making it less cumbersome to develop robust solutions.

It should be noted that many smaller enhancements to the API have been made that were not addressed in the chapter. For a complete list of changes, please see the Servlet 3.1 documentation, which can be found at the JSR 340 Specification website: (`http://jcp.org/en/jsr/detail?id=340`).

CHAPTER 2

JavaServer Faces and Facelets

The release of Java EE 7 embodies incremental updates for the JavaServer Faces (JSF) API, making it easier to use and more compliant with modern technology. The JSF web framework originated in the early 2000s, and the web landscape has changed much since its inception. The incremental releases of JSF 1.*x* added more features to help build out the framework, but JSF 1.*x* was still very much a work in progress that, although it worked fine by itself, was even better when paired with other third-party frameworks, such as JBoss Seam. When Java EE 6 was released, the JSF 2.0 framework became more self-sufficient and required no third-party frameworks to be fully functional. When utilized along with the new EJB infrastructure that was part of Java EE 6, JSF 2.0 worked seamlessly but still had a few rough edges. The JSF 2.1 release repaired bugs and helped smooth some of the rough edges that remained.

The JSF 2.2 release brings with it even more incremental updates that aim to complete the framework even further, bringing it into alignment with the next generation of web applications using HTML5. This chapter covers many of the new features that will be important to a wide range of developers. The updated release brings forth better integration with HTML5, less XML configuration, better page flow, and more security.

View Actions

In JSF 2.1 and prior, it was difficult to invoke action methods within a managed bean unless they were bound to a command component. Sometimes it makes sense to invoke a method when the page is loading, after the page has been fully loaded, and so on. In the past, this was done by using a `preRenderView` event listener, which causes the method bound within a managed bean to be invoked before the view is rendered. Utilization of the `preRenderView` event listener works, but it does not provide the level of control that is required to invoke a method during different phases of the view life cycle. The `preRenderView` event listener also requires developers to programmatically check the request type and work with the navigation handler.

In the JSF 2.2 release, you can use a new technique to invoke action methods within a managed bean during specified life-cycle events that occur within the view. A new tag, `f:viewAction`, can be bound to a view, and it can be incorporated into the JSF life cycle in both non-JSF (initial) and JSF (postback) requests. To use the tag, it must be a child of the metadata facet. View parameters can be specified within the metadata facet as well, and they will be available from within the managed bean when the action method is invoked.

The following simple JSF view demonstrates the use of the `viewAction`, because it will cause the `viewActionManagedBean.viewActionExample()` method to be invoked before the view is built:

```
<html xmlns="http://www.w3.org/1999/xhtml"
      xmlns:h="http://xmlns.jcp.org/jsf/html"
      xmlns:f="http://xmlns.jcp.org/jsf/core"
      xmlns:ui="http://xmlns.jcp.org/jsf/facelets">
    <h:head>
        <title>Chapter 2 - ViewAction Example</title>
    </h:head>
```

```
    <h:body>
        <ui:composition template="../layout/custom_template.xhtml">
            <ui:define name="content">
        <f:metadata>
            <f:viewAction action="#{viewActionManagedBean.viewActionExample()}"/>
        </f:metadata>
        Please look in the server log to see the message that is being
        printed via the viewActionManagedBean.viewActionExample() method.
            </ui:define>
        </ui:composition>
    </h:body>
</html>
```

In the ViewActionManagedBean controller, the action method named viewActionExample is invoked using the viewAction. In the following example method, a String is returned, which enables implicit navigation from the action method. If null is returned, the navigation handler is invoked, but the same view will be rendered again so long as there are no navigation condition expressions that change the navigation. If a String-based view name is returned, then the navigation handler will render that view once the method has completed. This can come in handy for situations such as authentication handling, where an action method is used to check the user's role, and then the appropriate view is rendered based upon the authenticated user role.

```
public String viewActionExample(){
    System.out.println("This is being written to the server log when the "
            + "view is accessed...");
    return null;
}
```

As mentioned previously, the viewAction facet can be customized to allow the action method to be invoked at different stages within the view life cycle. By default, the viewAction will be initiated before postback because they are expected to execute whether the request was Faces or non-Faces. However, this can be changed by setting the onPostback attribute of the viewAction tag to true.

```
<f:viewAction action="#{viewActionManagedBean.viewActionExample()}" onPostback="true"/>
```

If you need to get even more granular and invoke a view action during a specified life-cycle phase, it is possible by setting the phase attribute to the phase required. Table 2-1 specifies the different phases along with their phase value.

Table 2-1. *JSF Life-Cycle Phases*

Phase	Tag Value
Restore View	RESTORE_VIEW
Apply Request Values	APPLY_REQUEST_VALUES
Process Validations	PROCESS_VALIDATIONS
Update Model Values	UPDATE_MODEL_VALUES
Invoke Application	INVOKE_APPLICATION
Render Response	RENDER_RESPONSE

The following example demonstrates the viewAction facet that will cause the action to be invoked during the Process Validations phase:

```
<f:viewAction action="#{viewActionManagedBean.viewActionExample()}"
                phase="PROCESS_VALIDATIONS"/>
```

Faces Flow

The concept of session management has been a difficult feat to tackle since the beginning of web applications. A *web flow* refers to a grouping of web views that are interrelated and must have the ability to share information with each view within the flow. Many web frameworks have attempted to tackle this issue by creating different solutions that would facilitate the sharing of data across multiple views. Oftentimes, a mixture of session variables, request parameters, and cookies are used as a patchwork solution.

In JSF 2.2, a solution has been adopted for binding multiple JSF views to each other, allowing them to share information among each other. This solution is called *faces flow*, and it allows a group of interrelated views to belong to a "flow instance," and information can be shared across all of the views belonging to that flow instance. Flows contain separate navigation that pertains to the flow itself, and not the entire application. As such, flows contain their own configuration, and custom navigation can be defined in an XML format or via code using a builder pattern.

In this section, you will take a brief tour of faces flow technology and learn how to get started using it right away. However, this section will hardly scratch the surface because entire chapters could be written on the topic, and you are encouraged to learn about all features of faces flow so that you can decide what works best for your applications.

Defining a Flow

Before a flow can be defined within an application, some configuration must be made. You can designate a flow by creating a folder structure to encapsulate all nodes belonging to a flow. By convention, a directory that has the same name as a flow can be used to contain all nodes belonging to that flow. Moreover, the start node for a flow can optionally be designated as such by naming it the same as the flow (and the enclosing folder). For instance, if your flow were named exampleFlow, then each of the views that belonged to the flow should be placed inside a folder named exampleFlow, which resides at the root of the application web directory. Figure 2-1 shows how a flow directory structure might look.

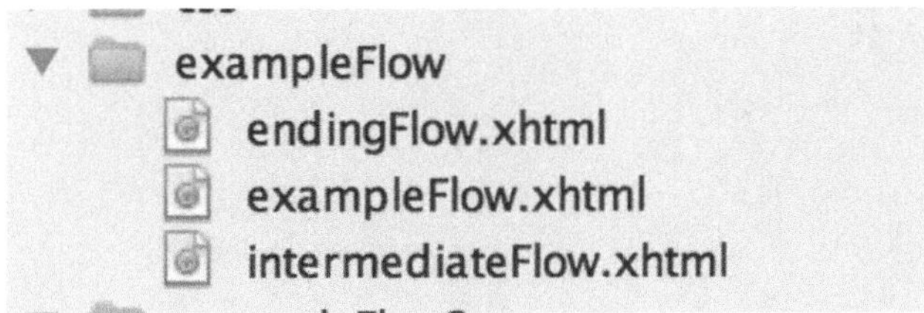

Figure 2-1. *Faces flow directory structure*

If you need to add custom navigation to your flows, you must decide upon the means by which your flow configurations will be defined. As mentioned previously, flows can contain their own navigation rules. As such, each flow can specify a set of navigational rules in some format, be it XML or code. If using XML, the flow configuration can be placed within the faces-config.xml file, or it can be placed within an XML file that has the same name as the flow, along with a flow.xml suffix, also referred to as a flow definition. Placing flow rules in their own separate files can be handy if your application has more than one flow, because it tends to make maintenance a bit easier. It can also be handy if you plan to package your flow for inclusion in another application, as described later in this chapter.

However, if you have only a small number of flows in an application, it may be simpler to include the flow navigation rules in the `faces-config.xml` file. If flow definition XML files are utilized, they must be placed within either a directory at the web root of the application that is named after the flow (`/<flow-name>/<flow-name>-flow.xml`), or a directory named after the flow that resides at the root of the `WEB-INF` directory (`/WEB-INF/<flow-name>/<flow-name>-flow.xml`). If you prefer to not use XML, then building out flow navigational rules in Java code is possible using the Flow API, which utilizes a builder pattern.

Each flow should include two or more views, which we will refer to as *nodes*. As such, each flow has a beginning node, an ending node, and optional intermediate nodes, which are also known as *view nodes*. Importantly, a flow also contains its own CDI managed bean, which is used to define methods and variables for use by each view node in the flow. The managed bean must be annotated with `@FlowScoped` to signify that it exists within the flow scope, and the annotation should specify an `id` attribute that contains the name of the flow to which the managed bean belongs. The following Java class, named `FlowBean`, demonstrates how to define a managed bean for use with a flow named `exampleFlow`:

```
import javax.faces.flow.FlowScoped;
import javax.inject.Named;

@Named
@FlowScoped(id="exampleFlow")
public class FlowBean implements java.io.Serializable {

    private String beanValue = "From the flowBean";

    /**
     * Creates a new instance of FlowBean
     */
    public FlowBean() {
    }

    public void initializeIt(){
        System.out.println("Initialize the flow...");
    }

    public void finalizeIt(){
        System.out.println("Finalize the flow...");
    }

    public String navMethod(){
        return "nextViewNode";
    }

    /**
     * @return the beanValue
     */
    public String getBeanValue() {
        return beanValue;
    }
```

```
    /**
     * @param beanValue the beanValue to set
     */
    public void setBeanValue(String beanValue) {
        this.beanValue = beanValue;
    }
}
```

A standard JSF command component can be used to enter a flow, specifying the flow name for the action. For instance, if you want to use a link to enter into a flow named `exampleFlow`, you can do something like the following:

```
<h:commandLink value="Enter flow" action="exampleFlow" />
```

Specifying the flow name for the action works because the flow has the same name as the folder containing the flow view nodes, so the action simply causes navigation to that folder. As mentioned previously, by convention, the first view node within the flow should have the same name as the enclosing folder. Using this convention causes the first view node within the flow to be accessed when specifying the flow name as the action for a command component. The code below shows what the `exampleFlow.xhtml` view contains.

```
<?xml version="1.0" encoding="UTF-8"?>
<!DOCTYPE html PUBLIC "-//W3C//DTD XHTML 1.0 Strict//EN"
"http://www.w3.org/TR/xhtml1/DTD/xhtml1-strict.dtd">
<html xmlns="http://www.w3.org/1999/xhtml"
      xmlns:f="http://xmlns.jcp.org/jsf/core"
      xmlns:h="http://xmlns.jcp.org/jsf/html"
      xmlns:ui="http://xmlns.jcp.org/jsf/facelets">
    <h:head>
        <meta http-equiv="Content-Type" content="text/html; charset=UTF-8"/>
        <title>Faces Flow Example #1, Page 1</title>

    </h:head>
    <h:body>
         <ui:composition template="../layout/custom_template.xhtml">
            <ui:define name="content">

            <h:form prependId="false">
        <p>
            This is the first view of the flow.
            <br/>
            Is this page contained within the flow? #{null
                                                  != facescontext.application.flowHandler.currentFlow}
            <br/>
            Message: #{flowBean.beanValue}
            <br/><br/>
            <h:commandLink value="Go to another view in the flow" action=”intermediateFlow"/>
        </p>
            </h:form>
```

```
            </ui:define>
        </ui:composition>
    </h:body>
</html>
```

Navigation to other nodes within a flow can occur normally, by simply placing the name of the node that you want to navigate to next within the `action` attribute of a command component. Optionally, navigation can be definition within the flow configuration, via either code or XML. We will discuss navigation more in the following sections. The next lines of code show you what `intermediateFlow.xhtml` looks like.

```
<?xml version="1.0" encoding="UTF-8"?>
<!DOCTYPE html PUBLIC "-//W3C//DTD XHTML 1.0 Strict//EN"
"http://www.w3.org/TR/xhtml1/DTD/xhtml1-strict.dtd">
<html xmlns="http://www.w3.org/1999/xhtml"
      xmlns:f="http://xmlns.jcp.org/jsf/core"
      xmlns:h="http://xmlns.jcp.org/jsf/html"
      xmlns:ui="http://xmlns.jcp.org/jsf/facelets">
    <h:head>
        <meta http-equiv="Content-Type" content="text/html; charset=UTF-8"/>
        <title>Faces Flow Example #1 - Second Page in Flow</title>

    </h:head>
    <h:body>
        <ui:composition template="../layout/custom_template.xhtml">
            <ui:define name="content">
                <h:form prependId="false">
                    <p>
                        This is the intermediate view of the flow.
                        <br/>
                        <h:commandLink value="Go to another final view in flow" action="endingFlow"/>
                        <br/>
                        <h:commandLink value="Go to first view in the flow" action="exampleFlow"/>
                        <br/>
                        <h:commandLink value="Exit Flow" action="/index"/>
                    </p>
                </h:form>
            </ui:define>
        </ui:composition>
    </h:body>
</html>
```

To determine when a flow will exit, either navigate to a view that resides outside of the flow using standard JSF navigation or specify an element entitled `<faces-flow-return>` in the flow definition. This `<faces-flow-return>` element can contain a `<navigation-case>` that will lead to the exit of the flow. For example, the following demonstrates a single exit navigational case for a flow:

```
<faces-flow-return id="intermediateFlow">
                <navigation-case>
                    <from-outcome>nextViewNode</from-outcome>
                </navigation-case>
</faces-flow-return>
```

You will learn more about the flow definition in the section below entitled "Navigating View Nodes". The code that was previously listed for intermediateFlow.xhtml demonstrates how a link could be utilized to exit a flow.

The Flow Managed Bean

A flow contains its own managed bean annotated as @FlowScoped, which differs from @SessionScoped because the data can be accessed only by other view nodes belonging to the flow. The @FlowScoped annotation relies upon contexts and dependency injection (CDI), because FlowScope is a CDI scope that causes the runtime to consider classes with the @FlowScoped annotation to be in the scope of the specified flow. A @FlowScoped bean maintains a life cycle that begins and ends with a flow instance. Multiple flow instances can exist for a single application, and if a user begins a flow within one browser tab and then opens another, a new flow instance will begin in the new tab. This solution resolves many lingering issues around sessions and modern browsers, allowing users to open multiple tabs without causing session-based issues. To maintain separate flow instances, the ClientId is used by JSF to differentiate among multiple instances.

Each flow can contain an initializer and a finalizer, that is, a method that will be invoked when a flow is entered, and a method that will be invoked when a flow is exited, respectively. To declare an initializer, specify a child element named <initializer> within the flow definition <faces-flow-definition>. The initializer element can be an EL expression that declares the managed bean initializer method, as such:

```
...
<initializer>#{flowBean.initializeIt}></initializer>
...
```

Similarly, a <finalizer> element can be specified within the flow definition to define the method that will be called when the flow is exited. The following demonstrates how to set the finalizer to an EL expression declaring the managed bean finalizer method:

```
...
<finalizer>#{flowBean.finalizeIt}></finalizer>
...
```

Flows can contain method calls and variable values that are accessible only via the flow nodes. These methods and variables should be placed within the FlowScoped bean and used the same as standard managed bean methods and variables. The main difference is that any variable that is instantiated within a FlowScoped bean is available only for a single flow instance.

Navigating View Nodes

Flows contain their own navigational rules. These rules can be straightforward and produce a page-by-page navigation, or they can be complex and include conditional logic. There are a series of elements that can be specified

Table 2-2. *Flow Navigational Nodes*

Element	Description
view	Navigates to a standard JSF view.
switch	One or more EL expressions that conditionally evaluate to true or false. If true, then navigation occurs to the specified view node.
flow-return	Outcome determined by the caller of the flow.
flow-call	A call to another flow; creates a nested flow.
method-call	Arbitrary method call that can invoke a method that returns a navigational outcome.

within the navigation rules, which will facilitate conditional navigation. Table 2-2 lists the different elements, along with an explanation of what they do.

As mentioned previously, flow navigation can be specified in XML format by placing it inside an XML file entitled `flowName-flow.xml`. Within this file, specify an `html` element that contains standard JSF taglib declarations. However, an additional taglib must be declared to enable flow configuration access. The new taglib, `xmlns:j="http://xmlns.jcp.org/jsf/flow"`, allows access to those navigational elements listed in Table 2-2. The following flow configuration is an example containing flow navigation that using conditional logic:

```
<?xml version="1.0" encoding="UTF-8"?>
<html xmlns="http://www.w3.org/1999/xhtml"
      xmlns:f="http://xmlns.jcp.org/jsf/core"
      xmlns:h="http://xmlns.jcp.org/jsf/html"
      xmlns:j="http://xmlns.jcp.org/jsf/flow">

    <f:metadata>
        <j:faces-flow-definition>

            <j:initializer>#{flowBean.initializeIt}</j:initializer>
            <j:start-node>exampleFlow</j:start-node>

            <j:switch id="startNode">
                <j:navigation-case>
                    <j:if>#{flowBean.someCondition}</j:if>
                        <j:from-outcome>newView</J;from-outcome>
                </j:navigation-case>
             </j:switch>

             <j:flow-return id="exit">
                 <j:navigation-case>
                     <j:from-outcome>exitFlow</j:from-outcome>
                 </j:navigation-case>
             </j:flow-return>

             <j:finalizer>#{flowBean.finalizeIt}</j:finalizer>

        </j:faces-flow-definition>
    </f:metadata>
</html>
```

As mentioned previously, flow navigation can also be defined within Java code by utilizing the flow builder API. To use this technique, create a new Java class that is named the same as the flow identifier, and annotate it with `@FlowDefinition`, which will earmark it as a flow definition class. Within the class, a method named `defineFlow` should be implemented, which will accept `FacesContext` and `FlowBuilder` objects. The `FlowBuilder` can then be used to construct the rules for the flow.

```
import javax.faces.context.FacesContext;
import javax.faces.flow.Flow;
import javax.faces.flow.FlowDefinition;
import javax.faces.flow.builder.FlowBuilder;
import javax.inject.Named;
```

```
/**
 *
 * @author Juneau
 */
@Named("exampleFlow2")
@FlowDefinition
public class ExampleFlow {
    private static final long serialVersionUID = -7623501087369765218L;

    public Flow defineFlow(FacesContext context, FlowBuilder builder){
        String flowId = "example2";

        builder.id("",flowId);
        builder.viewNode(flowId, "/" + flowId + ".xhtml").markAsStartNode();

        builder.returnNode("returnFromFlow").fromOutcome("#{flowBean.returnValue}");

        return builder.getFlow();
    }
}
```

Table 2-3 specifies the different methods that are available via the FlowBuilder.

Table 2-3. *FlowBuilder Methods*

Method	Description
`finalizer(MethodExpression)`	Specifies the finalizer method for the flow
`finalizer(String)`	
`flowCallNode(String string)`	Specifies a call node for the flow
`getFlow()`	Retrieves an instance of the flow
`id(String, String)`	Specifies the flow identifier
`inboundParameter(String, ValueExpression)`	Specifies an inbound parameter for the flow
`inboundParameter(String, String)`	
`initializer(MethodExpression)`	Specifies the initializer method for the flow
`initializer(String)`	
`methodCallNode(String)`	Specifies a method call node
`returnNode(String)`	Specifies the name of the exiting node
`switchNode(String)`	Specifies the name of a switch node
`viewNode(String, String)`	Specifies a view node

Either technique, XML or Java, works in the same manner. However, it is a good idea to specify the flow configuration within XML if you plan to change the way that the flow is configured, because using the Java API will mandate a recompile.

Flow EL

Flows contain a new EL variable named facesFlowScope. This variable is associated with the current flow, and it is a map that can be used for storing arbitrary values for use within a flow. The key-value pairs can be stored and read via a JSF view or through Java code within a managed bean. For example, to display the content for a particular map key, you could use the following:

```
The content for the key is:  #{facesFlowScope.myKey}
```

Java API for Flow Context

It is possible to gain access to an application's Flow context via the Java API by calling the javax.faces.application.Application getFlowHandler() method. Calling the method will return a thread-safe singleton instance of the FlowHandler for the application. A FlowHandler can then be used to gain access to the current flow, start a new flow, and so on. The following Java code demonstrates some of the possibilities:

```
FacesContext context = FacesContext.getCurrentInstance();
Application app = context.getApplication();

// Obtain the FlowHandler
FlowHandler handler = app.getFlowHandler();
// Obtain the current Flow
Flow flow = handler.getCurrentFlow();
// Obtain the current facesFlowScope Map content
Map flowScope = handler.getCurrentFlowScope();
// Add a new flow
Flow newFlow = new ExampleFlow();
handler.addFlow(context, newFlow, flow);
```

■ **Note** Flows cannot be altered once they are defined because they are immutable. The FlowHandler can gain access to a current flow to see information regarding the flow, but it cannot be used to dynamically alter the flow.

To learn the complete Java API, the best resource is to study the Javadoc for flows, which can be found at http://www.oracle.com/technetwork/java/javaee/javaserverfaces-139869.html.

Packaging a Flow

If a flow can be useful for more than one application, it can be made portable by packaging it up inside a JAR file. Once packaged, the flow can be brought into applications by simply including the JAR file in the application CLASSPATH. To package a flow, create a specific directory structure that includes the flow views, navigational XML, and any managed beans that may be used by the flow.

To create the directory structure, place a META-INF folder at the root, and then create a subdirectory for each of the flows that are packaged in the JAR. The subdirectory should be entitled flows, and it should contain a directory for each flow that will be packaged. Each of the flow directories should have the same name as the flow identifier. The flows must be explicitly defined in a faces-config.xml file that resides within the META-INF folder. Each of the nodes within a flow should be placed within the flow subdirectory. All Java code that belongs to a flow, such as the @FlowScoped and

`@FlowDefinition` beans, should be packaged into their corresponding Java packages and accompanied by a `beans.xml` file. The following outlines at the directory structure for a flow that is going to be packaged:

```
META-INF/faces-config.xml
META-INF/flows/exampleFlow/exampleFlow.xhtml
META-INF/flows/exampleFlow/intermediateFlow.xhtml
META-INF/flows/exampleFlow/endingFlow.xhtml
META-INF/beans.xml
org.javaee7.chapter02.jsf.ExampleFlow.java
org.javaee7.chapter02.jsf.FlowBean.java
```

Ajax Queues

By default, JSF Ajax requests are held in an Ajax request queue on the client in order to ensure that requests are sent to the server in the correct order. When a request is sent, it goes to the queue and waits until its turn to be sent to the server. After the request is sent to the server, a callback method is invoked that will remove that request from the queue.

A new `delay` attribute for the `f:ajax` tag allows a developer to specify a value in milliseconds that will be used to meter the time between server requests. If multiple requests arrive to the queue within the specified delay period, then only the most recent request is sent to the server. This prevents multiple unnecessary server requests from being sent, which can help performance in your application and reduce network traffic. Using the new attribute would be similar to the following example:

```
<h:commandButton value="Send Message" action="#{ajaxBean.sendMessage()}">
    <f:ajax delay="500"/>
</h:commandButton>
```

File Upload

JSF 2.2 includes a new file upload component that relies upon new Servlet 3.1 file upload support. The file upload support can be Ajax enabled or non-Ajax enabled. A new JSF component named `inputFile` has been added to the list of standard JSF components. This component can be used with or without the `f:ajax` tag, so files can be uploaded with a page refresh (non-Ajax) or without (Ajax).

To utilize the `inputFile` component, it must be placed within a JSF form that has an `enctype` set to multipart/form-data and no ID prepended. The `h:form` element contains the attributes `enctype` and `prependId`, which can be used to set these values, respectively. The following line of code demonstrates how to set the attributes for a form containing an `inputFile` component:

```
<h:form prependId="false" enctype="multipart/form-data">
```

The value of an `inputFile` component must be set to a managed bean variable that has a type of `javax.servlet.http.Part` (named `ajaxBean.upFile` in the following example). A JSF command component or the `f:ajax` tag should be set to an action method within the managed bean, which will save the file to disk.

The following JSF view demonstrates the use of the `inputFile` component in a non-Ajax solution:

```
<h:form prependId="false" enctype="multipart/form-data">
    Choose a file to upload to the server:
    <br/>
    <h:inputFile id="uploadFile" value="#{ajaxBean.upFile}">
        <f:validator validatorId="FileValidator"/>
```

```
    </h:inputFile>
    <br/>
    <h:commandButton action="#{ajaxBean.uploadFile}" value="Upload File"/>
</h:form>
```

The value attribute of the inputFile component is set to a variable of type javax.servlet.http.Part within the AjaxBean managed bean, and the commandButton has an action set to the managed bean's uploadFile method. In this particular example, a validator is applied to the file, which can contain code that is necessary to ensure the file for upload meets the standards for your application. The following example validator class, org.javaee7.chapter02.FileValidator, demonstrates how to write such a validator:

```
@FacesValidator(value = "FileValidator")
public class FileValidator implements Validator {

    public FileValidator() {
    }

    @Override
    public void validate(FacesContext context, UIComponent component, Object value)
throws ValidatorException {
        Part file = (Part) value;
        String text = null;
        try {
            InputStream is = file.getInputStream();
            text = new Scanner(is).useDelimiter("\\A").next();
        } catch (Exception ex) {
            throw new ValidatorException(new FacesMessage("Exception thrown"));
        }
    }
```

In the uploadFile method, the file is being stored into a directory named /Java_Dev/ on the server. The sources for the uploadFile method are as follows:

```
public void uploadFile() {
        try(InputStream is = file.getInputStream()) {

            int i = is.available();
            byte[] b = new byte[i];
            is.read(b);
            String fileName = getFileName(upFile);
            FileOutputStream os = new FileOutputStream("/Java_Dev/" + fileName);
            os.write(b);
            is.close();
        } catch (IOException ex) {
            Logger.getLogger(AjaxBean.class.getName()).log(Level.SEVERE, null, ex);
        }
}

    private String getFileName(Part part) {
    String partHeader = part.getHeader("content-disposition");
```

```
    for (String cd : part.getHeader("content-disposition").split(";")) {
      if (cd.trim().startsWith("filename")) {
        return cd.substring(cd.indexOf('=') + 1).trim()
            .replace("\"", "");
      }
    }
    return null;

  }
```

To make the file upload component work with Ajax, simply embed the `f:ajax` tag and provide the same action as the `commandButton` that is used in this example:

```
<h:inputFile id="ajaxUploadFile" value="#{ajaxBean.file}">
    <f:ajax execute="@form" listener="#{ajaxBean.uploadFile}"/>
</h:inputFile>
```

The new file upload component is a welcome addition to the JSF family of components. Since a file upload component is very oftentimes required within enterprise applications, it is now much easier because there are no third-party libraries to depend upon for acquiring this functionality.

Stateless Views

In JSF, every view by default carries some amount of statefulness. That is, when users navigate from view to view, some amount of state is persisted from view to view so that components can be rendered accordingly. In JSF, the component tree state is initialized upon the first Facelet request. Upon each subsequent request, only partial state changes are made, meaning that only the components within a view's component tree that require updating would be added to the view state. This means that the view state is always changing, which may cause application issues, depending upon a particular application's requirements. Therefore, an enhancement has been made in JSF 2.2, allowing the existing "transient" attribute to be added to an `<f:view>` tag and set to a value of `true`, thereby marking the view as stateless. When JSF encounters a view that contains a true transient attribute, the view's component state saving is skipped.

Let's take a look at a simple example. The following JSF view has been flagged as `stateless` since the transient attribute has been added to the `<f:view>` tag with a `true` value.

```
<html xmlns="http://www.w3.org/1999/xhtml"
      xmlns:f="http://xmlns.jcp.org/jsf/core"
      xmlns:h="http://xmlns.jcp.org/jsf/html"
      xmlns:ui="http://xmlns.jcp.org/jsf/facelets">
    <h:head>
        <meta http-equiv="Content-Type" content="text/html; charset=UTF-8"/>
        <title>Chapter 2 - Stateless View Example</title>
    </h:head>
    <h:body>
        <ui:composition template="../layout/custom_template.xhtml">
            <ui:define name="content">
        <f:view transient="true">
            <h:form>
                <p>
                    <h:outputText value="This is a stateless view..." />
                    <br/>
```

```
                    <br/>
                </p>
            </h:form>
        </f:view>
            </ui:define>
        </ui:composition>
    </h:body>
</html>
```

Along with this enhancement, the `javax.faces.render.ResponseStateManager.isStateless(FacesContext context, String viewId)` method has been added to determine whether the previous state that was posted contains any state. All views that are marked as stateless cause a value of "`stateless`" to be assigned to the view state parameter "`javax.faces.ViewState`". Therefore, a call to the new isStateless method checks this parameter.

HTML5 and JSF

One of the most prominent new capabilities of JSF 2.2 is increased support for HTML5. There have been some significant improvements to JSF that help facilitate the use of HTML5 attributes with standard JSF components, as well as including HTML5 tags within JSF views. This section covers a couple of these new features, including passthrough attributes and HTML5-friendly markup. After reading these sections, you will be able to incorporate modern HTML5 abilities into your JSF views with ease.

Passthrough Attributes

One major hurdle for using HTML5 along with standard JSF components is that there are attributes required by HTML5 tags that are not supported by the JSF components. HTML5 tags include data attributes that have the purpose of attaching data to HTML elements. The JSF components do not support these data attributes, but with the JSF 2.2 release, a new approach, known as *passthrough attributes*, helps resolve this issue. JSF passthrough attributes allow for attributes to be set for JSF components, to be passed through to the client directly, and not be consumed and/or processed by the component at all.

There are a few different ways to implement passthrough attributes. The first way is to use the new taglib URI (`xmlns:p="http://xmlns.jcp.org/jsf/passthrough"`), along with the new attribute `p:placeholder` to set the attribute. Using this technique, any JSF component can accept a `p:placeHolder` attribute, and it will be ignored by the component. The following example demonstrates how to utilize the `p:placeHolder` attribute of an `inputText` component:

```
<h:inputText value="#{ptBean.ptValue1}" p:placeholder="Passthrough Attribute 1">
                <f:ajax execute="@this" update="ptValues"/>
</h:inputText>
```

Another way to make use of passthrough attributes is to utilize a tag handler by embedding the `f:passThroughAttribute` tag inside a JSF component. The following example demonstrates the use of the `f:passThroughAttribute` tag:

```
<h:inputText value="#{ptBean.ptValue2}" >
    <f:passThroughAttribute name="ptValue2" value="Passthrough Attribute 2" />
    <f:ajax execute="@this" update="ptValues"/>
</h:inputText>
```

How about the cases where multiple passthrough attributes need to be set? The JSF 2.2 specification takes care of these cases by embedding the `f:passThroughAttributes` inside a JSF component. To set the values for multiple attributes, store them into a `Map<String,Object>` that resides within a managed bean, or use EL to define a `Map` of key-value pairs.

First, let's take a look at the solution where the value is bound to a `Map` residing in the managed bean.

```
<h:outputText id="ptValues" value="Attribute Values" >
    <f:passThroughAttributes value="#{ptBean.ptValues}" />
</h:outputText>
```

Next, we will look at the case where EL is used to specify a `Map` of name-value pairs to set for the passthrough attributes.

```
<h:outputText id="ptValues2" value="Attribute Values" >
                <f:passThroughAttributes value="{'first':1,'second':2,'third':3}" />
</h:outputText>
```

The following code demonstrates the use of each passthrough attribute solution in a JSF view:

```
<html xmlns="http://www.w3.org/1999/xhtml"
      xmlns:f="http://xmlns.jcp.org/jsf/core"
      xmlns:h="http://xmlns.jcp.org/jsf/html"
      xmlns:p="http://xmlns.jcp.org/jsf/passthrough">
    <h:head>
        <meta http-equiv="Content-Type" content="text/html; charset=UTF-8"/>
        <title>Passthrough Attribute Examples</title>
    </h:head>
    <h:body>
        <h:form>
            Using the passthrough placeholder attribute:
            <h:inputText value="#{ptBean.ptValue1}" p:placeholder="Passthrough Value 1">
                <f:ajax execute="@this" update="ptValues"/>
            </h:inputText>
            <br/><br/>
            Using the f:passThroughAttribute taghandler:
            <h:inputText value="#{ptBean.ptValue2}" >
                <f:passThroughAttribute name="ptValue2" value="Passthrough Value 2" />
                <f:ajax execute="@this" update="ptValues"/>
            </h:inputText>
            <br/><br/>
            Multiple Passthrough Attributes
            <h:outputText id="ptValues" value="Attribute Values" >
                <f:passThroughAttributes value="#{ptBean.ptValues}" />
            </h:outputText>
        </h:form>
    </h:body>
</html>
```

HTML5-Friendly Markup

The JSF 2.2 release includes the ability to utilize HTML5 markup within JSF views. As a matter of fact, the markup is not limited to HTML5; it can also include HTML4, and so on. The addition of a new tag URI makes this possible because it allows existing HTML tags to be bound to the JSF life cycle via new namespace attributes. It is now possible to develop entire JSF views without using any JSF tags at all.

To utilize the new namespace attributes, your JSF view must import the new taglib URI `jsf="http://xmlns.jcp.org/jsf"`. The new taglib can then be referenced as attributes within existing HTML tags, setting the underlying JSF attributes that are referenced. For instance, to utilize an HTML input tag with JSF, you would add the `jsf:id` attribute and set it equal to the JSF ID that you want to assign to that component. You would then set an attribute of `jsf:value` equal to the managed bean value. The following source code demonstrates a complete implementation of HTML5 code in a JSF view.

■ **Note** There is no need to import the `http://xmlns.jcp.org/jsf/html` taglib because you are no longer utilizing JSF component tags in the view.<?xml version="1.0" encoding="UTF-8"?>

```
<!DOCTYPE html PUBLIC "-//W3C//DTD XHTML 1.0 Strict//EN"
"http://www.w3.org/TR/xhtml1/DTD/xhtml1-strict.dtd">
<html xmlns="http://www.w3.org/1999/xhtml"
      xmlns:f="http://xmlns.jcp.org/jsf/core"
      xmlns:jsf="http://xmlns.jcp.org/jsf">
    <head jsf:id="head">
        <meta http-equiv="Content-Type" content="text/html; charset=UTF-8"/>

    </head>
    <body jsf:id="body">
        <form jsf:id="form" jsf:prependId="false">
            <input type="email" jsf:id="value1" jsf:value="#{ajaxBean.value1}">
                <f:ajax execute="@this" render="status"/>
            </input>
            <br/><br/>
            <input type="text" jsf:id="value2" jsf:value="#{ajaxBean.value2}">
                <f:ajax execute="@this" render="status"/>
            </input>
            <br/>
            <br/>
            <label for="status">Message: </label>
            <output jsf:id="status">#{ajaxBean.status}</output>
        </form>
    </body>
</html>
```

The new syntax provides several benefits for web developers. Although not all web developers are familiar with JSF component tags, HTML tags are well known. Utilizing the new syntax, both JSF and HTML developers alike can create web views that utilize the power of JSF along with the flexibility of HTML. The new syntax also makes it easier to bind HTML tags with JavaScript, if needed. You no longer need to worry about JSF view IDs getting in the way when working with HTML and JavaScript. With the addition of the new JSF taglib namespace for use with HTML tags, both JSF and HTML alike have been improved.

Facelets Enhancements

There have been a handful of updates to the Facelets implementation for JSF 2.2. Improvements and updates include the following:

- The ability to omit XML taglib files for custom components
- Facelets resource resolver annotation

This section covers each of these updates briefly and includes examples of each.

Exclude XML from Custom Components

The creation of custom components just got easier with the JSF 2.2 release. In previous versions, Facelets required the creation of a `*-taglib.xml` file that contained the name for the component. Once again, we have been mixing XML configurations into Java applications, making management more tedious. With the release of JSF 2.2, it is now possible to get rid of the taglib XML and use the `@FacesComponent` annotation instead, specifying the `createTag` attribute.

The `@FacesComponent` annotation should be placed on the custom component class. Table 2-4 lists possible attributes. To omit the taglib XML, the `createTag` attribute must be set to `true`.

Table 2-4. *@FacesComponent Attributes*

Attribute	Description
`createTag`	Set to `true` to make component directly usable via a tag on a Facelet.
`tagName`	Optional tag name.
`namespace`	Optional explicit namespace for tag. If omitted, the namespace of `http://xmlns.jcp.org/jsf/component` will be used.
`value`	Custom-component fully qualified name.

An example custom component class is as follows:

```
import javax.faces.component.FacesComponent;
import javax.faces.component.UIComponentBase;

@FacesComponent(value="components.SpecialComponent", createTag=true,
                namespace="http://www.apress.com/jsf/components")
public class SpecialComponent extends UIComponentBase {

    @Override
    public String getFamily() {
        // Do something here throw new UnsupportedOperationException("Not supported yet.");
        //To change body of generated methods, choose Tools | Templates.
    }

    //...
}
```

@FaceletsResourceResolver Annotation

In some cases, developers require the ability to influence the way that Facelets loads templates. In these circumstances, developers can specify the javax.faces.FACELETS_RESOURCE_RESOLVER environment parameter in the web.xml deployment descriptor. Since JSF 2.2 is steering more toward getting away from XML configuration and more toward annotation usage, the @FaceletsResourceResolver annotation has been created to take place of the old configuration. While the specification of javax.faces.FACELETS_RESOURCE_RESOLVER in the deployment descriptor still works, the new annotation makes it easy to register a Facelets resource resolver.

To use the annotation, specify it on a Java class that is intended for use as a resource resolver. By doing so, Facelets will automatically register the class as a resource resolver. The following source demonstrates the use of the new annotation.

```
import java.io.IOException;
import java.net.URL;
import javax.faces.application.Resource;
import javax.faces.view.facelets.FaceletsResourceResolver;
import javax.faces.context.FacesContext;
import javax.faces.view.facelets.ResourceResolver;

@FaceletsResourceResolver
public class AppResourceResolver extends ResourceResolver {
    private ResourceResolver parent;
    public AppResourceResolver(ResourceResolver parent) {
        this.parent = parent;
    }

    public URL resolveUrl(String path) {
        System.out.println("Using Custom Resource Resolver");
        URL url = parent.resolveUrl(path);
        if (url == null) {

            if (path.startsWith("/")) {
                path = path.substring(1);
            }
            url = parent.resolveUrl(path);
        }
        return url;
    }

}
```

Resource Library Contracts

An enhancement to the JSF resource library has made it easier to include new and/or additional templates for use within an application. The new enhancement enables multiple templates to be utilized within an application, with the ability to dynamically or statically define which template is to be applied to specified views. Let's start with the basics of setting up a resource library contract, and then we'll dive into the various means of applying one or more templates to views.

JSF allows templates to be created by adding a folder named /contracts to the root of an application's web directory, or into the /META-INF directory. Once added, one or more template directories can be placed inside of the contracts folder, each containing an associated template file and any optional resource files (CSS, JavaScript, etc.)

to be used along with the template. The template file must be named `template.xhtml`. For instance, to generate a template named "mocha" for an application, one could construct a hierarchy such as in Figure 2-2.

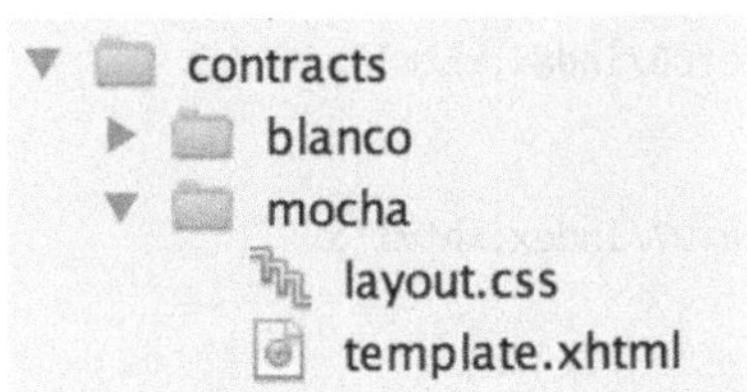

***Figure 2-2.** Resource Library Contracts Hierarchy*

If only one template directory resides within an application's `/contracts` or `/META-INF/contracts` directory, then that template can be applied to any view within the application by simply referencing the template as `/template.xhtml` within the template annotation of a view. For example, the contents of the `template.xhtml` file residing within the mocha directory are as follows:

```
<!DOCTYPE html PUBLIC "-//W3C//DTD XHTML 1.0 Transitional//EN"
"http://www.w3.org/TR/xhtml1/DTD/xhtml1-transitional.dtd">
<html xmlns="http://www.w3.org/1999/xhtml"
      xmlns:ui="http://xmlns.jcp.org/jsf/facelets"
      xmlns:h="http://xmlns.jcp.org/jsf/html">

    <h:head>
        <meta http-equiv="Content-Type" content="text/html; charset=UTF-8" />
        <h:outputStylesheet name="layout.css"/>
        <title>Introduction to Java EE 7 - Mocha Style</title>

    </h:head>

    <h:body>

        <div id="top">
            <h2>Intro to Java EE 7</h2>
        </div>
        <div>
            <div id="left">
                <h:form id="navForm">
                    <h:outputLink  value="/IntroToJavaEE7/faces/chapter01/index.xhtml" >
                     Chapter 1</h:outputLink>
                    <br/><br/>
                    <h:outputLink value="/IntroToJavaEE7/faces/chapter02/index.xhtml">
                     Chapter 2</h:outputLink>
                    <br/><br/>
                    <h:outputLink value="/IntroToJavaEE7/faces/chapter03/index.xhtml">
                     Chapter 3</h:outputLink>
                    <br/><br/>
                    <h:outputLink value="/IntroToJavaEE7/faces/chapter04/index.xhtml">
                     Chapter 4</h:outputLink>
```

```
                    <br/><br/>
                    <h:outputLink value="/IntroToJavaEE7/faces/chapter05/index.xhtml">
                     Chapter 5</h:outputLink>
                    <br/><br/>
                    <h:outputLink value="/IntroToJavaEE7/faces/chapter06/index.xhtml">
                     Chapter 6</h:outputLink>
                    <br/><br/>
                    <h:outputLink value="/IntroToJavaEE7/faces/chapter07/index.xhtml">
                     Chapter 7</h:outputLink>
                    <br/><br/>
                    <h:outputLink value="/IntroToJavaEE7/faces/chapter08/index.xhtml">
                     Chapter 8</h:outputLink>
                    <br/><br/>
                    <h:outputLink value="/IntroToJavaEE7/faces/chapter09/index.xhtml">
                     Chapter 9</h:outputLink>
                    <br/><br/>
                    <h:outputLink value="/IntroToJavaEE7/faces/chapter10/index.xhtml">
                     Chapter 10</h:outputLink>
                    <br/><br/>
                    <h:outputLink value="/IntroToJavaEE7/faces/chapter11/index.xhtml">
                     Chapter 11</h:outputLink>

                </h:form>
            </div>
            <div id="content" class="left_content">
                <ui:insert name="content">Content</ui:insert>
            </div>
        </div>
        <div id="bottom">
            Written by Josh Juneau, Apress Author
        </div>

    </h:body>

</html>
```

The following view can reside within any other folder within the application's web directory, and it can still simply specify "/template.xhtml" in order to make use of the "mocha" template.

```
<?xml version="1.0" encoding="UTF-8"?>
<!DOCTYPE html PUBLIC "-//W3C//DTD XHTML 1.0 Strict//EN"
"http://www.w3.org/TR/xhtml1/DTD/xhtml1-strict.dtd">
<html xmlns="http://www.w3.org/1999/xhtml"
      xmlns:f="http://xmlns.jcp.org/jsf/core"
      xmlns:h="http://xmlns.jcp.org/jsf/html"
      xmlns:ui="http://xmlns.jcp.org/jsf/facelets">
    <h:head>
        <meta http-equiv="Content-Type" content="text/html; charset=UTF-8"/>
        <title>Mocha Style</title>
    </h:head>
```

```
    <h:body>
        <ui:composition template="/template.xhtml">
            <ui:define name="content">
                <f:view>
                    <h:form>
                        ...content here
                    </h:form>
                </f:view>
            </ui:define>
        </ui:composition>
    </h:body>
</html>
```

If more than one template directory resides within an application's contracts directory then the desired template must be specified using one of a couple techniques. To dynamically or statically specify a view's template from directly within a view, utilize the new contracts annotation within the `<f:view>` tag of a view, specifying the desired template name. The following view demonstrates how to utilize this technique to specify a template named mocha for the view.

```
<?xml version="1.0" encoding="UTF-8"?>

<!DOCTYPE html PUBLIC "-//W3C//DTD XHTML 1.0 Strict//EN"
"http://www.w3.org/TR/xhtml1/DTD/xhtml1-strict.dtd">
<html xmlns="http://www.w3.org/1999/xhtml"
      xmlns:f="http://xmlns.jcp.org/jsf/core"
      xmlns:h="http://xmlns.jcp.org/jsf/html"
      xmlns:ui="http://xmlns.jcp.org/jsf/facelets">
    <h:head>
        <meta http-equiv="Content-Type" content="text/html; charset=UTF-8"/>
        <title>Mocha Style</title>
    </h:head>
    <h:body>
        <ui:composition template="/template.xhtml">
            <ui:define name="content">
                <f:view contracts="mocha">
            <h:form>
                <p>
                    <h:commandLink value="Enter flow" action="exampleFlow" />
                    <br/>
                    <br/>
                    <h:commandLink value="Enter flow #2" action="exampleFlow2" />
                </p>
            </h:form>
        </f:view>
            </ui:define>
        </ui:composition>
    </h:body>
</html>
```

JSF expresssion language could be utilized in-place of the static value for the contracts attribute in order to dynamically determine the name of the template to use. In this scenario, the value of the contracts annotation could be bound to a backing bean value, such as the following demonstrates:

```
<f:view contracts="#{myBean.chosenTemplate}">
    ...
</f:view>
```

It is also possible to statically define the templates within the faces-config.xml configuration file, associating a specified template to a URL path. To use this solution, add a <resource-library-contracts> section within the <application> configuration of the faces-config.xml. List each resource mapping within the <resource-library-contracts> section, mapping the templates that reside within the application's contracts directory to static URLs. The following is an excerpt from the faces-config.xml file, which ships with the book sources. The excerpt demonstrates how to facilitate a static URL mapping for two different templates named "mocha" and "blanco".

```
<application>
        <resource-library-contracts>
            <contract-mapping>
                <url-pattern>/chapter02/blanco/*</url-pattern>
                <contracts>blanco</contracts>
            </contract-mapping>
            <contract-mapping>
                <url-pattern>/chapter02/mocha/*</url-pattern>
                <contracts>mocha</contracts>
            </contract-mapping>
        </resource-library-contracts>
</application>
```

The full multi-templating implementation that was planned for inclusion in JSF 2.2 was cut from the final specification. However, the resource library contracts implementation, which is a scaled-down version of the previously planned implementation, is a step in the right direction.

Security Enhancements

The JSF 2.2 API includes security enhancements, and one of the most prominent of those is the ability to prevent cross-site forgery. It is possible for someone to alter a web site in such a way that when users input information into an application, they are redirected to some harmful server resource where information can be compromised. Oftentimes web site users do not even know that they've been redirected and end up providing personal information to a malicious site. JSF takes measures to prevent this type of attack because state is saved on the server side instead of on a client.

With the JSF 2.2 release, additional and stricter protection has been provided against this type of attack. By default, all postback requests are encrypted. If the page is not a postback request, then the following process occurs:

1. ViewHandler looks to see whether the view is listed within the <protected-views> element. If so, then the request is processed normally.

2. If the view is not listed under <protected-views>, the ViewHandler looks at the response header to determine whether the request is coming from another view within that same application. If so, then the request is processed.

3. If the request header is not present, then the ViewHandler checks to see whether there is a ResponseStateManager.NON_POSTBACK_VIEW_TOKEN_PARAM available. This query parameter should be present, by default, if the view is valid.

If a nonprotected page attempts to access a protected page without being validated by the ViewHandler as a secure view, then a javax.faces.application.ProtectedViewException will be raised. To specify a view manually, place the <protected-views> element in the faces-config.xml file, as shown here:

```
...
<protected-views>
    <url-pattern>/my_view.xhtml</url-pattern>
</protected-views>
```

Summary

The JSF 2.2 release adds great value to an already robust web framework. The addition of viewActions enables developers to invoke server side actions when views are accessed, which can be useful in any number of scenarios. The inclusion of faces flows helps to make web conversations even tighter, allowing scope to be maintained throughout the lifecycle of a conversation. HTML5 is becoming a prevalent option for web application development, and JSF 2.2 binds JSF with HTML5 more closely than in previous releases. This enables developers with more options for including HTML5 content within existing JSF applications, and even building entire JSF applications using HTML5 for the entire front end. Resource library contracts help to bring the concept of multi-templating into fruition, and security enhancements help to make JSF applications even more solid. The JSF 2.2 release is a very important release in the evolution of JSF, and it should enable the world of Java Enterprise to become even more widespread and a top choice for web development for the HTML5 era.

CHAPTER 3

Expression Language (EL)

The Expression Language (EL) 3.0 release is full of features that help enrich the language by making the language more powerful and by increasing productivity for developers. EL has always been a sweet spot for JSP and JSF developers, allowing the use of a very productive scripting language that provides the ability to interact directly with server-side Java within web views. This release enhances the language by adding features such as collection support and lambda expressions, which helps bring EL in line with more modern scripting languages. The release also adds support for working within a stand-alone environment. It is now possible to evaluate expressions, set variables, work with static fields and methods, and define functions.

Lambda Expressions

The EL 3.0 release brings support for lambda expressions. Simply put, a *lambda expression* behaves much like a function, because it accepts parameters and returns a value. Lambdas provide a way to encapsulate a function by assigning it to an identifier. That said, using lambdas, functions can be passed around as objects and even used as parameters to other functions. A lambda expression accepts parameters that go on the left side of the `->` operator, and the function or body of the expression is placed on the right side of the `->` operator. Lambda expressions in EL look much like those that are part of JDK 8, but the difference is that the body portion of an EL lambda is an EL expression that can utilize all the features provided by EL 3.0. For instance, all the reserved words that are available to EL, such as `gt`, `lt`, and `eq`, are available for use within a lambda expression. That said, let's take a look at some examples!

Lambda Concept and Examples

The following lambda expression accepts two parameters and returns the product:

```
((a,b) -> a * b (3,4))  -- Returns 12
```

Breaking down the example, the `(a,b)` part of the expression consists of the parameters that are accepted by the lambda. The `->` operator separates the parameters from the body of the lambda, which is `a * b`. Lastly, `(3,4)` are the values that are passed to the expression, and then the entire expression is surrounded by parentheses. The values being passed to the expression are optional, because the lambda could be assigned to an identifier instead. If a lambda is assigned to an identifier, that identifier can later be treated as a function, passing the values you want to utilize within the lambda as parameters. You'll see an example of this in the following section.

As mentioned previously, EL can be used within lambda expressions. Therefore, any of the EL operators are valid for use, so something like the following is possible:

```
a -> a == 0 ? 1 : a * a
```

The preceding example demonstrates a couple of concepts. First, the expression accepts a parameter (a), and the ternary operator says that if a is equal to 0, then 1 will be returned; otherwise, the product of a * a will be returned. Therefore, this example demonstrates the use of EL operators within a lambda expression. Second, note that this expression contains no parentheses. That is because parentheses are optional if there is only one parameter being passed into a lambda. If there are two or more parameters in use, then parentheses are required.

Variable Assignment

Sometimes it is useful to assign expressions to variables so that they can be passed around and utilized at a later time. This holds true for lambda expressions, because it allows for the encapsulation of a function, much like the concept of closures. The following EL demonstrates this concept by creating a lambda that returns the square root of a value that is passed in as a parameter:

```
// Assign the lambda to an identifier
sqrt = x -> x * x
// Use the lambda at a later point
sqrt(10) // returns 100
```

Nesting

Nesting a lambda expression inside another can produce very useful results. It is important to note that the scope within lambda functions is to the body of the lambda itself. Therefore, any identifiers, variables, or arguments that are defined inside a lambda body are available only within the scope of that expression. This can be useful for nesting because objects that are defined within a lambda can be passed to nested expressions but not vice versa. Take the following example, for instance:

```
c->[(c.num1, c.num2) -> x + y ]
```

In the previous expression, the c identifier would be an object that contains num1 and num2. Within the lambda, the c object is broken out and then used to find the sum of the two numbers, and then the result is returned.

Passing Lambdas to Java

It is possible to pass lambda expressions to Java code for evaluation, which can be beneficial to developers for a couple of reasons. First, having the ability to pass lambda expressions written in EL to a Java class provides the option to change that lambda at a later date without recompiling the Java code. This means that in a production environment, lambda expressions can be changed without redeploying an application.

Another good reason to pass lambdas to Java is so that you can utilize lambdas in code bases that are compiled using pre-Java 8 versions of the JDK. Lambdas are not available for use within Java code prior to the release of JDK 8; therefore, in order to benefit from the use of lambdas in Java, code bases will need to be migrated to JDK 8. This may not always be possible for a multitude of reasons. Therefore, for backward compatibility, lambda expressions may be written an EL and then passed to Java code that is compiled under JDK 7. Lastly, passing lambdas from EL to Java can aid in situations such as when there is a need to support query expressions on collections.

Let's take a look at how you can utilize EL lambda expressions from Java. Suppose you are using an EL lambda expression in a JSF view; then it could be passed to a managed bean method for evaluation, and a result could be returned. To accept a lambda expression, the Java method must accept a javax.el.LambdaExpression as a parameter. The lambda expression can then be invoked by calling its invoke method, which will return the result of the lambda.

The following EL is contained in a JSF view named chapter03\PassToJava.xhtml. The lambda expression in the EL is passed to a managed bean function named elExampleBean.

```
The employee makes more than 50,000:
            #{elExampleManagedBean.displayResult(x -> x.wage gt 50000)}
```

Next, you'll take a look at the `eLExampleManagedBean.displayResult` method, which accepts a `javax.el.LambdaExpression` as a parameter.

```
public boolean displayResult(javax.el.LambdaExpression le){
        Employee e = new Employee();  // Grab an employee instance
        if (le.invoke(e)){
            return true;
        } else {
            return false;
        }
}
```

Collections Enhancements

Collections have been reworked for EL 3.0, bringing them more in line with Java SE 8. Collections (sets, maps, and lists) can be constructed dynamically in EL. EL collections can be constructed from literals or from EL expressions. This can be a huge advantage when dynamically constructing a collection. In this section, I will briefly cover examples for creating and using each type of collection.

Sets

Sets are surrounded by curly braces, as in {}, and elements of the set are separated by commas. The following are examples of `Set` objects:

```
{a, b, c}
{1, "two", 3}
{a * b, 3, 5 * c}
```

Maps

Maps are key-value pairs, just like in the Java language. They are surrounded by curly braces, as in {}, just like `Set` objects. In a `Map` element, a colon is used to separate the key from the value. The following are examples of `Map` objects:

```
{"one":1, "two":2, 3:"three"}
{"first":"Josh", "last":"Juneau}
```

Lists

Lists are very similar to `Set` objects, but they have a different syntax because they are enclosed by brackets, [], rather than braces. The following are examples of `List` objects:

```
[a, b, c]
[1, "two", 3]
[d, [e, f, g, h], x]
```

Supporting Operations

A collection of data is represented in EL as `java.lang.Iterable<Object>`. Collections of data can be iterated over, and EL provides operations to perform on data while iterating over it. There are operations that can be performed on collections to accomplish a myriad of tasks, including filtering, sorting, selecting a subset of elements, and so forth. In this section, you will learn each of the collection operations and how they work.

There are two different types of collection operations: lazy and eager. *Lazy* operations tend to iterate only when necessary, and they avoid the creation of new collections (Table 3-1). *Eager* operations iterate over the entire collection each time they are performed (Table 3-2). The following sections break the collection operations into each of these two categories.

Table 3-1. *Lazy Collection Operations*

Operation	Description
`take`	Iterates over the source elements and yields the number of elements specified by the given argument. Elements are yielded from the front of the collection. If the count is greater than the number of source elements, all the elements are yielded; otherwise, if the count is less than or equal to zero, no elements are yielded. **Example:** `employees.take(2)`
`skip`	Iterates over the source elements, skipping the number of elements specified by the argument and yielding all of the remaining elements. If the source collection contains fewer elements than the number specified by the argument, nothing is yielded. If count is less than or equal to zero, all elements are yielded. **Example:** `employees.skip(2)`
`takeWhile`	Iterates over the source elements, applying the given predicate function to each element and yielding the elements that return a `true` result. The iteration stops the first time the predicate function returns `false` or when all of the elements have been processed. The predicate function takes two arguments. The first argument represents the element to test. The second argument, if present, represents the zero-based index of the element within the source collection. **Example:** `employees.takeWhile(Boolean predicate)`
`skipWhile`	Iterates over the source elements, applying the given predicate function to each element and skipping those elements that return a `true` result. The first element that returns a `false` result is yielded, along with all remaining elements. No elements are yielded if the predicate function returns `true` for all elements. The predicate function takes two arguments. The first argument represents the element to test. The second argument, if present, represents the zero-based index of the element within the source sequence. **Example:** `employees.skipWhile(Boolean predicate)`
`first`	Iterates the source elements, and if a predicate function is specified, then the first element returning a `true` result is yielded. Otherwise, if no predicate function is specified, the first operator simply returns the first element in the collection. An `InvalidOperationException` is thrown if no element matches the predicate or if the source collection is empty. **Example:** `employees.first()`

(*continued*)

Table 3-1. (*continued*)

Operation	Description
`firstOrDefault`	Iterates over the source elements, and if a predicate function is specified, then the first element returning a `true` result is yielded. Otherwise, if no predicate function is specified, the `firstOrDefault` operator simply returns the first element in the collection. If no element matches the predicate or if the source sequence is empty, a `null` is returned. **Example:** `employees.firstOrDefault()`
`last`	Iterates over the source elements, and if a predicate function is specified, then the last element returning a `true` result is yielded. Otherwise, if no predicate function is specified, the last operator simply returns the last element in the collection. An `InvalidOperationException` is thrown if no element matches the predicate or if the source collection is empty. **Example:** `employees.last()`
`lastOrDefault`	Iterates over the source elements, and if a predicate function is specified, then the last element returning a `true` result is yielded. If no predicate function is specified, the `lastOrDefault` operator simply returns the last element in the collection. If no element matches the predicate or if the source sequence is empty, a `null` is returned. **Example:** `employees.lastOrDefault()`
`single`	Iterates over the source elements and returns the single element that returns `true` from the predicate function. If no predicate function is specified, the single operator simply returns the single element of the collection. An `InvalidOperationException` is thrown if the source sequence is empty or contains no matching element or more than one matching element. **Example:** `employees.single()`
`singleOrDefault`	Iterates over the source elements and returns the single element that returns `true` from the predicate function. If no predicate function is specified, the `singleOrDefault` operator simply returns the single element of the collection. An `InvalidOperationException` is thrown if the source sequence contains more than one matching element. If no element matches the predicate or if the source sequence is empty, `null` is returned. **Example:** `employees.singleOrDefault()`
`elementAt`	The `List.get()` method is used to obtain the element at the specified `index` if the collection is a `List`. Otherwise, the elements in the collection are iterated `index` number of times, and the element found at the specified position is returned. An `IndexOutOfBoundException` is thrown if the index is less than zero or greater than or equal to the number of elements in the collection. **Example:** `employees.elementAt(12)`

(*continued*)

Table 3-1. (*continued*)

Operation	Description
elementAtOrDefault	The `List.get()` method is used to obtain the element at the specified `index` if the collection is a `List`. Otherwise, the elements in the collection are iterated `index` number of times, and the element found at the specified position is returned. A `null` is returned if the index is less than zero or greater than or equal to the number of elements in the collection. **Example:** `employees.elementAtOrDefault(10)`
any	Iterates over the source elements to determine if any of the elements satisfy the predicate function test. If so, then `true` is returned. If no predicate function is specified, the any operator simply returns `true` if the source collection is greater than zero in size. The iteration stops as soon as the result is known. **Example:** `employees.any()`
all	If the collection is empty, then `null` is returned. Otherwise all elements that satisfy the test given by the predicate are returned. The iteration halts when the result is known. **Example:** `employees.all()`
contains	The `Collection.contains()` method is invoked to obtain the result if the source implements the collection type. Otherwise the elements of the collection are iterated to determine if the element is found. The iteration stops as soon as a matching element is found. **Example:** `employees.contains(elem) // where elem is an element`

Table 3-2. *Eager Collection Operations*

Operation	Description
where	Iterates over the source elements yielding each one for which the specified predicate function returns true. The predicate function can accept two arguments. The first argument of predicate function represents the element to test. The second optional argument represents the zero-based index of the element within the source collection. **Example:** `employees.where(e->e.wage >= 50000)`
select	Iterates over the source and yields the results of applying the selector function for each element. The first argument of selector represents the element to process. The second argument, if any, represents the zero-based index of the element within the source collection. **Example:** `employees.select(e->e.first)`
selectMany	Iterates over the source elements, producing an `Iterable` for each element by evaluating the selector function. If the result of evaluating the selector function is not an `Iterable`, the behavior is undefined. The inner `Iterable` is then iterated, and if there is no `resultSelector` function then its element is yielded. If there is a `resultSelector` function, it is invoked, passing the outer and inner elements as its arguments, and the result is yielded. The second optional argument to the selector function represents the zero-based index of the element within the source collection. **Example:** `employees.selectMany(e->e.position)`

(*continued*)

Table 3-2. (*continued*)

Operation	Description
`join`	Iterates over the source elements, and for each element (referred to as *outer element*), the `outerKeySelector` function is evaluated to a value (referred to as `key1`). For each non-null `key1`, `innerKeySequence` is iterated, and for each element (referred to as *inner element*), the `innerKeySelector` function is evaluated to a value (referred to as `key2`). The value `key1` is compared with `key2`, and if equal, the `resultKeySelector` function is evaluated (with the outer element and the inner element as its arguments), and the result is yielded. A comparator can be used for the comparison `key1` to `key2`. **Example:** `employees.join(positions, e->e.positionId, p->p.positionId,` `(e, p) -> [e.first, e.last, p.position])`
`groupJoin`	Iterates over the source elements, and for each element (referred to as *outer element*), the `outerKeySelector` function is evaluated to a value (referred to as `key1`). If `key1` is non-null, `innerSequence` is iterated, and for each element (referred to as *inner element*), the `innerKeySelector` function is evaluated to a value (referred to as `key2`). The inner elements whose `key2` equals `key1` are collected in a list. The `resultSelector` function is then evaluated, with the outer element and the list (can possibly be empty) as its arguments, and the result is yielded. A comparator can be used for the comparison of `key1` and `key2`. The operator preserves the order of the outer elements, and for each outer element, the order of the matching inner elements is preserved. **Example:** `employees.select(e ->` `[e.first, e.last, e.yearsOfService.sum(y->y.years)])`

`concat`	Iterates over the source elements, yields each element in the collection, and then iterates over the second collection, yielding each element in the collection.
	Example: `employees.concat(positions)`
	`orderBy`, `thenBy`, `orderByDescending`, `thenByDescending`
	These operators can be used together to order a collection via multiple keys. A composition of the operators has the form
	`source.orderBy(...).thenBy(...).thenBy(...) ...`
	where `orderBy(...)` is an invocation of `orderBy` or `orderByDescending` and each `thenBy(...)`, if any, is an invocation of `thenBy` or `thenByDescending`. The primary ordering is established by the initial `orderBy` or `orderByDescending`, the first `thenBy` or `thenByDescending` establishes the secondary ordering, the second `thenBy` or `thenByDescending` establishes the tertiary ordering, and so on.
	Example: `employees.orderBy(p->p.position)`
	`thenByDescending(p->p.salary)`

`reverse`	Iterates over the source elements, collecting all elements in a list. Each element in the resulting list is then yielded in reverse order. **Example:** `employees.reverse()`

(*continued*)

Table 3-2. (*continued*)

Operation	Description
groupBy	Iterates over the collection and, for each element, evaluates the keySelector and elementSelector functions, if present. The keySelector and the elementSelector select a key and a destination element, respectively, from the source elements. If no elementSelector is specified, elements of the collection become the destination elements. The destination elements with the same key value are grouped in a Grouping, which is then yielded. The groupings are yielded in the order in which their key values first occurred in the original collection, and destination elements within a grouping are ordered by their occurrences in the source elements. A comparator can be used for comparison of the key values. **Example:** employees.groupBy(p->p.position, p->p.salary)
distinct	Iterates over the source elements, yielding each element that has not previously been yielded. A comparator can be used to compare the elements. **Example:** employees.distinct()
union	Iterates over the elements of the source and second collections, in that order. Each element that has not yet been yielded is returned. A comparator can be used to compare the elements. **Example:** [1,3,5,7,9].union([2,4,6,8,10])
intersect	Iterates over the source elements, and each element that is contained in the second collection and has not yet been yielded is returned. A comparator can be used to compare the elements. **Example:** [1,3,5,7,9].intersect([2,4,6,8,10])
except	Iterates over the source elements, and each element that is contained in the second collection and has not yet been yielded is returned. A comparator can be used to compare the elements. **Example:** [1,3,5,7,9].except([1,2,3,4,5]) //returns 2,4,7,9
toArray	Iterates over the collection and returns an array containing the elements.
toSet	Iterates over the collection and returns a Set containing the elements.
toList	Iterates over the collection and returns a List containing the elements.
toMap	Iterates over the collection and evaluates the keySelector and elementSelector functions for each element, producing a key and a value. The resulting key and value pairs are returned in a Map. If no elementSelector was specified, the value is the element itself.
toLookup	Iterates over the source elements and evaluates the keySelector and elementSelector functions for each element, producing a key and a value. The values with the same key are grouped together in a Grouping, and the resulting key and the Grouping pairs are returned in a Map. If no elementSelector is specified, the value for each element is the element itself. **Example:** employees.toLookup(e->e.last, e->e.positionId)

(*continued*)

Table 3-2. (*continued*)

Operation	Description
sequenceEqual	Iterates over the two source elements in parallel and compares their corresponding elements. If all corresponding elements are equal and the collection sizes are equal, then `true` is returned. Otherwise, the method returns `false`. If a comparator is specified, it is used to compare the elements. **Example:** `seqA.sequenceEqual(seqB)`
defaultIfEmpty	Iterates over and yields all elements of the source collection. If the source collection is empty, the `defaultValue` is yielded. If `defaultvalue` is not specified, a `null` is yielded. **Example:** `employees.defaultIfEmpty()`
count	`Collection.size()` is used to obtain the count if there is no predicate function specified and if the source implements `Collection`. If the source does not implement `Collection`, then the count operator iterates over the source elements, counting the total number. If a predicate is specified, the `count` operator iterates over the source elements and counts the number of elements for which the predicate function returns `true`. **Example:** `employees.count()`
sum	Iterates over the source elements, invoking the selector function for each element. Computes the sum of the returned values. If no selector function is specified, the sum of the elements in the collection is computed. Zero is returned for an empty collection. Furthermore, the operator does not include `null` values in the result. **Example:** `[3,5,7,10].sum()`
min	Iterates over the source elements, invoking the selector function for each element. Finds the minimum of the returned values. If no selector function is specified, the minimum of the elements in the collection is computed. The values to be compared must implement `Comparable`. `null` is returned for an empty collection. **Example:** `[3,5,7,10].min()  // returns 3`
max	Iterates over the source elements, invoking the selector function for each element. Finds the maximum of the returned values. If no selector function is specified, the maximum of the elements in the collection is computed. The values to be compared must implement `Comparable`. The `max` operator returns `null` for an empty collection. **Example:** `[3,5,7,10].max()  // returns 10`
average	Iterates over the source elements, invoking the selector function for each element. Computes the average of the returned values. If no selector function is specified, the average of the elements in the collection is calculated. The `average` operator returns `null` for an empty collection. **Example:** `[3,5,7].average()`

(*continued*)

Table 3-2. (*continued*)

Operation	Description
`aggregate`	If a seed value is specified, then it is assigned to an internal accumulator variable. Iterates over the source elements, repeatedly computing the next accumulator value by invoking the specified function and passing the current accumulator value as the first argument and the current element as the second argument. At the end of the iteration, if a `resultSelector` is not specified, the final accumulator value is returned; otherwise, `resultSelector function` is invoked, passing the final accumulator as its argument, and the result is returned. If no seed value is specified, then the value of the first element is used as the seed value. If the source collection is empty, the aggregate operator without a seed value throws an `InvalidOperationException`.
`forEach`	Iterates over the source elements and applies the action function to each element. The action can take two arguments. The first argument of action represents the element to process. The second argument, if present, represents the zero-based index of the element within the source collection. The `forEach` operators always return `null`.

■ **Note** It is important to note that zero or more operators can be chained together to achieve the desired result. For instance, you can apply a `select` operator to a collection and then apply a `where` operator to that same collection.

New Operators

New operators have been added to EL in order to bring new features to the language. This section will cover each of the new operators and provide a brief example for each. Lastly, there have been some operator precedence changes in order to accommodate the new additions to the language, so I'll cover them as well.

String Concatenation Operator

The `String` concatenation operator works if and only if one of the operands is a `String`. The new operators for concatenation are + and `cat`. Since the + operator has been overloaded, if both operands are numeric values, then it adds the two together; otherwise, if one operand is a `String`, then concatenation will occur.

The following examples demonstrate the use of the new + operator for concatenation:

```
${"Hello " + emp.name}
${100 + "3"}  // produces: 1003
```

The other concatenation operator, `cat`, is used in the following way:

```
${"Hello ".cat(emp.name)}
```

Assignment Operator

The assignment operator can be applied to expressions, and it assigns the rvalue to the lvalue.

■ **Note** An *lvalue* refers to the value or expression on the left side of the = sign, and the *rvalue* refers to the value or expression on the right side of the = sign. If the lvalue is not writable, then a `PropertyNotWriteableException` will be thrown.

In the case of `X = Y`, `X` would be assigned the value of `Y`. If there are more than one equal signs present in an expression, then when read from left to right, the first equal sign divides the lvalue and rvalue. All remaining equal signs are part of the rvalue. For instance, the parentheses in the following example surround the rvalue:

```
y = (a = z -x * 10)
```

The `ELResolver.setValue` method determines how assignment is made. If an assignment is illegal in a given circumstance, then the `ELResolver.setValue` method will not make the assignment. In a stand-alone environment, the `ELResolver` is part of a class named the `StandardELContext`. If an assignment is made to an identifier that has not yet been declared, then a new bean is created in the local bean repository, and it is named the same as the newly specified identifier.

Semicolon Operator

The semicolon operator (;) is used to return from an expression. The semicolon operator is much like the semicolon in Java, whereas it is used to end a statement or expression. Therefore, if there were more than one expression on the same line and the expressions were separated by semicolons, then the first expression would be evaluated, followed by the second, and so on. After each expression is evaluated, it is discarded, and the next expression is evaluated separately.

Precedence Changes

Operator precedence can become important if more than one operator exists in the same expression. It is important to understand which operator will be evaluated first so that the correct expression will be evaluated first. Table 3-3 lists each of the operators that are part of EL, from highest precedence to lowest precedence, given that an expression is evaluated from left to right. If more than one operator has the same precedence, then each of those operators will be listed in the same table line.

Table 3-3. *EL Operator Precedence*

	Operator
1	`[] .`
2	`()`
3	`-` (unary) `not ! empty`
4	`* / div % mod`
5	`+ -` (binary)
6	`cat`
7	`< > <= >= lt gt le ge`
8	`== != eq ne`
9	`&& and`
10	`|| or`
11	`? :`
12	`->`
13	`=`
14	`;`

Static Field and Methods

A static field or method can be referenced by referring to the class that embodies the field or method and then using the dot (.) operator to denote the static field or method. To refer to a given class, use the following notation, where `className` refers to the fully qualified name of the class:

```
T(className)
```

Therefore, the following references would be valid:

```
T(classA).myVar
T(java.lang.Boolean).FALSE
```

■ **Note** `T` is used with Java generics to specify a type whenever there is nothing more specific about the type to distinguish it.

Stand-Alone API

The 3.0 release provides a stand-alone API for the Expression Language (EL). Utilization of such an API can be handy in various situations. In the forefront, a stand-alone API can be useful if you are interested in making use of Expression Language within a Java SE environment. However, it can also be useful when developing EL that will be later utilized within JSPs or JSF views.

The stand-alone API makes use of the `javax.el.ELProcessor` class to obtain an instance of the ELProcessor for working with the EL. To use this class, instantiate a new instance and then call upon its methods to utilize different components of the EL stand alone API. Table 3-4 lists the different methods that can be called upon from an instance of the ELProcessor class, along with a description of each.

Table 3-4. *ELProcessor Methods*

Method	Description
`defineBean(String, Object)`	Defines a variable within the EL environment and assigns a specified JavaBean to that variable. This makes the bean available in the local bean repository.
`defineFunction(String, String, Method)` `defineFunction(String, String, String, String)`	Defines an EL function in the local function mapper.
`eval(String)`	Evaluates an EL Expression.
`getELManager()`	Returns an EL Manager that can be used for EL Processing.
`getValue(String, Class)`	Evaluates a given EL expression, coerces it into the specified type, and returns the result.
`setValue(String, Object)`	Sets an expression with a value.
`setVariable(String, String)`	Assigns an EL expression to an EL variable.

Most of the methods that can be called upon from the `ELProcessor` class can be called upon to work with the EL processor and achieve the desired effect. The `getELManager()` method is different in that it returns an instance of the `ELManager` class, which allows one to further configure the EL environment. The following sections will further outline the functionality of the EL Processor.

Defining a Bean

Consider the case where you have a Java class that you would like to make available for use within an EL expression. The `ELProcessor defineBean` method can be utilized for doing just that. This method takes two parameters, the first being a string that will be used to declare the EL variable name, and the second being the JavaBean object that you'd like to make available from within the EL. The following example demonstrates how to make a bean named `TestBean` available for use within an EL context. First, let's take a look at the `TestBean` source to see that it is a simple JavaBean that contains no additional extras to facilitate the `ELProcessor`.

```
public class TestBean {

    private int num1 = 5;
    private int num2 = 7;

    /**
     * @return the num1
     */
    public int getNum1() {
        return num1;
    }
```

```
    /**
     * @param num1 the num1 to set
     */
    public void setNum1(int num1) {
        this.num1 = num1;
    }

    /**
     * @return the num2
     */
    public int getNum2() {
        return num2;
    }

    /**
     * @param num2 the num2 to set
     */
    public void setNum2(int num2) {
        this.num2 = num2;
    }

    public static String obtainMessage(){
        return "Hello from the function";
    }
}
```

Next, we'll take a look at the code that can be utilized to bring an instance of TestBean into an EL context for use with EL expressions. To do so, an instance of ELProcessor must be obtained, and then the defineBean method is invoked, passing the String-based variable name along with the String-based fully qualified class name of the bean that we wish to make available. Once the bean has been made available, it can be utilized in an EL expression and evaluated by calling the ELProcessor eval method, as demonstrated in the following code.

```
ELProcessor el = new ELProcessor();
// Assign a bean instance to a variable
el.defineBean("c", new TestBean());
el.setVariable("adder", "(x,y) -> x + y");
// Utilize the bean instance variables
Object result = el.eval("adder(c.num1, c.num2)");
```

Declaring a Variable

The stand-alone API makes it easy to declare an EL variable and assign an expression to it. This can be done by first obtaining an instance of ELProcessor, and then calling the setVariable method, passing the String-based name of the desired variable, along with the String-based expression. The following lines of code demonstrate this functionality by assigning a lambda expression to a String-based variable.

```
ELProcessor el = new ELProcessor();
el.setVariable("sqrt", "x -> (x * x)");

Object result = el.eval("sqrt(150)");
```

Defining a Function

If you wish to assign a Java-based function to an EL expression variable, you can do so by calling one of the ELProcessor defineFunction methods. These two methods both achieve the same result, but they each accept different parameters to get there. First, you can call the defineFunction(String, String, Method) function by passing the following parameters:

- String-based prefix (Java package) that should be utilized to fully qualify the function
- String-based name of the Java class that contains the method you would like to assign to the function
- Method object that you'd like to invoke

The second defineFunction method accepts four String-based parameter values, those being the following:

- Prefix (Java package) that should be utilized to fully qualify the function
- Name identifier to which you would like to assign the method call
- Name of the Java class that contains the method that you would like to assign to the function
- Name of the static Java method to utlize

The following lines of code demonstrate how to define a function named obtainMessage to a Java-based method named obtainMessage, which belongs within the TestBean class.

```
ELProcessor el = new ELProcessor();
try {
    el.defineFunction("org", "obtainMessage", "org.javaee7.chapter03.el.client.TestBean",
"obtainMessage");
} catch (ClassNotFoundException|NoSuchMethodException ex) {
    // handle error
}

Object result = el.eval("org:obtainMessage()");
```

Utilizing the ELManager

The ELManager class can be used to set configurations for the EL environment. For instance, it can be used to import Java packages or classes for use within EL expressions. Table 3-5 lists the methods that can be useful within the ELManager for configuring the EL environment. It should be noted that some of the methods mirror those that are available from the ELProcessor.

Table 3-5. ELManager Methods

Method	Description
addBeanNameResolver	Registers a bean-name resolver
addELResolver	Registers an EL Resolver
addEvaluationListener	Registers an EvaluationListener
defineBean	Defines a bean with the local bean repository
getELContext	Returns ELContext that can be used for parsing and evaluating expressions
importClass	Imports a Java class
importMethod	Imports a Java method
importStatic	Imports a static field or method
mapFunction	Maps a static method to a function name
setELContext	Used to set the ELContext
setVariable	Assigns a value or expression to an EL variable

The following code listing demonstrates how to make use of the ELManager for importing a Java class into the EL context.

```
ELProcessor el = new ELProcessor();
ELManager elMgr = el.getELManager();
elMgr.importClass("org.javaee7.chapter03.el.client.TestBean");
el.setVariable("bean", "new TestBean()");
Object result = el.eval("bean.num1 + bean.num2");
```

Incompatibilities with Previous Releases

Most of the EL 3.0 release is backward compatible; however, there are a few incompatibilities with previous releases, mostly because of the nature of the new features. The list of incompatibilities is as follows:

- The new keywords are T and cat.
- The + operator is overloaded for String concatenation.
- Non-primitive types are coerced to null by default.

Summary

Expression Language provides a binding between web views and server side logic. The Expression Language 3.0 release brings with it many great enhancements, including a stand-alone API, and more modern coding techniques such as lambda expressions. Brushing up with the latest enhancements to the API will enhance any developer's productivity, and it can also increase the availability of the API for those who wish to utilize EL within Java SE applications.

CHAPTER 4

Object Relational Mapping and JPA

Object Relational Mapping (ORM) is the process of mapping entity classes to underlying database tables, and using those entities to work with data, rather than direct SQL. Many developers have adopted ORM solutions over the years, and a variety of different ORM technologies have emerged due to the uptake. The Java EE platform contains the Java Persistence API (JPA), which is the standard ORM technology for Java enterprise development. Over the years, JPA has changed significantly, making development easier and opening more options to developers with each release. The latest release, JPA 2.1, is no exception, as it brings forth many incremental updates to the API, allowing developers more flexibility and ease of development than ever before.

In this chapter, you will learn about the updates that have been made to JPA in an effort to expand the API. Such updates include: ON Conditions, the ability to invoke database functions, bulk updates and deletions via the Criteria API, and so on. You will also learn about enhancements to JPA that make development even easier and more productive, such as schema generation.

Support for Joins with ON Conditions

When writing Java Persistence Query Language (JPQL) queries, it is sometimes beneficial to join two or more tables to acquire related information. Furthermore, it is usually helpful to filter information based upon certain specified criteria so that the number of records returned can be manageable. JPQL joins typically include `INNER`, `OUTER`, and `FETCH` joins. To review, an `INNER` join allows retrieval from two tables such that records being returned contain at least one match in both tables. For instance, you may wish to query an `Employee` entity join it to `the Jobs` entity to return only employees that have a specific job title. An `OUTER` join allows retrieval from two tables such that all of the records from one of the entities (left entity) are returned, regardless if they match with a record in the other entity. Lastly, a `FETCH` join enables the fetching of an association as a side effect of the query execution. In JPA 2.1, JPQL has been updated to include the `ON` condition, which allows one to perform an `OUTER` join and include a specified condition with the join. This capability has always been available with the `WHERE` clause of the JPQL query . . . but what about the cases when you wish to return all matching records along with those that may not match, as with an `OUTER` join? The JPA 2.1 release provides this functionality in a concise manner with the addition of `ON` conditions. Simply put, an `ON` condition modifies a join query such that it will incorporate better control over the data that is returned in a concise manner.

In order to demonstrate this new syntax, let's take a look at an SQL query and then we will compare it to its JPQL counterpart. The following SQL will join the `EMPLOYEE` table with the `JOBS` table on the `JOB_ID` field. It will also limit the returned records to those that include a salary of >= 50,000 with the specification in the `WHERE` clause.

```
SELECT J.TITLE, COUNT(E.ID)
FROM JOBS J LEFT JOIN EMPLOYEE E
   ON J.JOB_ID = E.JOB_ID and E.STATUS = 'ACTIVE'
WHERE J.SALARY >= 50000
GROUP BY J.TITLE;
```

This will return all of the JOB records, grouped by job title, listing the number of each job that contains an Employee whose status is ACTIVE, as shown below.

```
HR TITLE A     1
HR TITLE B     0
IT TITLE A     0
IT TITLE B     0
TITLE A        0
```

The following method includes the JPQL that is the equivalent of the SQL above, and it uses the new ON condition. This method, named activeEmployeeCount, can be found within the org.javaee7.jpa.session.EmployeeSession file.

```
public List obtainActiveEmployeeCount() {
        TypedQuery<Object[]> qry = em.createQuery("SELECT j.title, count(e) "
                  + "FROM Jobs j LEFT JOIN j.employees e "
                  + "ON e.status = 'ACTIVE' "
                  + "WHERE j.salary >= 50000 "
                  + "GROUP BY j.title", Object[].class);

        List data = new ArrayList();
         if (!qry.getResultList().isEmpty()) {
              List<Object[]> tdata = qry.getResultList();
             for (Object[] t : tdata) {
                 HashMap resultMap = new HashMap();
                 resultMap.put("title", t[0]);
                 resultMap.put("count", t[1]);
                 data.add(resultMap);
             }
         }
         return data;

    }
```

In the end, the ON condition helps to make JPQL outer joins more concise and easy to use. Although the same capability has been available in previous versions of JPQL, but the ON clause helps to make record filtering with joins much easier.

Invocation of Database Functions

It is possible to invoke database functions directly within a JPQL query using the new function invocation syntax. Both predefined database functions or user-defined database functions are supported for use via this feature. The FUNCTION keyword can be used within a query to invoke a database function using the following syntax:

```
FUNCTION(function_name {,args}*)
```

When calling a database function, zero or more arguments can be passed to the function by listing them after the String-based name of the function, separated by commas. The following example JPQL invokes a function named "aboveTaxBracket", passing the employee salary as an argument.

```
SELECT e FROM Employee e WHERE FUNCTION('aboveTaxBracket', e.salary)
```

■ **Note** If an application utilizes FUNCTION invocation, it may not be portable across databases.

Bulk Updates and Deletions

The Criteria API has been enhanced to support bulk updates and deletions. The Criteria API allows developers to utilize Java language syntax in order to perform database queries and manipulations, rather than JPQL or SQL. A `javax.persistence.criteria.CriteriaUpdate` object can be used to perform bulk update operations, and a `javax.persistence.critera.CriteriaDelete` object can be used to perform bulk deletion operations. How do we obtain such objects? The Criteria API is dependent upon the `javax.persistence.criteria.CriteriaBuilder` interface, which is used to return objects that can be used to work with specified Entity classes. In the JPA 2.1 release, the `CriteriaBuilder` has been updated to include the methods `createCriteriaUpdate` and `createCriteriaDelete`, which will return the `CriteriaUpdate` or `CriteriaDelete` objects, respectively.

To make use of the `CriteriaBuilder`, you first need to obtain a `CriteriaBuilder` from the `EntityManager`. You can then use the `CriteriaBuilder` to obtain the `CriteriaUpdate` or `CriteriaDelete` object of your choosing. In the following lines of code, a `CriteriaUpdate` object is obtained for use with an `Employee` entity.

```
CriteriaBuilder builder = em.getCriteriaBuilder();
CriteriaUpdate<Employee> q = builder.createCriteriaUpdate(Employee.class);
```

Once obtained, the `CriteriaUpdate` can be used to build a query and set values, as desired, for making the necessary updates or deletions. In the following excerpt, the `CriteriaUpdate` object is used to update all `Employee` objects that have a status of `INACTIVE`, changing that status to `ACTIVE`.

```
Root<Employee> e = q.from(Employee.class);
q.set(e.get("status"), "ACTIVE")
        .where(builder.equal(e.get("status"), "INACTIVE"));
```

Let's break this down a bit to explain what exactly is going on. First, the query root is set by calling the `q.from` method and passing the entity class for which we wish to obtain the root, where `q` is the `CriteriaUpdate` object. Next, the `q.set` method is invoked, passing the `Path` to the `Employee status` attribute, along with the `ACTIVE` String. The `q.set` method is performing the bulk update. To further refine the query, a `WHERE` clause is added by adding a chained call to the `.where` method, and passing the `Employee` objects that have a status of `INACTIVE`. To see an entire example, please visit the `org.javaee7.chapter04.jsf.CriteriaUpdates` class. The entire Criteria update looks as follows:

```
CriteriaBuilder builder = em.getCriteriaBuilder();
CriteriaUpdate<Employee> q = builder.createCriteriaUpdate(Employee.class);
Root<Employee> e = q.from(Employee.class);
q.set(e.get("status"), "ACTIVE")
    .where(builder.equal(e.get("status"), "INACTIVE"));
```

Finally, to complete the transaction, you must create the `Query` object and then execute it using the following lines of code:

```
Query criteriaUpd = em.createQuery(q);
criteriaUpd.executeUpdate();
```

The complete code for the bulk update in this example resides within a method named `updateEmployeeStatusInactive`, which is listed below.

```
    ...
    @Resource
    private UserTransaction ut;
    ...
    public String updateEmployeeStatusInactive {
        try {
            CriteriaBuilder builder = em.getCriteriaBuilder();
            CriteriaUpdate<Employee> q = builder.createCriteriaUpdate(Employee.class);
            Root<Employee> e = q.from(Employee.class);
            q.set(e.get("status"), "INACTIVE")
                    .where(builder.equal(e.get("status"), "ACTIVE"));
            ut.begin();
            Query criteriaUpd = em.createQuery(q);
            criteriaUpd.executeUpdate();
            ut.commit();
        } catch (NotSupportedException | RollbackException | SystemException |
HeuristicMixedException | HeuristicRollbackException ex) {
            Logger.getLogger(CriteriaUpdates.class.getName()).log(Level.SEVERE, null, ex);
        }
        return null;
    }
    ...
```

The bulk deletion is very similar, except instead of using the `CriteriaBuilder` to obtain a `CriteriaUpdate` object, use it to obtain a `CriteriaDelete` object instead. To obtain a `CriteriaDelete` object, call the `CriteriaBuilder` `createCriteriaDelete` method, as follows.

```
CriteriaBuilder builder = em.getCriteriaBuilder();
CriteriaDelete<Employee> q = builder.createCriteriaDelete(Employee.class);
```

Once a `CriteriaDelete` object has been obtained, then the conditions for deletion need to be specified by filtering the results using a call (or chain of calls) to the `.where` method. When using the bulk delete, all objects that match the specified condition will be deleted. For example, the following lines of code demonstrate how to delete all `Employee` objects that have the status attribute equal to `INACTIVE`.

```
Root<Employee> e = q.from(Employee.class);
q.where(builder.equal(e.get("status"), "INACTIVE"));
```

The complete code for the bulk deletion in this example resides within a method named `deleteEmployeeOnStatus`, which is listed below.

```
...
@Resource
private UserTransaction ut;
...
public String deleteEmployeeOnStatus(String condition) {
        try {
            CriteriaBuilder builder = em.getCriteriaBuilder();
            CriteriaDelete<Employee> q = builder.createCriteriaDelete(Employee.class);
            Root<Employee> e = q.from(Employee.class);
            q.where(builder.equal(e.get("status"), condition));
            ut.begin();
```

```
            Query criteriaDel = em.createQuery(q);
            criteriaDel.executeUpdate();
            ut.commit();
        } catch (NotSupportedException | RollbackException | SystemException |
HeuristicMixedException | HeuristicRollbackException ex) {
            Logger.getLogger(CriteriaUpdates.class.getName()).log(Level.SEVERE, null, ex);
        }
        return null;
}
...
```

■ **Note** Both the `CriteriaUpdate` and `CriteriaDelete` examples that we've demonstrated can be made more type-safe by making use of the `MetaModel` API. For each entity class in a particular persistence unit, a metamodel class is created with a trailing underscore, along with the attributes that correspond to the persistent fields of the entity class. This metamodel can be used to managed entity classes and their persistent state and relationships. Therefore, instead of specifying an error prone String in the `Path` to obtain a particular attribute, you could specify the metamodel attribute instead, as follows: `e.get(Employee_.status)`

For more information on using the MetaModel API to create type-safe queries, please refer to the online documentation.

The Criteria API can be very detailed, and it is also very powerful. To learn more about the Criteria API, please see the documentation online at `http://docs.oracle.com/javaee/6/tutorial/doc/gjitv.html`.

Downcasting in the FROM and WHERE clauses

The act of downcasting is defined as the casting of a base type or class reference to one of its derived types or classes. The Java EE 7 platform introduces the concept of downcasting to JPA by providing the ability to obtain a reference to a subclass of a specified entity within a query. In other words, you can explicitly query one or more entities and retrieve the attributes from each of the entities as well as any attributes from entities that are subclasses of those that are explicitly declared in the query. In order to provide this ability, the new `TREAT` keyword has been added to JPA.

The use of the `TREAT` operator is supported for downcasting within path expressions in the `FROM` and `WHERE` clauses. The first argument to the `TREAT` operator should be a subtype of the target type, otherwise the path is considered to have no value, attributing nothing to the end result. The `TREAT` operator can filter on the specified types and subtypes, as well as perform a downcast.

The syntax for use of the `TREAT` operator is as follows:

```
SELECT b.attr1, b.attr2
FROM EntityA a JOIN TREAT(a.referenceToEntityB as EntityBType) b
```

In the above JPQL, the `TREAT` operator contains an attribute from the specified entity (`EntityA`) that relates to a subtype (`EntityB`). The downcast takes place when attributes from `EntityBType`, a subclass of `EntityB`, are specified within the `SELECT` clause. The `TREAT` operator performs the downcast and allows access to subtype entities. The following lines of code demonstrate this technique in action. This method is taken from the class `org.javaee7.session.ProductSession`, and it is used to obtain the `name` and `color` of `WidgetA` entities, which are a sub-type of the `Product` entity.

```
public List obtainProduct() {
        TypedQuery<Object[]> qry = em.createQuery("select a.name, a.color " +
                 "from Factory f JOIN TREAT(f.product as WidgetA) a", Object[].class);

        List data = new ArrayList();
         if (!qry.getResultList().isEmpty()) {
              List<Object[]> tdata = qry.getResultList();
             for (Object[] t : tdata) {
                 HashMap resultMap = new HashMap();
                 resultMap.put("name", t[0]);
                 resultMap.put("color", t[1]);
                 data.add(resultMap);
             }
         }
         return data;

    }
```

To better understand this concept, let's talk a bit about the underlying database. The `Factory` entity class is the object relational mapping for the `FACTORY` database table. The `Product` entity class is the object-relational mapping for the `PRODUCT` database table. Lastly, the `WidgetA` entity class is a sub-type of the `Product` entity, so the `PRODUCT` table is also utilized for storage of `WidgetA` object types. The overall structure of the `PRODUCT` database table is as follows:

```
CREATE TABLE PRODUCT (
ID              NUMERIC PRIMARY KEY,
NAME      VARCHAR(150),
PRODUCT_TYPE VARCHAR(50),
DESCRIPTION VARCHAR(2000),
COLOR           VARCHAR2(100),
FACTORY_ID NUMERIC);
```

The `Product` entity class contains a few annotations that help to facilitate the entity relationship. First, the `@Inheritence` annotation denotes that this entity is capable of `SINGLE_TABLE` inheritence. Next, the `@DiscriminatorColumn` annotation declares the database column of `PRODUCT_TYPE` as a discriminator column for the entity. This means that the `PRODUCT_TYPE` column is used to determine which entity sub-type object to utilize for working with the data.

```
package org.javaee7.entity;

import java.io.Serializable;
import javax.persistence.Column;
import javax.persistence.DiscriminatorColumn;
import javax.persistence.DiscriminatorType;
import javax.persistence.DiscriminatorValue;
import javax.persistence.Entity;
import javax.persistence.FetchType;
import javax.persistence.GeneratedValue;
import javax.persistence.GenerationType;
import javax.persistence.Id;
import javax.persistence.Inheritance;
import javax.persistence.InheritanceType;
import javax.persistence.JoinColumn;
```

```
import javax.persistence.ManyToOne;
import org.glassfish.internal.embedded.ScatteredArchive.Builder.type;

@Entity
@Inheritance(strategy=InheritanceType.SINGLE_TABLE)
@DiscriminatorColumn(name="PRODUCT_TYPE", discriminatorType=DiscriminatorType.STRING,length=20)
@DiscriminatorValue("A")
public abstract class Product implements Serializable {
    private static final long serialVersionUID = 1L;
    @Id
    @GeneratedValue(strategy = GenerationType.AUTO)
    private Long id;
    @Column(name="NAME")
    String name;
    @Column(name="DESCRIPTION")
    String description;
    @ManyToOne(fetch=FetchType.LAZY)
    @JoinColumn(name="FACTORY_ID", referencedColumnName="ID")
    private Factory factory;
    public Long getId() {
        return id;
    }

    public void setId(Long id) {
        this.id = id;
    }

    @Override
    public int hashCode() {
        int hash = 0;
        hash += (getId() != null ? getId().hashCode() : 0);
        return hash;
    }

    @Override
    public boolean equals(Object object) {
        // TODO: Warning - this method won't work in the case the id fields are not set
        if (!(object instanceof Product)) {
            return false;
        }
        Product other = (Product) object;
        if ((this.getId() == null && other.getId() != null) || (this.getId() != null && !this.
id.equals(other.id))) {
            return false;
        }
        return true;
    }

    @Override
    public String toString() {
        return "org.javaee7.entity.Factory[ id=" + getId() + " ]";
    }
```

```
    /**
     * @return the name
     */
    public String getName() {
        return name;
    }

    /**
     * @param name the name to set
     */
    public void setName(String name) {
        this.name = name;
    }

    /**
     * @return the description
     */
    public String getDescription() {
        return description;
    }

    /**
     * @param description the description to set
     */
    public void setDescription(String description) {
        this.description = description;
    }

    /**
     * @return the factory
     */
    public Factory getFactory() {
        return factory;
    }

    /**
     * @param factory the factory to set
     */
    public void setFactory(Factory factory) {
        this.factory = factory;
    }

}
```

The WidgetA entity class is a sub-class of Product, and therefore all attributes that are part of the Product entity can be utilized within the WidgetA entity. This entity class also defines the color attribute, which maps to the column within the PRODUCT database table of the same name. The @DiscriminatorValue annotation denotes the value of the PRODUCT_TYPE database column for this type of entity. Since it is a sub-class of Product, the @DiscriminatorValue helps to determine the "category" for this relation.

```
package org.javaee7.entity;

import java.io.Serializable;
import javax.persistence.Column;
import javax.persistence.DiscriminatorValue;
import javax.persistence.Entity;

/**
 *
 * @author Juneau
 */
@Entity
@DiscriminatorValue("A")
public class WidgetA extends Product implements Serializable {

    @Column(name="COLOR")
    private String color;

    public WidgetA(){

    }


    /**
     * @return the color
     */
    public String getColor() {
        return color;
    }

    /**
     * @param color the color to set
     */
    public void setColor(String color) {
        this.color = color;
    }


}
```

The following JSF view excerpt demonstrates how to display the results of the downcast. The `dataTable` references `productBean.productType()` for the value, which initiates the invocation of the `obtainProduct` method within the `ProductSession` EJB.

```
...
        <h:dataTable var="product" border="1" value="#{productBean.productType()}">
            <h:column>
                <f:facet name="header">
                    Product Name
                </f:facet>
                <h:outputText value="#{product.name}"/>
            </h:column>
```

```
            <h:column>
                <f:facet name="header">
                    Product Color
                </f:facet>
                <h:outputText value="#{product.color}"/>
            </h:column>

        </h:dataTable>
...
```

As mentioned previously, the TREAT operator can also be used within the WHERE clause in order to filter a query based upon subtype attribute values. In the following example, the query will return all employees that are from the IT department and have a status of ACTIVE. The assumption is that the ItEmployee entity is a subtype of the Employee entity.

```
SELECT e FROM Employee
WHERE TREAT(e as ItEmployee).status = "ACTIVE";
```

Downcasting support adds yet another feature to the scope of JPA, making it even more flexible for developers to use. This technique will make it easier to obtain values from related entities or subtypes, without the need to issue an extra query.

Schema Generation

Schema generation refers to the creation of underlying database tables, views, constraints, and other database artifacts. Prior to the Java EE 7 release, schema generation has only been automated via the use of an IDE such as Netbeans or Eclipse. However, the EE 7 release takes a step towards breaking this dependency on an IDE by allowing schema generation to become automated by configuring an appropriate persistence.xml for an application.

Schema generation can be applied directly to the database or it can generate SQL scripts that can be manually applied to the database (or both), depending upon which options are configured for the application. Schema generation may occur prior to application deployment, or when an EntityManagerFactory is created as part of the application deployment and initialization. To perform schema generation, the container may call the PersistenceProvider generateSchema method separate from and/or prior to the entity manager factory for the persistence unit. The createContainerEntityManagerFactory call can accept additional information to cause generation of schema constructs to occur as part of the entity manager factory creation or initialization process. Furthermore, this information can determine whether the database is manipulated directly or if SQL scripts are created, or both.

■ **Note** Schema generation is also available outside of a managed container (eg., application server) in Java SE environments. To perform schema generation in an SE environment, the application may call the Persistence generateSchema method separately from and/or prior to the creation of the entity manager factory or may pass information to the createEntityManagerFactory method to cause schema generation to occur as part of the entity manager factory creation.

Schema generation is determined by the object/relational metadata of the persistence.xml file unless custom scripts are provided for the generation. The application developer can package scripts as part of the persistence unit or can supply URLs to the location of the scripts for schema generation. The execution of such scripts can be carried out by the container itself, or the container may direct the persistence provider to take care of script execution.

Table 4-1 lists the different `persistence.xml` or `EntityManagerFactory` properties that are used to configure schema generation. These properties are passed as a `Map` argument from the container to the `PersistenceProvider` `generateSchema` method, or the `createContainerEntityManagerFactory` method. Each of the properties resides within the `javax.persistence` package, and therefore, should be prefixed with `javax.persistence`.

Table 4-1. *Schema Generation Properties*

Property	Purpose
`schema-generation.create-script-source`	Name of script that is packaged as part of application, or a string corresponding to file URL string that designates a script.
`schema-generation.drop-script-source`	Name of script that is packaged as part of application, or a string corresponding to file URL string that designates a script
`sql-load-script-source`	Name of script that is packaged as part of application, or a string corresponding to file URL string that designates a script
`schema-generation.database.action`	Controls action to be taken by persistence provider with regard to database access **Values**: "none," "create," "drop-and-create," "drop"
`schema-generation.scripts.action`	Controls action to be taken by persistence provider with regard to script generation **Values**: "none," "create," "drop-and-create," "drop"
`schema-generation.create-source`	Specifies whether the creation of database artifacts should occur on the basis of the ORM metadata, DDL script, or both **Values**: "metadata," "script," "metadata-then-script," "script-then-metadata"
`schema-generation.drop-source`	Specifies whether the dropping of database artifacts should occur on the basis of ORM metadata, DDL script, or both **Values**: "metadata," "script," "metadata-then-script," "script-then-metadata"
`schema-generation.scripts.create-target`	When generating scripts, these properties specify the
`schema-generation.scripts.drop-target`	the target locations in String format.

The schema generation is controlled by utilization of the properties that are listed in Table 4-1 within the `persistence.xml`. The following example of `persistence.xml` demonstrates how to have database artifacts and scripts generated for creation of both.

```
<?xml version="1.0" encoding="UTF-8"?>
<persistence version="2.0" xmlns="http://java.sun.com/xml/ns/persistence" xmlns:xsi="
http://www.w3.org/2001/XMLSchema-instance" xsi:schemaLocation="http://java.sun.com/xml/ns/
persistence http://java.sun.com/xml/ns/persistence/persistence_2_0.xsd">
  <persistence-unit name="IntroToJavaEE7PU" transaction-type="JTA">
    <provider>org.eclipse.persistence.jpa.PersistenceProvider</provider>
    <jta-data-source>jdbc/DerbyConnection</jta-data-source>
    <exclude-unlisted-classes>false</exclude-unlisted-classes>
    <properties>
       <properties>
            <property name="javax.persistence.schema-generation.database.action" value="create"/>
            <property name="javax.persistence.schema-generation.scripts.action" value="create"/>
```

```
            <property name="javax.persistence.schema-generation.scripts.create-target"
value="/ddl-scripts/create-trarget-script.ddl"/>
            <property name="eclipselink.deploy-on-startup" value="true"/>
        </properties>
    </properties>
  </persistence-unit>
</persistence>
```

Programmatically, schema generation is determined by a series of annotations that are placed in entity classes. The @Table annotation denotes an entity mapping to an underlying database table. By default, a table is generated for each top-level entity and includes columns based upon the specified attributes for that entity. Therefore, the @Column and @JoinColumn annotations are used for generating such columns for a table. Column ordering is not determined based upon the ordering of @Column or @JoinColumn annotations. If column ordering is important then a Data Definition Language (DDL) script must be supplied for generation of the table. Other annotations and annotation attributes, such as @Id, also play important roles in schema generation. Table 4-2 lists the different annotations that are involved in schema generation, along with a brief description and the elements that can be populated for further control over the generated schema.

Table 4-2. *Schema Generation Annotations*

Annotation	Description	Elements
@Table	Used for generating tables. By default, the table name is generated from the entity name, and the entity name is defaulted from the class name.	
@SecondaryTable	A secondary table is created to partition the mapping of entity state across multiple tables.	
@CollectionTable	A colletion table is created for mapping of an element collection. The Column, AttributeOverride, and AssociationOverride annotations may be used to override CollectionTable mappings.	
@JoinTable	By default, join tables are created for the mapping of many-to-many relationships and unidirectional one-to-many relationships.	
@TableGenerator	Table generator tables are used to store generated primary key values.	
@Column	Determines the name and configuration for a column within a table.	unique nullable columnDefinition table length precision scale name

(*continued*)

Table 4-2. (*continued*)

Annotation	Description	Elements
`@MapKeyColumn`	The MapKeyColumn annotation specifies the mapping of a key column of a map when the key is of basic type.	name unique nullable columnDefinition table length precision scale
`@Enumerated,` `@MapKeyEnumerated`	Control whether string- or integer-valued columns are generated for basic attributes of enumerated types and therefore impact the default column mapping of these types.	
`@Temporal,` `@MapKeyTemporal`	Control whether date-, time-, or timestamp-value columns are generated for basic attributes of temporal types, and therefore impact the default column mappings for these types.	
`@Lob`	Specifies that a persistent attribute is to be persisted to a database large object type.	
`@OrderColumn`	Specifies the generation of a column that is used to maintain the persistent ordering of a list that is represented in an element collection, one-to-many, or many-to-many relationship.	name nullable columnDefinition
`@DiscriminatorColumn`	A discriminator column is generated for the SINGLE_TABLE mapping strategy and may optionally be generated by the provider for use with the JOINED inheritance strategy.	
`@Version`	Specifies the generation of a column to serve as an entity's optimistic lock.	
`@Id`	Specifies attributes whose database columns correspond to a primary key. Use of the Id annotation results in the creation of a primary key consisting of the corresponding column or columns.	
`@EmbeddedId`	Specifies an embedded attribute whose corresponding columns correspond to a database primary key. Use of the EmbeddedId annotation results in the creation of a primary key consisting of the corresponding columns.	
`@GeneratedValue`	Indicates a primary key whose value is to be generated by the provider. If a strategy is indicated, the provider must use it if it is supported by the target database.	
`@JoinColumn`	The JoinColumn annotation is typically used in specifying a foreign key mapping. In general, the foreign key definitions created will be provider-dependent and database-dependent. Applications that are sensitive to the exact mapping that is used should use the foreignKey element of the JoinColumn annotation or include DDL files that specify how the database schemas are to be generated.	name referencedColumnName unique nullable columnDefinition table foreignKey

(*continued*)

Table 4-2. (*continued*)

Annotation	Description	Elements
`@MapKeyJoinColumn`	Specify foreign key mappings to entities that are map keys in map-valued element collections or relationships. In general, the foreign key definitions created should be expected to be provider-dependent and database-dependent. Applications that are sensitive to the exact mapping that is used should use the foreignKey element of the MapKeyJoinColumn annotation or include DDL files that specify how the database schemas are to be generated.	name referencedColumnName unique nullable columnDefinition table foreignKey
`@PrimaryJoinKeyColumn`	Specifies that a primary key column is to be used as a foreign key. This annotation is used in the specification of the JOINED mapping strategy and for joining a secondary table to a primary table in a OneToOne relationship mapping. In general, the foreign key definitions created should be expected to be provider-dependent and database-dependent. Applications that are sensitive to the exact mapping that is used should use the foreignKey element of the PrimaryKeyJoinColumn annotation or include DDL files that specify how the database schemas are to be generated.	
`@ForeignKey`	Used within the JoinColumn, JoinColumns, MapKeyJoinColumn, MapKeyJoinColumns, PrimaryKeyJoinColumn, and PrimaryKeyJoinColumns annotations to specify or override a foreign keyconstraint.	
`@SequenceGenerator`	Creates a database sequence to be used for Id generation. The use of generators is limited to those databases that support them.	
`@Index`	Generates an index consisting of the specified columns. The ordering of the names in the columnList element specified in the Index annotation must be observed by the provider when creating the index.	
`@UniqueConstraint`	Generates a unique constraint for the given table. Databases typically implement unique constraints by creating unique indexes. The ordering of the columnNames specified in the UniqueConstraint annotation must be observed by the provider when creating the constraint.	

As per Table 4-2, there are a couple of new annotations that have been created specifically to facilitate schema generation. The new annotations are `@Index` and `@ForeignKey`, where `@Index` is responsible for generating an index of the specified columns. `@ForeignKey` is used to define a foreign key on a table.

Support for Database Stored Procedures

In some applications, database stored procedures are used to encapsulate logic for performing database-specific transactions. Many times, these database stored procedures need to be invoked from an application. Historically, the only way to work with database-stored procedures from JPA was to utilize a native query. To create a native query, a SQL string needs to be created, which can then be passed to the EntityManager createNativeQuery method. The returned Query object can then be used to invoke the stored procedure.

Suppose that there was a database procedure named CREATE_EMP, and it accepted three arguments: first, last and status. You could invoke the CREATE_EMP procedure by calling it via a native SQL query. The following method, named createEmpOld, accepts a first, last, and status as arguments, and passes them to the underlying database procedure and executes it.

```
public void createEmpOld(String first,
                         String last,
                         String status) {

        Query qry = em.createNativeQuery("select CREATE_EMP(:first, :last, :status) from dual")
                .setParameter("first", first)
                .setParameter("last", last)
                .setParameter("status", status);
        qry.executeUpdate();


    }
```

Using this technique, the EntityManager's createNativeQuery method is called, and a SQL String that performs a SELECT on the stored procedure is passed to the method. In SQL, performing a SELECT on a stored procedure will cause the procedure to be executed. Notice that the DUAL table is being referenced in the SQL. The DUAL is a dummy table in Oracle that can be used when you need to apply SELECT statements to different database constructs, such as a stored procedure. One could also issue the following SQL string to do the same thing.

```
"begin create_emp(:first, :last, :status); end; "
OR
"exec create_emp(:first, :last, :status) ";
```

Execution of native SQL is an acceptable solution for invoking stored procedures that have no return values, or when you only have a limited number of SQL statements to maintain. However, in most enterprise situations that require an application with multiple stored procedure calls or calls that require a return value, the better technique is to utilize the new @NamedStoredProcedureQuery annotation within an entity class to specify the name and parameters of a stored procedure.

```
@NamedStoredProcedureQuery(name="createEmp", procedureName="CREATE_EMP")
```

Execution of the stored procedure occurs within the EJB by calling the EntityManager object's createNamedStoredProcedureQuery method, and passing the name that was specified within the @NamedStoredProcedureQuery annotation. The following method, which resides within the org.javaee7.jpa.session.EmployeeSession, can be used to invoke the underlying database's CREATE_EMP procedure.

```
public boolean createEmp(String firstName, String lastName, String status){
        boolean result = false;
        System.out.println("executing the stored procedure");
        StoredProcedureQuery qry = em.createNamedStoredProcedureQuery("createEmp");
```

```
        qry.registerStoredProcedureParameter(1, String.class, ParameterMode.IN);
        qry.setParameter(1, firstName);
        qry.registerStoredProcedureParameter(2, String.class, ParameterMode.IN);
        qry.setParameter(2,lastName);
        qry.registerStoredProcedureParameter(3, String.class, ParameterMode.IN);
        qry.setParameter(3, status);

        try {
            qry.execute();
            String response = qry.getOutputParameterValue(1).toString();
            System.out.println("stored procedure executed..." + response);
        } catch (Exception ex) {
            System.out.println(ex);
        }
        return result;
    }
```

Using a native query works fine for executing stored procedures, but it can become more difficult since it must return a cursor object or read an OUT parameter when attempting to return values from a stored procedure. It can also become a maintenance nightmare if too many native SQL Strings are embedded throughout an application's codebase. It is best to use JPQL or the Critiera API when working with JPA.

Let's dig a bit deeper into the @NamedStoredProcedureQuery annotation. Metadata or annotations can be used to declare stored procedures and their associated parameters. The @NamedStoredProcedureQuery can be specified within an entity class to assign a name to a particular stored procedure. The @NamedStoredProcedureQuery accepts the following parameters:

- name: The String-based name that will be used to call the stored procedure
- procedureName: The name of the underlying stored procedure
- resultClass: The entity object that can be used to return the stored procedure result
- resultSetMapping: SqlResultSetMapping if needed
- returnsResultSet: boolean value indicating whether or not a resultSet is returned
- parameters: zero or more @StoredProcedureParameter annotations, one for each of the parameters accepted by the stored procedure.

In the example, the CREATE_EMP stored procedure is configured using an @NamedStoredProcedureQuery annotation. Since there are three parameters that are accepted by the stored procedure, all three of them must be passed to the stored procedure within the EJB stored procedure call. Execution of a named stored procedure is much like the execution of a named query. A StoredProcedureQuery object is obtained by calling the EntityManager's createStoredProcedureQuery method, passing the name specified for the @NamedStoredProcedureQuery annotation. Parameter values are set by calling both the Query object's registerStoredProcedureParameter method, and the setParameter method against the StoredProcedureQuery, and passing the name of the parameter along with the value to be substituted. The registerStoredProcedureParameter method accepts the parameter position as the first argument, the parameter type as the second, and the type of ParameterMode as the third. The subsequent call to setParameter registers the parameter value with the corresponding parameter position. Finally, to invoke the stored procedure, call the StoredProcedureQuery object's execute method.

A dynamic stored procedure can also be constructed using the StoredProcedureQuery API, rather than using a named stored procedure. To construct a StoredProcedureQuery object dynamically, pass the name of the underlying database stored procedure to the EntityManager's createStoredProcedureQuery method. Parameters for a dynamic stored procedure invocation must be registered using the registerStoredProcedureParameter method, rather than the StoredProcedureQuery interface. The following code shows how to call the CREATE_EMP stored procedure dynamically:

```
StoredProcedureQuery qry = em.createStoredProcedureQuery("CREATE_EMP");
qry.registerStoredProcedureParameter("FIRSTNAME", firstName);
qry.registerStoredProcedureParameter("LASTNAME", lastName);
qry.registerStoredProcedureParameter("STATUS", status);
qry.executeUpdate();
```

■ **Note** Utiliztion of database stored procedures can be beneficial because they allow for separation between the compiled Java code and the database procedure. That is, if a database stored procedure implementation needs to change, it can be adjusted without redeploying the Java application, so long as the procedure name or number of parameters stays the same.

Synchronization of Persistence Contexts

By default, persistence contexts are synchronized, meaning that the context is automatically joined to the current JTA transaction, and that any updates that are made are propagated accordingly. In JPA 2.1, a persistence context can be specified as unsynchronized, meaning that it be not enlisted in any JTA transaction unless explicitly joined to a transaction by the application. One may wish to create an entity manager as unsynchronized if an application needed to perform work against Entity classes, without having the changes flushed to the database until the work was complete. To create an unsynchronized persistence context, specify a synchronization attribute of type SynchronizationType.UNSYNCHRONIZED. The following demonstrates how to create such a persistence context:

```
@PersistenceContext(synchronization=SynchronizationType.UNSYNCHRONIZED) EntityManager em;
```

To join an unsynchronized persistence context to a JTA transaction, invoke the EntityManager joinTransaction method. After a persistence context has been joined to a transaction, it remains enlisted until a transaction either commits or is rolled back. An application can make use of an unsynchronized persistence context's persist, remove, merge, and refresh entity lifecycle operations without being joined to a JTA transaction. This makes it possible to perform work against Entities without affecting the underlying data store. If an unsynchronized persistence context has had lifecycle operations invoked, it can later flush those operations to a database by being joined to a transaction.

Entity Listeners using CDI

It is possible to create a listener for an entity class; which handle lifecycle events. In JPA 2.1, entity listeners became even more powerful via the support of Contexts and Dependency Injection (CDI). An entity listener can be registered with an entity class, and that listener can have resources injected into it via CDI. Note that resources are not injected via the Java EE container, so you can only inject resources available via CDI.

An entity listener class must have a public, no argument constructor. The entity listener class can optionally define lifecycle callback methods annotated with the PostConstruct and PreDestroy methods. The following entity listener class, org.javaee7.entity.listener.EmployeeEntityListener, is registered on the org.javaee7.entity.Employee entity. It demonstrates the new functionality by injecting a mail session into the listener.

```
public class EmployeeEntityListener {

    @Resource(name="jndi/AcmeMail")
    javax.mail.Session mailSession;

    @PrePersist
    public void prePersist(Employee employee){
        System.out.println("The following Employee enity is about to be persisted: "
+ employee.getLast());
        // use the mail session
    }

}
```

To register this entity listener on the entity, utilize the @EntityListeners annotation on the entity itself, as follows:

```
@Entity
@Table(name = "EMPLOYEE")
@EntityListeners(EmployeeEntityListener.class)
public class Employee implements Serializable {
...
}
```

Summary

Object-relational mapping is a natural way of mapping database tables to Java objects. Coding against Java objects, rather than writing standard SQL to work with databases, can be beneficial for a number of reasons. Not only does it make an application easier to maintain, but it also makes it less error prone. The JPA 2.1 release includes some incremental enhancements that help to make it even more productive and enable even more features, such as the ability to utilize stored database procedures more easily. Furthermore, schema management has never been easier than it is now with the new JPA schema generation. Although the JPA 2.1 release is incremental, it brings forth many improvements that help to solidify object-oriented development for Java Enterprise applications.

CHAPTER 5

Business Logic Using EJB

The EJB 3.2 specification has been included as part of the Java EE 7 release, and with it will come more enhancements to further solidify the Java enterprise platform. Although the EJB 3.2 release does not include any radical redesigns, it helps improve developer productivity and flexibility by adding a few new features and bringing the specification into alignment with other EE 7 technology updates. The updates include minor enhancements to the transactional life cycle, bean passivation, timers, and more. New features have been added to EJB Lite, a subset of features for those who do not need the entire EJB stack. Better alignment with the Java Message Service (JMS) has also been added, making it even easier to configure message-driven beans (MDBs). Lastly, a handful of features that are rarely used, or induce overhead, have been pruned from the release to make it even easier to use. This chapter will focus on each area of the updates and show examples of how to utilize the latest features.

General Updates and Improvements

Many of the changes made in the EJB specification for 3.2 are considered incremental updates and improvements. That said, these features are a nice addition and will certainly come in handy in certain situations. This section will cover these enhancements.

Transaction Life-Cycle Callbacks in Session Beans

Session beans have callback methods that are invoked when certain stages of a bean's life cycle occur. For instance, a method can be registered within a session bean via annotation to invoke after the bean is constructed (`@PostConstruct`), before it is destroyed (`@PreDestroy`), and so on. Sometimes it makes sense to start a new transaction when one of these events occurs. It is possible to specify the transactional status of an annotated life-cycle callback method within a session bean, when using container-managed transactions. In the following excerpt from `org.javaee7.jpa.session.AcmeFacade`, a new transaction is started upon creation of the bean and also upon destruction of the bean:

```
@Stateful
public class AcmeFacade {

    @PersistenceContext(unitName = "IntroToJavaEE7PU", type = PersistenceContextType.EXTENDED)
    private EntityManager em;

    @TransactionAttribute(TransactionAttributeType.REQUIRES_NEW)
    @PostConstruct
    public void init() {
        System.out.println("The Acme Bean has been created");
    }
```

```
    @TransactionAttribute(TransactionAttributeType.REQUIRES_NEW)
    @PreDestroy
    public void destroy() {
        System.out.println("The Acme Bean is being destroyed...");
        em.flush();
    }
}
```

Note that the @TransactionAttribute annotation is used to specify the transaction type of the callback method, if needed. The annotation accepts a transaction type as per the values listed in Table 5-1.

Table 5-1. *Container-Managed Transaction Demarcation*

Attribute	Description
MANDATORY	The container must invoke an enterprise bean method whose transaction is set to this attribute in the client's transaction context. The client is required to call with a transaction context.
REQUIRED	The container must invoke an enterprise bean method whose transaction is set to this attribute value with an unspecified transaction context.
REQUIRES_NEW	The container must invoke an enterprise bean method whose transaction is set to this attribute value with a new transaction context.
SUPPORTS	If the client calls with a transaction context, then the container treats it as REQUIRED. If the client calls without a transaction context, the container treats it as NOT_SUPPORTED.
NOT_SUPPORTED	The container invokes an enterprise bean method whose transaction attribute is set to this value with an unspecified transaction context.
NEVER	The container invokes an enterprise bean method whose transaction is set to this value without a transaction context defined by the EJB specification.

By default, the life-cycle callback methods are not transactional in order to maintain backward compatibility. By annotating the callback method with the @TransactionAttribute and the preferred demarcation type, the callback method has opted in to be transactional.

To see the complete example of a transactional life-cycle callback, deploy the demo application for this book and look at the Chapter 5 transactional examples. When you visit the web page for the example, the AcmeFacade session bean is initialized, and the message is printed to the system log.

Passivation Made Optional

When a stateful session bean has been inactive for a period of time, the container may choose to passivate the bean in an effort to conserve memory and resources. Typically, the EJB container will passivate stateful session beans using a least recently used algorithm. When passivation occurs, the bean is moved to secondary storage and removed from memory. Prior to the passivation of a stateful session bean, any methods annotated with @PrePassivate will be invoked. When a stateful session bean that has been passivated needs to be made active again, the EJB container activates the bean, then calls any methods annotated with @PostActivate, and finally moves the bean to the ready stage. In EJB 3.2, stateful session beans can opt out of passivation so that they will remain in memory instead of being transferred to secondary storage if inactive. This may be helpful in situations where a bean needs to remain active for application processes or where the bean contains a nonserializable field, since these fields cannot be passivated and are made null upon passivation.

To opt out of passivation, set the passivationCapable attribute of the @Stateful annotation to false, as demonstrated in the following excerpt:

```
@Stateful(passivationCapable=false)
public class AcmeFacade {
    ...
}
```

Explicitly Denoting Local and Remote Business Interfaces

The release of EJB 3.0 greatly simplified development with EJBs because it introduced the no-interface view for making local business interfaces optional. The no-interface view automatically exposes all public methods of a bean to the caller. By default, a no-interface view is automatically exposed by any session bean that does not include an implements clause and has no local or remote client views defined. The EJB 3.2 release aims to provide further granularity for those situations where local and remote interfaces need to be explicitly specified.

A business interface cannot be made both the local and remote business interfaces for a bean. Therefore, a new API has been developed to specify whether a business interface is intended as local or remote. The following rules pertain to business interfaces implemented by enterprise bean classes:

- The java.io.Serializable interface, the java.io.Externalizable interface, and interfaces defined by the javax.ejb package are always excluded when the determination of local or remote business interfaces are declared for a bean.
- If a bean class contains the @Remote annotation, then all implemented interfaces are assumed to be remote.
- If a bean class contains no annotation or if the @Local annotation is specified, then all implemented interfaces are assumed to be local.
- Any business interface that is explicitly defined for a bean that contains the no-interface view must be designated as @Local.
- Any business interface must be explicitly designated as local or remote if the bean class explicitly specifies the @Local or @Remote annotation with a nonempty value.
- Any business interface must be explicitly designated as local or remote if the deployment descriptor specifies as such.

Let's break down these rules a bit so that they are easier to understand. First, if an EJB exposes local interfaces, then there is no need to explicitly denote a bean as such. For instance, the following bean contains a local interface, although it is not explicitly denoted:

```
@Stateless
public class AcmeSession implements interfaceA {
    ...
}
public interfaceA { ... }
```

If a bean class is annotated with @Remote, then any interfaces that it implements are assumed to be remote. For instance, the following bean class implements two interfaces, and both are assumed to be remote although they do not contain any annotation to indicate as such:

```
@Remote
@Stateless
public class AcmeSession implements interfaceA, interfaceB {
    ...
}
```

If a bean class contains the @Local annotation, then any interfaces that it implements are assumed to be local. For instance, the following bean class implements two interfaces, and both are assumed to be local although they do not contain any annotation to indicate as such:

```
@Local
@Stateless
public class AcmeSession implements interfaceA, interfaceB {
    ...
}
```

If a bean class contains the @Local or @Remote annotation and specifies an interface name within the annotation, then the specified interface is designated the same designation as the annotated bean. For instance, the following bean is annotated to include a local business interface, and the name of the interface is specified in the annotation, thereby making the interface local:

```
@Local(interfaceA.class)
@Stateless
public class AcmeSession implements interfaceA {
    ...
}
```

These new designation rules make it easier to designate and determine the type of business interface that is implemented by a bean.

Extended TimerService API

The TimerService API has been extended to include a new convenience method that allows you to obtain information about all active timers. The TimerService API is a facility that allows time-based method invocations to occur within a session bean. Using the API, it is possible to create scheduled tasks, programmatically timed tasks, and automated tasks based upon a specified time and/or date. In this section, you'll take a brief look at creating a couple of timers, and then you will see how to utilize the newly added getAllTimers method to return all active timers within the same bean.

Utilize dependency injection to obtain an instance of the TimerService for use within your bean. A TimerService can be an injected using the @Resource annotation, as follows:

```
@Resource
TimerService timerService;
```

As mentioned, you can create different types of timers, depending upon the use case. To programmatically create a timer, use the TimerService API to return the type of timer desired. Table 5-2 describes the types of programmatic timers that can be created by the TimerService API .

Table 5-2. Programmatic TimerService Methods for Timer Creation

Method	Description
`createCalendarTimer`	Creates a calendar timer based upon the input schedule expression.
`createIntervalTimer`	Creates an interval timer whose first expiration occurs at a given point in time or duration and whose subsequent expirations occur after a specified interval.
`createSingleActionTimer`	Creates a single-action timer that expires after a specified period of time or duration.
`createTimer`	Creates a timer whose type depends upon the parameters that are passed to the `createTimer` method.

The following excerpt, taken from `org.javaee7.jpa.session.AcmeTimerFacade`, demonstrates how to create a programmatic timer that will expire in 6,000 milliseconds:

```
public String createProgrammaticTimer() {
    long duration = 6000;
    Timer timer = timerService.createTimer(duration, "Created new programmatic timer");
    return "TimerExamples";  // Used for Navigation
}
```

When creating a programmatic timer, such as demonstrated in the previous example, the method within the bean that is annotated with `@Timeout` will be invoked when the programmatic timer expires and then again upon each duration expiration. The following code demonstrates an example of one such method that will be invoked when a bean's programmatic timer expires:

```
@Timeout
    public void timeout(Timer timer){
        System.out.println("The timer was just invoked...");
    }
```

To schedule a timer based upon a given calendar time and date, annotate the session bean method that you want to invoke with the `@Schedule` annotation, which was introduced in EJB 3.1. The following method demonstrates a timer that will expire every minute:

```
@Schedule(minute="*, hour="*")
    public void scheduledTimerExample(){
            System.out.println("This timer will go off every minute");
    }
```

In the previous example, the `@Schedule` annotation accepts two attributes: minute and hour. In the example, the minute value is indicated by the wildcard character *, meaning that the timer is scheduled to go off every hour of every minute. Suppose that you have each of these timers (and possibly more) specified within a given session bean. At any given point it may make sense to check which timers are active. You can do so by calling the `TimerService.getAllTimers` method, which returns a `Collection` of `Timer` instances. The following method demonstrates how to obtain all the active timers and build a `String` that provides the current information for each of them:

```
public String getTimerInfo(){
    Collection<Timer> timers = timerService.getAllTimers();
    StringBuffer sb = new StringBuffer();
    int x = 0;
```

```
    for (Timer timer:timers){
        sb.append("Time Remaining on timer #" + x );
        sb.append(" " + timer.getTimeRemaining());
        sb.append("    ");
        x++;
    }
    timerInfo = sb.toString();
    return timerInfo;
}
```

JMS Alignment

Message-driven beans (MDBs) are Enterprise JavaBeans that are utilized for processing messages in an asynchronous manner. Most often MDBs are JMS message listeners, receiving messages and processing accordingly. In brief, a message-driven bean is created by annotating a bean with the @MessageDriven annotation and implementing the MessageListener interface. When a message is received in the container queue, the container invokes the bean's onMessage method, which contains the business logic that is responsible for processing the message accordingly. The following class, org.javaee7.session.AcmeMessageDrivenBean, demonstrates a simple MDB implementation:

```
@MessageDriven(mappedName = "jms/Queue", activationConfig = {
    @ActivationConfigProperty(propertyName = "destinationType", propertyValue = "javax.jms.Queue")
})
public class AcmeMessageDrivenBean implements MessageListener {

    public AcmeMessageDrivenBean() {
    }

    @Override
    public void onMessage(Message message) {
        System.out.println("The following message has been received: " + message);
    }
}
```

In this example, when a message is sent to the bean, the onMessage method is invoked, which prints a message to the system log. As shown in the example, bean providers may provide special configurations for MDBs to the deployers, such as information regarding message selectors, acknowledgment modes, and so on, by means of the activationConfig element of the @MessageDriven annotation. The EJB 3.2 release provides a standard list of activationConfig properties for JMS 2.0 alignment. Table 5-3 describes the new properties.

Table 5-3. JMS 2.0 Aligned activationConfig Properties

Property	Description
destinationLookup	Provides advice to the deployer regarding whether the message-driven bean is intended to be associated with a Queue or Topic. Values for this property are javax.jms.Queue and javax.jms.Topic.
connectionFactoryLookup	Specifies the lookup name of an administratively defined ConnectionFactory object that will be used for the connection to the JMS provider from which a message-driven bean will send JMS messages.
clientId	Specifies the client identifier that will be used for the connection to the JMS provider from which a message-driven bean will send JMS messages.
subscriptionName	If the message-driven bean is intended to be used with a topic, then the bean provider can specify the name of a durable subscription with this property and set the subscriptionDurability property to Durable.
shareSubscriptions	This property is to be used only when a message-driven bean is deployed to a clustered application server, and the value for this property can be either true or false. A value of true means that the same durable subscription name or nondurable subscription will be used for each instance in the cluster. A value of false means that a different durable subscription name or nondurable subscription will be used for each instance in the cluster.

Embeddable EJBContainer Now Autocloseable

The embeddable EJBContainer enables the use of EJBs within Java SE applications. The embeddable container cannot be used within a Java EE environment because it allows both the client-side code and EJBs to reside within the same JVM container. That said, it is noteworthy that the embeddable EJBContainer has been updated in EJB 3.2 in order to bring it inline with more current Java 7 coding techniques.

When using an EJBContainer, it is important to close it when finished. To do so, a client can directly invoke the container's close method. As of EJB 3.2, the close method can also be invoked via the try-with-resources statement because the EJBContainer now implements the java.lang.AutoCloseable interface.

New Features in EJB Lite

EJB Lite was introduced in the 3.1 release, and it allows developers to utilize a subset of EJB functionality, without the requirement to package the entire API. The EJB 3.2 release includes a couple of new features for the EJB Lite configuration. One of those features is asynchronous session bean invocation. In EJB 3.1, this ability was added to session beans; previously the only way to asynchronously invoke a method within an enterprise bean was to utilize a message-driven bean. When asynchronous session bean invocation was introduced, it was only made part of the EJB full implementation. However, it was later determined that those using EJB Lite would also benefit from the feature.

Although asynchronous session bean invocation has been around a while, I will go through a brief example for those who are not yet familiar with the topic. To mark an EJB method as asynchronous, simply annotate the method with @Asynchronous. When a method that is annotated with @Asynchronous is invoked, the call will return immediately, allowing other work to be performed while the method invocation runs in the background. The container ensures that the method is executed to completion. It is most common to see asynchronous methods with a void return type; however, it is certainly possible to return a value using a return type of java.util.concurrent.Future<V>, where V represents the type of the asynchronous return, an AsyncResult<V> object.

Let's take a look at an asynchronous method that includes a void return type. The following method has been excerpted from the org.javaee7.jpa.session.JobsSession class, and the asynchronous task involves querying the Jobs entity and returning all results:

```
@Asynchronous
    public void retrieveJobs(){
        Query qry = em.createQuery("select j from Jobs j");
        List<Jobs> jobs = qry.getResultList();

        for (Jobs job:jobs){
            System.out.println(job.getTitle());
        }
    }
```

The following is an example of an asynchronous method that returns a result. The same method that was used in the previous example has been altered to return a Boolean value to indicate whether any Jobs entities exist.

```
@Asynchronous
    public Future<Boolean> obtainJobListing(){
        Query qry = em.createQuery("select j from Jobs j");
        List<Jobs> jobs = qry.getResultList();
        if(jobs.size() > 0){
            this.jobList = jobs;
            return new AsyncResult<Boolean>(true);
        } else {
            return new AsyncResult<Boolean>(false);
        }
    }
```

Another new feature for EJB Lite is that it is now possible to specify a nonpersistent timer service. To specify a timer as nonpersistent, specify the persistent attribute with a value of false for the @Schedule annotation. The following schedule-based timer demonstrates a nonpersistent timer designation:

```
@Schedule(minute="*/1", hour="*", persistent=false)
    public void scheduledTimerExample(){
            System.out.println("This timer will go off every minute");
    }
```

Optional Features

As the EJB specification grows and matures, a number of older API features are no longer required. As a result, it is prudent to make such features optional in order to maintain backward compatibility. The following features have been made optional in the EJB 3.2 release:

- Entity bean component contract for CMP and BMP
- Client view of an EJB 2.1 and earlier entity bean
- EJBQL
- JAX-RPC web service endpoints and client view

Remember, these features are optional because they represent older APIs being phased out. You may want to stay away from these APIs when writing new code.

Summary

The EJB API has been incrementally enhanced with the 3.2 release. The enhancements that have been included in the release help developers create more integrated solutions. To summarize, the new features covered in this book include the following:

- Lifecycle callback interceptor methods of stageful session beans added option to be executed in transaction context that is determined by the lifecycle callback method's transaction attribute
- Ability to disable passivation of stageful session beans
- TimerService API enhancements
- Embeddable EJBContainer has been enhanced to implement AutoClosable
- Default rules for session bean to designate local or remote interfaces have been relaxed
- Enhanced JMS MDB activation properties
- EJB Lite enhancements

The inclusions in this release are not limited to those that have been presented in this book. To learn more about these additional features, please take a look at the specification, which is available at: `http://www.jcp.org/en/jsr/detail?id=345`. Additional features of the 3.2 release include:

- MDB contracts enhanced with a no-method message listener interface to expose any public methods as message listeners
- New security role named "**" which indicates any authenticated callers that are not assigned to a designated role name
- Local asynchronous session bean invocations and non-persistent EJB Timer Service has been added to the EJB Lite group

CHAPTER 6

Validating Data

The Bean Validation API is utilized for validating data values in both Java SE and EE applications. As of Java EE 6, Bean Validation was included in the platform, adding integrated validation capabilities for enterprise applications. JavaServer Faces applications can utilize bean validation for validating values that are entered on an input form or even for calculations that are processed on the server. The best part is that the validation can occur with minimal programming because annotations are utilized to declaratively apply constraints against data for validation.

The Bean Validation 1.1 API is included in the Java EE 7 platform, and it brings forth a handful of welcome enhancements, as well as some new features that make validation even more useful. This chapter covers those new features and provides brief overviews of how they are to be used.

An Overview of Bean Validation with Java EE

The Bean Validation API can be used with many different technologies in both SE and EE environments. In the context of Java EE, Bean Validation can be performed by placing annotations on a field, method, or class such as a JSF managed bean or entity class. For instance, in a Java EE application that utilizes the JSF framework, validation occurs when a user enters values into a view and those values are propagated to the server via either a form submit or Ajax. To validate a specified entity field, simply annotate that field within the managed bean with the appropriate annotation according to the validations that you want to apply. When the JSF Process Validations phase occurs, the value that was entered by the user will be validated based upon the specified validation criteria. At this point, if the validation fails, the Render Response phase is executed, and an appropriate error message is added to the `FacesContext`. However, if the validation is successful, then the life cycle continues normally.

Suppose you wanted to perform validation on the fields of an entity class, such that the values for each field will be validated accordingly when a user has entered the values for creating a new entity object. In the following example, the `AuthorWork` entity has been enhanced to include bean validation for the `id`, `address1`, `state`, and `zip` fields, by incorporating some of the built-in constraint validation annotations:

```
...
@Entity
@Table(name = "AUTHOR_DETAIL")

public class AuthorDetailBeanValidation implements Serializable {
    private static final long serialVersionUID = 1L;
    @Id
    @Basic(optional = false)
    @SequenceGenerator(name="author_detail_s_generator",sequenceName="author__detail_s",
initialValue=1, allocationSize=1)
    @GeneratedValue(strategy=GenerationType.SEQUENCE,
    generator="author_detail_s_generator")
    @NotNull
```

```
    @Column(name = "ID")
    private BigDecimal id;
    @Size(max = 200)
    @Pattern(regexp="", message="Invalid Address")
    @Column(name = "ADDRESS1")
    private String address1;
    @Size(max = 200)
    @Column(name = "ADDRESS2")
    private String address2;
    @Size(max = 250)
    @Column(name = "CITY")
    private String city;
    @Size(max = 2)
    @Column(name = "STATE")
    @Pattern(regexp="^(?-i:A[LKSZRAEP]|C[AOT]|D[EC]|F[LM]|G[AU]|HI|I[ADLN]|K[SY]|LA|M[ADEHINOPST]
|N[CDEHJMVY]|O[HKR]|P[ARW]|RI|S[CD]|T[NX]|UT|V[AIT]|W[AIVY])$",
            message="Invalid State")
    private String state;
    @Size(max = 10)
    @Column(name = "ZIP")
    @Pattern(regexp="^\\d{5}\\p{Punct}?\\s?(?:\\d{4})?$",
            message="Invalid Zip Code")
    private String zip;
    @Column(name = "START_DATE")
    @Temporal(TemporalType.DATE)
    private Date startDate;
    @Lob
    @Column(name = "NOTES")
    private String notes;
    @ManyToOne
    private AuthorBeanValidation author;
...
```

As you can see, the @Size, @Pattern, and @NotNull constraint annotations are specified on various fields within the example entity class. These annotations check to ensure that the values entered for these fields adhere to the specified rules, namely, that the size does not exceed a certain limit, a String matches a specified pattern, and a String is not empty, respectively. This example barely scratches the surface of the types of validation that are possible; for an in-depth tutorial on bean validation or for detailed documentation on the constraint annotations, please refer to the online documentation. This chapter aims to cover the new additions in the Bean Validation 1.1 release, but it will compare those changes with the previous functionality, where possible.

Constraint Validation Annotations

Annotations are the heart of the Bean Validation API because they are used to decorate any fields, methods, or classes that are being validated. By utilizing annotations, the validation can be specified in a declarative manner, rather than by coding conditional logic by hand. The Bean Validation API comes prepackaged with some constraint validation annotations that are most commonly used. Table 6-1 includes an overview of the full list of built-in constraint annotations that can be used to perform validation, along with a description of what they validate.

Table 6-1. Built-in Bean Validation Constraints

Annotation Type	Description
@AssertFalse	The annotated element must be false.
@AssertTrue	The annotated element must be true.
@DecimalMax	The annotated element must be a number that cannot have a value that is greater than the specified maximum value. Supported types: BigDecimal BigInteger CharSequence byte, short, int, long, and their wrappers
@DecimalMin	The annotated element must be a number that cannot have a value that is less than the specified minimum value. Supported types: Same as @DecimalMax
@Digits	The annotated element must be a number within the accepted range. Supported types: Same as @DecimalMax
@Future	The annotated element must be a date that will occur at some point in the future. Supported types: java.util.Date java.util.Calendar
@Max	The annotated element must be a number that contains a value that is lower than or equal to the specified maximum value. Supported types: Same as @DecimalMax
@Min	The annotated element must be a number that contains a value that is greater than or equal to the specified minimum value. Supported types: Same as @DecimalMax
@NotNull	The annotated element must not be NULL.
@Null	The annotated element must be NULL.
@Past	The annotated element must be a data that occurred at some point in the past. Supported types: Same as @Future

(continued)

Table 6-1. (*continued*)

Annotation Type	Description
@Pattern	The annotated CharSequence must match the specified regular expression. The regular expression follows the conventions of java.util.regex.Pattern.
@Size	The annotated element must be sided between the specified boundaries. Supported Types: CharSequence Collection Map Array

What happens when you'd like to perform some validation that is not covered by one of the built-in constraint annotations? Well, it is easy to build custom constraint annotations to incorporate validations that are not available with the built-ins. Let's briefly review how this is done.

Suppose that employees in your organization have a customized employee identifier and want to include validation to ensure that a given employee identifier complies with the standard for your organization. There are a couple of ways to implement custom validation.

- Implementing a managed bean method that has the task of performing validation
- Creating a custom Validator class by implementing the javax.faces.validator.Validator interface

Review: Utilizing Different Validation Techniques

In this section, I will review how to implement validation for a form using both bean validation as well as a JSF validator to compare the differences. The easiest way to write a custom JSF validator solution is to implement a managed bean method that performs the validation. To do so, create a method that accepts three arguments.

- FacesContext: The current context
- UIComponent: The component being validated (must be of type UIInput)
- Object: The value of the component being validated

The idea is that the value being passed into the method is validated against a custom constraint. If the validation fails, the FacesContext is utilized to create a message, and the UIComponent's valid attribute is set to null to indicate that the validation has failed. Once the method has been created within a managed bean, it can be bound to a JSF component via the component's validator attribute.

In the following example, method validation is used to process the value that is specified for an employee ID in a UIInput component. If the value does not match the pattern constraint, then the validation fails. The validator method in the following code excerpt is taken from a session-scoped JSF managed bean, org.javaee7.jsf.UsersBean:

```
public void validateUserId(FacesContext context,
                                UIComponent component,
                                Object value){
        String idValue = (String) value;
```

```
        boolean result = idValue.matches("[0-9]{7}[JJ]");
        if (!result) {
            FacesMessage message = new FacesMessage();
            message.setSeverity(FacesMessage.SEVERITY_ERROR);
            message.setSummary(component.getClientId()
            .substring(component.getClientId().indexOf(":") + 1) +
              " issue, please use the format XXXXXXXJJ");
            context.addMessage(component.getClientId(), message);
            // Set the component's valid attribute to false
            ((UIInput) component).setValid(false);
        }
    }
```

If the values passed into the validateUserId method do not match the regular expression pattern, then the validation fails, and a message is displayed to the user. Now, let's take a look at bean validation to see how it differs from the use of a JSF validator. Rather than implementing a separate validation method or class, an annotation is placed on the property field of the bean that you want to validate. The following entity, org.javaee7.entity.Users, contains bean validation constraint annotations on its fields. The same validation that is being utilized by the validateUserId method in the previous code listing can be achieved using an @Pattern annotation.

```
...
@Entity
@Table(name="USERS")
public class Users implements Serializable {

    @Id
    @Basic(optional = false)
    @NotNull
    @GeneratedValue(strategy = GenerationType.AUTO)
    @Column(name = "ID")
    private BigDecimal id;

    @Pattern(regexp="[0-9]{7}[JJ]")
    private String userId;

    @Size(min=8, groups=Authentication.class)
    private String username;

    @Size(min=8, groups=Authentication.class)
    @Pattern(regexp="^[a-zA-Z\\d_]{4,12}$")
    private String password;

    @NotNull
    private String firstname;

    @NotNull
    private String lastname;

    @NotNull()
    private String email;
...
```

The excerpt taken from the following JSF view demonstrates how to bind a UIInput component to this method for validation purposes. Note that the userid field does not use bean validation since the JSF validator method is registered with it.

```
...
<h:form prependId="false">
                        <h1>Create User</h1>
                        <br/>
                        <h:messages infoStyle="color: green;" errorStyle="color:red;"/>

                        <h:panelGrid columns="2" width="50%" cellspacing="5px;">
                            <h:outputLabel for="userid" value="User ID "/>
                            <h:panelGroup>
                                <h:inputText id="userid" value="#{usersBean.users.userId}"
                                             validator="#{usersBean.validateUserId}"/>
                                <h:message for="userid" errorStyle="color: red;"
                                    infoStyle="color: green"/>
                            </h:panelGroup>

                            <h:outputLabel for="username" value="Username: "/>

                            <h:panelGroup>
                                <h:inputText id="username" value="#{usersBean.users.username}"/>
                                <h:message for="username" errorStyle="color: red;"
                                    infoStyle="color: green"/>
                            </h:panelGroup>

                            <h:outputLabel for="firstname" value="First:  "/>
                            <h:panelGroup>
                                <h:inputText id="firstname"
                                   value="#{usersBean.users.firstname}"/>
                                <h:message for="firstname" errorStyle="color: red;"
                                   infoStyle="color: green"/>
                            </h:panelGroup>

                            <h:outputLabel for="lastname" value="Last:  "/>
                            <h:panelGroup>
                                <h:inputText id="lastname" value="#{usersBean.users.lastname}"/>
                                <h:message for="lastname" errorStyle="color: red;"
                                   infoStyle="color: green"/>
                            </h:panelGroup>

                            <h:outputLabel for="password" value="Password: "/>
                            <h:panelGroup>
                                <h:inputSecret id="password"
                                  value="#{usersBean.users.password}"/>
                                <h:message for="password" errorStyle="color: red;"
                                  infoStyle="color: green"/>
                            </h:panelGroup>
                        </h:panelGrid>
```

```
                    <br/>
                    <h:commandButton action="#{usersBean.createUser()}"
                                     value="Create User"/>

                </h:form>...
```

If the form is entered with incorrect values, then error messages are displayed to the user. Figure 6-1 shows what a user may see if invalid values are entered.

Figure 6-1. *Validation errors on input*

Review: Writing a Custom Constraint Annotation

To create a custom constraint annotation, simply create a Java interface that contains the customized constraint code. In the following code example, a custom constraint annotation is developed that will provide the same level of validation as the method validator and bean validation annotation used in the previous section for validating a `userid` field:

```
@Pattern(regexp = "[0-9]{7}[JJ]")
@Documented
@Target({ElementType.METHOD, ElementType.FIELD, ElementType.ANNOTATION_TYPE})
@Retention(RetentionPolicy.RUNTIME)
public @interface UserIdValidator {

    String message() default "{invalid.userid}";

    Class<?>[] groups() default {};

    Class<? extends Payload>[] payload() default {};
}
```

To apply this custom constraint annotation to a field, indicate the interface name after the annotation character, as follows:

```
@UserIdValidator
private String userId;
```

Contexts and Dependency Injection Integration

There have been several integration points between Bean Validation and CDI added with the 1.1 release. This section will cover each of these integration points and provide examples of how to utilize the integrations.

ValidatorFactory and Validator Injection

The @ValidatorFactory is used to provide initialized instances of Validator to Bean Validation clients. You would want to obtain a Validator instance so that you could obtain metadata related to a given object or perform manual validations on bean classes and other objects. If using Bean Validation prior to 1.1, the ValidatorFactory had to be obtained by calling the Validation.buildDefaultValidatorFactory() method. However, it has been made easier because the ValidatorFactory can now be injected, as follows:

```
@Inject ValidatorFactory;
```

For a bit of background, you may want to obtain a Validator instance so that manual validation can be performed. The following lines of code demonstrate how to perform manual validation and then parse out the results:

```
Validator validator = factory.getValidator();
Set<ConstraintViolation<Object>> constraintViolations = validator.validate(o);
        for (ConstraintViolation<Object> violation : constraintViolations) {
            // do something
        }
```

Depending upon the work that needs to be done, CDI integration makes this process easier once again by allowing the injection of a Validator as well. To inject a validator, use the same technique as was demonstrated with the ValidatorFactory injection.

```
@Inject Validator;
```

These injections can also be registered as provider-specific by adding a custom qualifier at the injection point. Using a custom qualifier will help reduce ambiguity in the event that more than one Validator or ValidationFactory is eligible for injection in a single application. For instance, if you wanted to ensure that injections pertained to a specific product name of MYPRODUCT, you could inject as follows:

```
@Inject @MYPRODUCT Validator;
```

Managed Instances of Requested Classes

If an application requests one of the following classes via XML configuration within the web.xml deployment descriptor, then an injected ValidationFactory will be configured with managed instances of each of the requested classes.

- ConstraintValidatorFactory
- MessageInterpolator
- ParameterNameProvider
- TransversableResolver

In cases where one or more of the listed classes is registered with an application, the aforementioned managed instance can be injected into a bean via the @Inject annotation.

Method Validation

Have you ever had the need to validate method parameters or return values without writing an extra layer of code? The Bean Validation 1.1 release aims to solve this issue by providing the capability to utilize a programming style known as Programming by Contract (PbC). This programming style adheres to a couple of key standards.

- Validations can be expressed declaratively, without writing an extra layer of code.
- Annotations are automatically included in any JavaDoc that is generated from a method that includes validation.

Method validation takes place in a couple of different contexts. A validation can be placed on the constructor of a class, a method of a class, or a method's parameters. All validation techniques that apply to methods of a class also pertain to the validation of a class constructor. For a method to be capable of validation, it must be nonstatic. Constraint annotations that are placed on a method are used to validate the return value of that method. To validate parameters for a method, constraint annotations can be placed directly on each parameter.

■ **Note** It is also possible to utilize a constraint mapping file, rather than annotations, for applying constraints to a method and/or its parameters. This technique is known as *method-level overriding*, and you can learn more about this technique by visiting the online documentation at `http://beanvalidation.org/1.1/spec/`.

Declaring Parameter Constraints

To declare constraints on the parameters of a method or constructor, place annotations on the parameter(s) you want to validate. For instance, to place a constraint on a method parameter that ensures the parameter is not null, utilize an `@NotNull` annotation in the method signature. The following method signature demonstrates how to validate parameters of a method named `placeOrder`:

```
public void createJob(
            @NotNull @Size(min = 3, max = 20) Integer jobId,
            @NotNull String jobTitle,
            @DecimalMin("35000") BigDecimal salary,
            @NotNull String division) {
        Jobs newJob = new Jobs();
        newJob.setDivision(division);
        newJob.setJobId(jobId);
        newJob.setTitle(jobTitle);
        newJob.setSalary(salary);
        jobsSession.create(newJob);
    }
```

In the case that a parameter fails validation, it is identified in the resulting `ConstraintViolation`. To gain access to the list of `ConstraintViolation` exceptions that are thrown, the Bean Validation API defines the `javax.validation.ParameterNameProvider` API to retrieve the parameter names. To retrieve the names of the parameters that were in violation, call the `getParameterNames()` method of the `ParamterNameProvider`.

```
ParameterNameProvider provider = // obtain the provider...
List<parameter name> pnames = provider.getParameterNames()
```

Declaring Return Value Constraints

To declare constraints on method return values, apply constraint annotation(s) directly on the method. In the following method named placeOrder, the return value will be validated to ensure that at least one order is placed:

```
@NotNull
public Order placeOrder(...) {
    ...
    return order;

}
```

Similarly, a return value constraint can be placed on the constructor of a class to ensure that the object being returned conforms to the specified constraints. For instance, to validate that the WidgetOrderingService in the following example is valid, the constructor can be decorated with a constraint annotation, which validates the rules to adhere as a valid service:

```
@ValidOrderingService
public WidgetOrderingService(){
        ...
}
```

Cascaded Validation

Marking a method or parameter with the @Valid annotation flags it for cascaded validation. This means that the validation is recursive, in that any parameter or return value marked with @Valid will be validated. For example, in the following example, any time that the placeOrder method is invoked, it will cause recursive validation to occur:

```
@NotNull @Valid
public Order placeOrder(...) {
    ...
    return order;

}
```

Customizing Method, Constructor, or Getter Validation

It is possible to customize whether a method, constructor, or getter is validated. To do so the @ValidateOnExecution annotation can be placed on a method, constructor, getter method, or type declaring the executable in order to validate the annotated executable upon execution. The same effect can also be achieved via configuration within the validation.xml file. First, let's take a look at how to make use of the @ValidateOnExecution annotation.

The @ValidateOnExecution annotation accepts an argument named type, which accepts an executable type that is used to specify the override you want to perform. Table 6-2 lists the different executable types that can be passed to the @ValidateOnExecution annotation.

Table 6-2. @ValidateOnExecution Executable Types

Type	Description
NONE	Parameters and return types are not validated upon execution.
CONSTRUCTORS	Parameters and return types are validated as long as the executable is a constructor.
NON_GETTER_METHODS	Parameters and return types are validated as long as the executable is not a getter method.
GETTER_METHODS	Parameters and return types are validated as long as the executable is a getter method.
IMPLICIT	When placed on a class or interface, it causes validation to be skipped; otherwise, the type attribute must match the type of executable being annotated. For instance, if on a constructor, then the type attribute must be equal to CONSTRUCTORS.
ALL	All parameters and return types are validated for all executables.

If a constructor or method is annotated with the @ValidateOnExecution annotation, and the annotation's type attribute is set to the executable type or IMPLICIT, then the executable will be validated upon execution. Otherwise, the validation will be skipped. Similarly, if a class or interface is annotated with @ValidateOnExecution, and the annotation's type attribute contains the executable type, then the class or interface will be validated. However, if the class or interface annotation contains a type attribute set to IMPLICIT, then the validation will be skipped.

Let's take a look at one of the use cases for specification of the @ValidateOnExecution annotation. By default, getter methods are not validated when method-level validation is being used. It is possible to change this default behavior by annotating any getter methods that you want to validate with the @ValidateOnExecution annotation and passing the appropriate type argument to the annotation. The following lines of code demonstrate how to enable a getter method for validation:

```
@ValidateOnExecution(type=GETTER_METHODS)
    public BigDecimal getTotal() {
        return total;
    }
```

It is also possible to specify more than one type for the @ValidateOnExecution annotation. To do so, enclose the type values within curly brackets, as demonstrated in the following example. Suppose that we have a service that it utilized for online catalog processing. The service class could include default impementations for performing common tasks, such as processing an order. It is possible to validate these methods utilizing the @ValidateOnExecution annotation, as follows:

```
public class CatalogService {
    ...

    @ValidateOnExecution(type={javax.validation.executable.ExecutableType.NON_GETTER_METHODS,
                               javax.validation.executable.ExecutableType.CONSTRUCTORS})
    public Order placeOrder(
            @NotNull @Size(min = 3, max = 20) String customerNumber,
            @NotNull @Valid Widget widget,
            @Min(1) int quantity) {
        Order order = new Order();
        order.setCustomerNumber(customerNumber);
```

```
        order.setProduct(widget);
        order.setQuantity(quantity);

        // Send the order to the database
        return order;
    }
    ...
}
```

Now let's consider a class that extends another class, overriding method(s) that contain the @ValidateOnExecution annotation. It is possible to override the validation type, or specify another validation type within the extending class. In the following example, WidgetOrderingService extends the CatalogService class that was previously presented. The @ValidateOnExecution annotation has been specified at the class level, indicating that any GETTER_METHODS or CONSTRUCTORS should be validated.

```
@ValidateOnExecution(type={javax.validation.executable.ExecutableType.GETTER_METHODS,
                           javax.validation.executable.ExecutableType.CONSTRUCTORS})
public class WidgetOrderingService extends CatalogService {

    public WidgetOrderingService(){
    }

    @Override
    public Order placeOrder(
            @NotNull @Size(min = 3, max = 20) String customerNumber,
            @NotNull @Valid Widget widget,
            @Min(1) int quantity) {
        Order order = new Order();
        order.setCustomerNumber(customerNumber);
        order.setProduct(widget);
        order.setQuantity(quantity);
        // Do something specific with widget order
        return order;

    }
}
```

Another way to achieve customizable validation is to utilize either the executable-validation or default-validated-executable-types elements within the validation.xml configuration file. If the executable-validation element is specified, and its enabled attribute is set to false, then executable validation is disabled. However, if the default-validated-executable-types element is specified as a sub-element to the executable-validation element, then specific executable types can be specified for executable validation. For example, the following excerpt from a validation.xml file demonstrates how to disable executable validation for all executables with the exception of getter methods:

```
...
<executable-validation>
        <default-validated-executable-types>
            <executable-type>GETTER_METHODS</executable-type>
        </default-validated-executable-types>
    </executable-validation>
...
```

Manual Method Level Validation Invocation

As mentioned previously, method validation is not automatic, and it must be implemented by the provider or manually invoked via code. The process for invoking method-level validation varies depending upon the type of validation you want to perform. In all cases, you must use the `javax.validation.ExecutableValidator` interface to manually invoke the execution. To obtain a handle on the `ExecutableValidator`, utilize the `Validation.buildDefaultValidatorFactory.getValidator().forExecutables()` call, as demonstrated in the following lines:

```
ExecutableValidator executableValidator = Validation
    .buildDefaultValidatorFactory().getValidator().forExecutables();
```

Depending upon the type of method-level validation that you want to invoke, make calls to the appropriate `ExecutableValidator` methods. Table 6-3 lists the different methods available for invoking validation.

Table 6-3. *ExecutableValidator Validation Methods*

Method and Description
`validateParameters(T object, Method method, Object[] parameterValues, Class<?>... groups)`
Validates the arguments (as given in `parameterValues`) for the parameters of a given method (identified by `method`)
`validateReturnValue(T object, Method method, Object returnValue, Class<?>... groups)`
Validates the return value (specified by `returnValue`) of a given method (identified by `method`)
`validateConstructorParameters(Constructor<T> constructor, Object[] parameterValues, Class<?>... groups)`
Validates the arguments (as given in `parameterValues`) for the parameters of a given constructor (identified by `constructor`)
`validateConstructorReturnValue(Constructor<T> constructor, T createdObject, Class<?>... groups)`
Validates the object (specified by `createdObject`) of a given constructor (identified by `constructor`)

The following example demonstrates how to manually invoke validation. The call will return a `Set` of `ConstraintViolation` objects, one for each violation that occurred. If no issues occurred, then there will be an empty set returned.

```
Set<ConstraintViolation> constraintViolations = executableValidator.validateParameters(
    widgetOrderingService, placeOrder, new Object[] { null, widget1, 5 })
```

Group Conversion

Group validation refers to the notion that constraints can belong to one or more groups that will be used for validation. A new feature of Bean Validation 1.1 is known as *group conversion*, which I will discuss within this section. First, we will summarize the concept of validation groups and their associated concepts. After a brief overview, I'll dig into group conversions.

Applications can elect to validate a specific "group" of constraints based upon an activity that is being performed. This means that instead of validating all constraints that belong to an object graph, a subset of those constraints can be validated, if so desired. Why would this be useful? Consider the case where a user is logging into an application and you want to validate the user name and password. The user object may contain several different constraint validations, perhaps constraints on e-mail address, street address, and so on, but you need to validate only the username and password. In such a case, the login process can validate a subset of those constraints by using the validation group.

Validation groups are Java interfaces, so to create a group, you simply create an interface. For instance, to create the authorization group that was mentioned in the previous paragraph, an interface such as the following could be created:

```
public interface Authentication {}
```

To apply one or more groups to a specified constraint annotation, use the `groups` attribute of the annotation constraint and indicate the class name of the interface. For instance, in the following example, the `User` class contains two fields that belong to the `Authentication` group:

```
public class Users {

    @Size(min=8, groups=Authentication.class)
    private String username;

    @Size(min=8, groups=Authentication.class)
    @Pattern(regexp="^[a-zA-Z\\d_]{4,12}$")
    private String password;

    @NotNull
    private String firstname;

    @NotNull
    private String lastname;

    @NotNull()
    private String email;

    ...
}
```

It is possible to specify more than one group for a constraint annotation by denoting a list of values for the `groups` attribute. For instance, if the `username` field needed to also belong to the `Authentication2` group, then it could be registered to both groups using the following notation:

```
@Size(min=8, groups={Authentication.class, Authentication2.class})
private String username;
```

■ **Note** The `Default.class` group is created automatically, and any validation constraint that does not have a group specified will belong to the `Default` group.

Group Validation

In some situations, it makes sense to have one group inherit another. In such cases, it is possible to apply group inheritance by performing interface inheritance. For example, if the `Authentication` group needs to inherit the `BaseAuthentication` group, it could be done by specifying the inheritance within the `Authentication` interface.

```
public interface Authentication extends BasicAuthentication {}
```

Specifying the Order of Group Validation

By default, the Bean Validation API will validate each constraint within a group in no particular order. In some cases, it may make sense to define an explicit ordering for validation, such as when one validation depends upon another. In such cases, explicit ordering can be implemented by creating a group sequence. To define a group sequence, declare a Java interface to create a new validation group, and then annotate that interface with the @GroupSequence annotation, specifying validation groups within the annotation in the order in which they should be validated. If a constraint that belongs to one group fails, then the validation halts, and all subsequent groups are not validated.

For example, the following group, named MasterAuthentication, specifies a group sequence in which all constraints belonging to the Authentication group are first validated, followed by the constraints belonging to the Authentication2 group:

```
@GroupSequence({Authentication.class, Authentication2.class})
public interface MasterAuthentication {}
```

■ **Note** If a group sequence is defined and there is a circular dependency with another sequence or group, then a GroupDefinitionException is raised.

Group Conversion

The brief overview that was given in the previous sections will help you understand group conversion, which is a new feature of Bean Validation 1.1. It is now possible to alter a validation group specification to use a group different from the one originally requested. To do so, specify the @ConvertGroup annotation, which can be used anywhere that @Valid can be used. If used without specifying the @Valid annotation, then a ConstraintDeclarationException is raised.

The @Valid annotation indicates that validation is to be propagated and groups are passed as nested elements unless the @ConvertGroup annotation is specified. You can think of group conversion as a conditional element of group validation. For instance, in one circumstance it may make sense to utilize one group of validations, whereas in another circumstance it may make sense to utilize a different group of validations. Let's say you wanted to apply a stronger authentication mechanism to administrator users and apply a lesser authentication mechanism to standard users. You could do so by indicating which validation group to use under each circumstance using group conversion.

To use this technique, specify the @ConvertGroup annotation on any field that may have multiple group designations, depending upon the circumstance. Specify the group that should be indicated by using the from attribute of the @ConvertGroup annotation, and specify the group that should be converted to with the to attribute. To indicate more than one case of group conversion, specify the @ConvertGroup.List annotation, and specify a List of @ConvertGroup annotations.

Perhaps the easiest way to understand this concept is to see an example. In the following example, the User group is going to utilize the Authentication validation group if a Default group is specified (standard user), and it will utilize the Authentiation2 validation group if a Admin group is specified:

```
public class User {
    @Valid
    @ConvertGroup.List( {
        @ConvertGroup(from=Default.class, to=Authentication.class),
        @ConvertGroup(from=Admin.class, to=Authentication2.class)
    } )
    private String getPassword() { ... }
}
```

By utilizing group conversion, you can achieve the full potential of validation groups. This allows applications to become more versatile and also enhances the validation of application objects since it allows for finer-grained control.

Message Interpolation via EL

The Bean Validation 1.1 release has made validation messaging much more flexible via the use of messaging within the unified expression language (EL). A formatter object and the validation values are now injected into the EL context, allowing nicely formatted messages to be made available for use within an application's views.

For example, suppose that you wished to print an error message if a @NotNull constraint was violated. It is possible to embed the EL within the error message, as in the following excerpt:

```
@NotNull(message="The message is dated ${today}, and the username should not be null")
@Size(min=8, groups=Authentication.class)
private String username;
```

A Truly Open API

Bean Validation 1.1 is an open source API. That is, the web site (http://beanvalidation.org) sources, discussions, and work are all performed in the open. As such, not only is the API tied into Java EE 7, but it can also be used with many other technologies outside of Java EE. Anyone can join the mailing lists and get involved in working with Bean Validation, if interested.

Summary

In the early days of web applications, one had to utilize a combination of JavaScript and server-side logic in order to validate data being entered into a web form. Applications using that kind of validation were difficult to develop and maintain because one had to jump back and forth between JavaScript, Java, and HTML, while paying careful attention to the DOM to ensure that everything was being referenced properly. Bean validation aims to make it easier to apply validation to applications by moving validation logic into the server-side bean and getting rid of the cumbersome JavaScript technique. The release of Bean Validation 1.1 makes this API even more robust, adding features such as CDI integration and method validation.

CHAPTER 7

Contexts and Dependency Injection

One of the most important features in Java EE is Contexts and Dependency Injection (CDI). CDI helps bind the web tier and the business logic or transactional tier of the Java EE platform together and makes it easy to utilize resources and objects throughout an application. CDI makes it easy to expose business objects for use within JSF web views so that developers can directly bind JSF view widgets to public JavaBean members and methods. It also provides facilities that make it possible to inject JavaBean classes and resources into other Java objects in a type-safe and efficient manner.

CDI is architected from two methodologies: contexts and dependency injection. *Contexts* provide the ability to bind the life cycle and interactions of stateful components to well-defined but extensive contexts, per Oracle's Java EE 7 tutorial. In the same tutorial, *dependency injection* is defined as the ability to inject components into an application in a type-safe manner, including the ability to choose at deployment time which implementation of a particular interface to inject. To use CDI, a developer should become familiar with a series of annotations that can be used to decorate objects and injected components. This chapter covers concepts that will demonstrate such annotations and where they should be used.

Since CDI provides a high level of loose coupling, it is an important piece of any Java EE application. Applications that use CDI in the right way can become very efficient because CDI provides decoupling of resources, as well as strong typing by eliminating the requirement to use `String`-based names for managed resources, and provides the use of declarative Java annotations to specify just about everything. Although it is possible to develop Java EE applications without the use of CDI, it is very easy to use and enables enterprise applications to become more robust and efficient than those that do not use CDI features.

This chapter will provide a brief overview of the concepts that comprise CDI, but it will focus on mostly those new features that are part of CDI 1.1 and the Java EE 7 platform. CDI 1.1 is an incremental release, which provides many small enhancements to help solidify the API. If you are unfamiliar with CDI, I recommend you learn more about it from the Oracle Java EE 7 tutorial online before reading this chapter. If you want to be on the cutting edge of CDI, you can learn much more about current and future CDI features by referencing Weld, a subset of the JBoss Seam web framework, which is the reference implementation for CDI. To learn more about Weld, please refer to the online documentation at `http://seamframework.org/Weld`.

Brief Overview of CDI

While CDI is part of Java EE 7 and is certainly utilized within Java EE applications, it is by no means available only within the Java EE ecosystem; it can also be utilized within Java SE applications. Of course, only a subset of the CDI API, such as bean injection and bean scope, is available for use within Java SE applications. The focus of this chapter is geared toward use within a Java EE environment; to learn more about using CDI within Java SE, please refer to the online documentation.

CDI is comprised of a variety of concepts and programming techniques. Let's break it down just a bit so you can more easily understand the scope of CDI. As mentioned in the introduction to this chapter, the *C* portion of CDI refers to the contextual scoping of resources within an application. Inherently, resources that are managed by CDI will have scope propagated to them in such a way that the container or application will automatically manage their scopes.

You can refer to resources that are instantiated and bound to CDI as *contextual instances*. When an application is deployed and enabled, a contextual instance of a resource that is denoted as `ApplicationScoped` can be created, and that same resource can be destroyed when an application is undeployed or disabled. The application developer does not need to do anything to manage the scope of such resources; the container simply takes care of the scope management. Similarly, a resource that is denoted as `SessionScoped` can be instantiated when a session begins, and then once the session ends, that resource will be destroyed. Contextual scoping makes CDI a very important piece of Java applications, especially for resource management.

Also mentioned in the introduction, the *DI* portion of CDI refers to the ability to inject resources, or *contextual instances*, into other resources. By use of dependency injection, objects and resources can be injected into other objects that are referred to as *injection targets*. Those injected objects and resources maintain their context, and therefore, if one `SessionScoped` managed bean is injected into another, all of the session-specific information is available and can be accessed/updated as needed.

CDI is one of those technologies that has a tendency to be a game changer, making the life of a programmer much easier once all of its benefits are utilized. This chapter will briefly cover some of the most widely used portions of CDI and delve into the enhancements that have been made in CDI 1.1.

Dependency Injection

The concept of dependency injection greatly reduces the amount of overhead that is necessary for a developer to gain reference to a Java object from within another Java class. The Java EE stack makes it very easy to gain reference to just about any Java object from within another class. *Dependency injection* refers to the ability to inject components into an application in a type-safe manner, including the ability to choose at deployment time which implementation of a particular interface to inject. CDI allows almost any Java class to be injected into another with very little configuration. This ability increases the usability of resources since such resource can be referenced from any number of different classes and maintain the same state wherever they are being used. In reality, just about any object can be injected anywhere with CDI. The following are some Java objects that can be injected:

- Almost any Java class
- Session beans
- Java EE resources, including data sources, JMS topics, queues, and connection factories
- Persistence contexts
- Producer fields
- Objects returned by producer methods
- Web service references
- Remote EJB references

To inject a resource into another, the application module or JAR file must contain a `META-INF` directory that includes a `beans.xml` configuration file. The `beans.xml` file may or may not be empty depending upon the configuration. However, for the purposes of this example (and for most general CDI use cases), the `beans.xml` file is usually an empty configuration file that is used as a placeholder to tell Java EE that the application wants to use CDI.

■ **Note** In previous versions of Java EE, most configuration and deployments were accomplished via XML.

Next, the `javax.inject.Inject` annotation (`@Inject`) must be used to denote the class being injected by annotating a class variable of the object type. For instance, if you want to inject a Java object of TypeA, you would declare a class variable of type TypeA and annotate it with `@Inject`, as follows:

```
@Inject
TypeA myTypeVar;
```

Once the injection is performed, the declared variable can be utilized throughout the class because it is a direct reference to the original class of the specified Java type. By defining a specific scope to the injection bean, you can indicate whether an injected object will cause the instantiation of a new object of that type or whether it will look up an existing object of that type and reuse it. By far, one of the most convenient and useful cases for using CDI is the ability to inject a managed bean into another object and make use of its current state, as if its contents existed everywhere.

CDI provides type-safe injection because there is no need to specify a String-based name in order to instantiate or refer to another object. By maintaining declared variables that are used as points of injection, the variable name itself provides for strong typing and thus reduces the number of errors that may arise. A couple new features have been added to make dependency injection even more useful, and the following sections aim to describe those enhancements.

Injection of Bean Metadata

The `Bean`, `Interceptor`, and `Decorator` interfaces provide metadata about a bean. As of CDI 1.1, it is possible for bean metadata to be injected into a bean instance. To obtain information using the `Bean` interface, inject it into the bean that needs to use it, and then call upon its methods to obtain the desired information. The following bean types can be injected using the `Bean` type:

- A bean with scope `@Dependent`, `@Default` as the qualifier, and type `Bean`
- A bean with scope `@Dependent`, `@Default` as the qualifier, and type `Interceptor`
- A bean with scope `@Dependent`, `@Default` as the qualifier, and type `Decorator`

Additionally, beans that allow interceptors and decorators can obtain information about the beans that they intercept and/or decorate. A definition error occurs if an `Interceptor` or `Decorator` instance is injected into any bean instance other than an interceptor or decorator instance, respectively.

The following example demonstrates the use of the `Bean` interface to retrieve metadata regarding the bean named `OrderProcessor`:

```
@Named("Order")
public class OrderProcessor {
    @Inject Bean<OrderProcessor> bean;

    public String getBeanName(){
        return bean.getName();
    }

    public Class<? extends Annotation> getScope(){
        return bean.getScope();
    }
}
```

In the previous example, the getBeanName method will return the String-based name of the bean, and getBeanScope will return the Annotation class for the bean scope. The Class<? extends Annotation> is a generic syntax that designates an Annotation type class. Table 7-1 lists the different methods available from the Bean interface for obtaining metadata, along with a brief description of each.

***Table 7-1.** Bean Interface Methods for Obtaining Metadata*

Method	Returns	Description
getBeanClass	Class<?>	Returns the bean class of the managed or session bean, or of the bean that declares the producer method or field.
getInjectionPoints	Set<InjectionPoint>	Returns the InjectionPoint objects of the bean.
getName	String	Returns the EL name of the bean, if it exists.
getQualifiers	Set<Annotation>	Returns the bean's qualifiers.
getScope	Class<? extends Annotation>	Returns the scope of the bean.
getStereotypes	Set<Class ? extends Annotation>	Returns the stereotypes of the bean.
getTypes	Set<Type>	Returns the types of the bean.
isAlternative	boolean	Determines whether the bean is an alternative.
isNullable	boolean	Determines whether the create() method may return a null value.

Injection of the ServletContext

It is now possible to inject ServletContext into application classes using the javax.servlet.ServletContext bean type. Doing so allows control of the servlet context for a particular application. As such, one can add listeners, create filters, work with attributes, and so on, just as if a bean were a standard Java servlet class. To inject the ServletContext, write the following code:

```
@Inject
ServletContext context;
```

Let's take a look at how you can use the ServletContext information from a JSF application. Suppose that you want to display the server information on a JSF view. In the following code for org.javaee7.jsf.AcmeBean, the ServletContext is injected using the new enhancement, and data from it is made available for use in a JSF view:

```
package org.javaee7.jsf;

...
import javax.servlet.ServletContext;

@ManagedBean(name = "acmeBean")
@SessionScoped
public class AcmeBean implements Serializable {

    @EJB
    private AcmeFacade facade;
```

```
    @EJB
    private AcmeTimerFacade timerFacade;

    @Inject
    ServletContext context;

    ...
    public String getContextInfo(){
        return context.getServerInfo();
    }
}
```

Now within a JSF view, the server information can be displayed by simply calling upon the `contextInfo` getter that was implemented in `AcmeBean`.

```
<h:outputText id="widget" style="font-weight: bold;" value="#{acmeBean.contextInfo}"/>
```

Marking Classes as Ignored by CDI

Almost any Java object can be injected using CDI, and injection is even possible into beans that are not managed by CDI. A managed bean in the context of CDI is a bean class that is implemented by a Java class. CDI utilization within managed beans serves a number of purposes. For instance, managed beans can be annotated for scoping, naming and referential purposes, and so forth. EJB session beans can also utilize CDI in a number of ways, similar to managed beans. The topic of CDI usage within managed beans and session beans is very large and out of scope for this book on new features. Therefore, to learn more about the ways CDI can be used in these bean types, please refer to the documentation or other books, such as *Java EE 7 Recipes* by Apress.

New to managed and session beans in CDI 1.1 is the ability to veto beans in a declarative manner by utilizing the `@Veto` and `@Requires` annotations. To veto a bean means to mark it as ignored by CDI. Therefore, if a bean contains the `@Veto` annotation, it cannot be processed by CDI. A vetoed class will not contain the life cycle of a contextual instance, nor can it be injected into other classes. In fact, if a managed bean or session bean contains the `@Veto` annotation, it cannot be considered a managed bean or session bean at all. In some cases, it makes sense to mark a bean as such to ensure that it cannot become managed by CDI. The following code demonstrates how to apply the `@Veto` annotation to a class:

```
@Veto
public class OrderFacade implements java.io.Serializable {
...
```

The `@Veto` annotation can also be placed on a package declaration, which will prevent all of the beans that are contained within that package from being processed via CDI.

```
@Veto
package org.javaee.chapter7.*;
...
```

Any of the following definitions on a vetoed type will not be processed:

- Managed beans, session beans, interceptors, decorators
- Observer methods, producer methods, producer fields

The @Requires annotation can be used to mark a class to be ignored by CDI if it does not meet the specified required criteria. The @Requires annotation accepts a String-based fully qualified class name of the dependency or dependencies. If the object is able to fulfill its dependencies, then it will be managed by CDI. For instance, the following class requires the dependency of javax.persistence.EntityManager in order to be managed by CDI:

```
@Requires("javax.persistence.EntityManager")
public class EmployeeFacade {
    ...
    @Produces
    public EntityManager getEntityManager(){
        ...
    }
    ...
}
```

Similarly to @Veto, the @Requires annotation can be placed on a package as well. If that package is unable to fulfill the dependency that is denoted by @Requires, then all classes contained within that package will be unmanaged by CDI.

Producers

CDI brings forth the concept of producers. According to the specification, a producer method acts as a source of objects to be injected, where the following are all true:

- Objects to be injected aren't required to be bean instances.
- Injected object types may vary at runtime.
- An initialization method is required, separate from the bean constructor.

In a nutshell, a producer method allows generation of an injectable object. They are very useful in situations where an application requires injection of an object that is not injectable or an object requires some custom initialization that the bean's constructor does not take care of. Producer methods are annotated with the javax.enterprise.inject.Produces annotation.

For instance, the following producer method can be called upon to obtain an injectable Widget bean, the type of which may vary depending upon the given criteria:

```
public class WidgetBean implements java.io.Serializable {

    private String widgetType = Widget.GENERIC;
    private Widget selectedWidget;

    public WidgetBean() {
    }

    @Produces
    public Widget getWidget() {
        switch (widgetType) {
            case Widget.PLASTIC:
                return new WidgetOne();
            case Widget.METAL:
```

```
                return new WidgetTwo();
            default:
                return new WidgetX();
        }
    }
...
```

In the next example, a list of widgets is returned for use via a JSF view.

```
...
@Produces
    @Named
    public List<Widget> getWidgets(){
        return widgets;
    }
...
```

The previous list of widgets can be displayed via a JSF view using the following markup:

```
<h:dataTable id="widgets" var="widget" value="#{widgetBean.widgets}">
    <h:column>
        <h:outputText value="#{widget.type}"/>
    </h:column>
</h:dataTable>
```

Producer fields are an alternative to producer methods. They are a field of a bean that can generate an object. Producer fields are commonly used for the declaration of resources, but they can be used for the generation of other objects as well.

A producer method can be used to generate an object that needs to be removed once it is no longer needed. Much like a finalizer for a class, an object that has been injected via a producer method can contain a method that is invoked when the injected instance is being destroyed. Such a method is known as a *disposer method*. To declare a method as a disposer method, create a method defined by the same class as the producer method. The disposer method must have at least one parameter, with the same type and qualifiers as the producer method. That parameter should be annotated with `@Disposes`. In CDI 1.1, this technique can now be applied to producer fields as well.

Programmatic Lookup

In some cases, programmatic lookup of contextual instances may not be convenient. For instance, injection may not be possible or convenient in the following circumstances:

- If a bean's type or qualifiers vary dynamically
- If there is no bean that satisfies the given type and/or qualifiers
- If an application needs to iterate over all beans of a specified type

In these situations, you can inject a `javax.enterprise.inject.Instance` interface in order to gain access to contextual references. For instance, in the following example, a contextual instance of AcmeBean is obtained. Once the instance of the bean has been injected, its `get` method can be invoked to obtain the contextual reference.

```
@Inject Instance<AcmeBean> acmeBean;
AcmeBean ab = acmeBean.get();
```

Similarly, the javax.enterprise.inject.spi.BeanManager interface provides operations for obtaining contextual references for beans, along with many operations that can be used with portable extensions. For instance, the BeanManager can be used to obtain a reference to a bean by calling its getReference method, as demonstrated in the following lines of code:

```
@Inject
BeanManager beanManager;

...
beanManager.getReference(bean, beanType, creationalContext);
...
```

Most recently, with the release of CDI 1.1, the BeanManager can be used to obtain programmatic access to a Producer, InjectionTarget, and AnnotatedType. To do so, the BeanManager must be obtained and then invoke the method corresponding to the object that needs to be obtained. Table 7-2 lists the different methods that can be called against the BeanManager in order to obtain access to these three types. By no means is the table an exhaustive list of all methods available via the BeanManager, but it lists the new BeanManager methods.

Table 7-2. *BeanManager Methods*

Method	Description
createAnnotatedType	Returns an AnnotatedType that may be used to read the annotations of the given Java class or interface
getAnnotatedType getAnnotatedTypes	Returns the AnnotatedType(s) discovered or added during container initialization
createInjectionTarget	Returns a container-provided implementation of InjectionTarget for a given AnnotatedType or throws an IllegalArgumentException if there is a definition error associated with any injection point of the type
getExtensions	Returns the container's instance of an Extension class that is declared in the META-INF/services file or throws an IllegalArgumentException if the container does not contain an instance of the specified class
createProducer	Returns a container provided implementation of Producer for a given AnnotatedMethod or AnnotatedField or throws an IllegalArgumentException if there is a definition error associated with the producer method or field

■ **Note** Please see the online documentation for comprehensive details regarding the BeanManager interface: https://javaee-spec.java.net/nonav/javadocs/javax/enterprise/inject/spi/BeanManager.html

Container Life-Cycle Events

The application server container fires a series of events that allow portable extensions to integrate with the container initialization process. This series of events is known as the *container life-cycle events*. For instance, before the container begins the bean discovery process, it must fire a BeforeBeanDiscovery event. After the bean discovery process has completed, the AfterBeanDiscovery event is fired.

New in CDI 1.1, the container must fire an event for each bean archive, before it processes the classes that have been packaged in that module. This event is known as the `AfterTypeDiscovery` event. Any observer, or class that listens for events, of the `AfterTypeDiscovery` event is permitted to add and/or remove classes from the set of alternatives, list of interceptors, or list of decorators. The `beans.xml` file is used to initialize values of the collections. The `AfterTypeDiscovery` interface contains the methods listed in Table 7-3.

Table 7-3. *`AfterTypeDiscovery` Interface Methods*

Method	Description
`getAlternatives`	Returns the set of enabled alternatives in the bean deployment archive
`getAnnotatedTypes`	Returns the set of enabled annotated types in the bean deployment archive
`getBeansXml`	Returns an `InputStream` that can be utilized for reading the `beans.xml` configuration file for the module
`getDecorators`	Returns a list of enabled decorators in the bean deployment archive
`getInterceptors`	Returns an Iterator that can be used to traverse over the `AnnotatedTypes` objects that represent the Java class or interfaces in the bean deployment archive

Priorities

The `@Priority` annotation has been added to CDI 1.1 to aid in the ordering of use for specific bean types. In Java EE, the `@Priority` annotation can be specified on a class to indicate that the class should be invoked before another class. In other words, the annotation allows one to indicate in what order classes should be invoked. In CDI, the `@Priority` annotation can be utilized to specify the ordering of Interceptors, Alternatives, and Decorators.

Interceptors

Interceptors are part of the EJB specification, and allow developers to invoke targeted tasks outside of the business logic of an application. Also known as *cross-cutting* tasks, interceptors can be bound to application events and specified business methods so that they become invoked when a specified event occurs upon the intercepted method. To review, interceptor methods contain one or more methods annotated with one of the following: `@AroundInvoke`, `@AroundTimeout`, `@PostContruct`, or `@PreDestroy`. These annotations indicate the time at which the interceptor method or class should be invoked within the event lifecycle. In order to bind an interceptor to a class or method, an interceptor binding type must also be declared.

The CDI 1.1 specification enhances interceptors by allowing developers to specify precedence for the invocation of interceptors if more than one has been defined for a particular class or method. The `@Priority` annotation can be specified on an interceptor in order to control interceptor invocation order. Let's take a look at an example.

Suppose that we had an interceptor named `MessageInterceptor`. Further suppose that it should be invoked before any other in an application. The priority specification may look as follows:

```
...
@Priority(Interceptor.Priority.APPLICATION+10)
  @Interceptor  public class MessageInterceptor { ... }
```

The `@Priority` annotation accepts a `Interceptor.Priority` value. Table 7-4 lists each of the priorites that are available for use. Each of the priority values are of type `static int`. According to the specification, the interceptor containing the highest priority value is invoked first.

Table 7-4. Interceptor.Priority Values

Priority Field	Description
APPLICATION	Start of the range for interceptors that are defined by applications. (Value: 2000)
LIBRARY_AFTER	Start of the range for late interceptors that are defined by extension libraries. (Value: 3000)
LIBRARY_BEFORE	Start of the range for early interceptors that are defined by extension libraries. (Value: 1000)
PLATFORM_AFTER	Start of the range for late interceptors that are defined by specifications of platforms. (Value: 4000)
PLATFORM_BEFORE	Start of the range for early interceptors that are defined by specifications of platforms. (Value: 0)

■ **Note** Since the `Interceptor.Priority` value is a constant `int`, another `int` can be added to it in order to ensure that a higher priority than other interceptors that are given the specified priority value. In the preceding example, the value 10 is added to `Interceptor.Priority.APPLICATION`. The resulting priority then has the value 2010. (2000 is from the `APPLICATION` priority. See Table 7-4).

For more information on utilization of interceptors, please refer to the documentation that can be found online.

Decorators

Decorators are Java classes that have the ability to intercept invocations for a particular Java interface, and therefore they are aware of any semantics that apply to the specified interface. Additional functionality can then be applied to the methods of the implementation class, and that additional functionality will be invoked and processed along with the standard implementation. Decorators entail operations that include business logic, so they differ from interceptors in that respect. In effect, the decorator class implementation surrounds the inner class. A decorator can be an abstract class, and it must contain a special injection point known as the delegate injection point. This point must be the same type as the beans being decorated, and it must be injected along with the `@Delegate` annotation. Let's look at an example.

In this example, a human resources department may choose to implement a specialized hiring process for employees in different departments. Rather than creating separate implementation classes, it would be easier to "wrap" additional functionality around the standard implementation. In this case, a decorator class is used to add functionality to the employee hiring process. The following class, `EmployeeProcessorDecorator`, demonstrates a decorator that has the ability to implement additional functionality around the standard implementations for the `Hire` interface.

```
package org.javaee7.chapter07;

import javax.decorator.Decorator;
import javax.decorator.Delegate;
import javax.enterprise.inject.Any;

import javax.inject.Inject;
```

```
/**
 * This decorator class is applied to the employee hiring process to implement
 * additional functionality to any of the methods implemented within are called.
 * @author Juneau
 */
@Decorator
public class EmployeeProcessorDecorator implements Hire{

    @Inject
    @Delegate
    @Any
    Hire hire;

    @Override
    public String badgeEmployee() {
        String result = null;
        // Perform a test implementation for badging an employee
        hire.badgeEmployee();
        return result;
    }

    @Override
    public String trainEmployee() {
        String result = null;
        // Perform a test implementation for training an employee
        hire.trainEmployee();
        return result;
    }
}
```

As of CDI 1.1, it is possible to define the ordering of decorator classes by applying the `@Priority` annotation. The following example demonstrates how to specify priority for a decorator class known as `EmployeeProcessorDecorator`:

```
@Decorator
@Priority(Interceptor.Priority.APPLICATION)
public class EmployeeProcessorDecorator implements Hire{
...
}
```

Please refer to Table 7-4 for more information regarding `Interceptor.Priority` values. Also, if you are unfamiliar with the concept of decorators, please refer to the documentation that can be found within the online Java EE 7 tutorial for more information.

Alternatives

Alternatives provide a good solution for implementing multiple versions of a bean that can be used for different purposes. Qualifiers can be utlilized during the development phase for injecting different bean implementations, whereas alternatives allow one to choose between different implementations at deployment time. Alternatives are useful for scenarios where an application may be deployed with some default functionality, but made configurable to utlize a different functionality if deployed in another environment. They can also be useful for testing different versions of beans, whereby a default implementation is written, but an alternate bean can be specified at deployment time.

To mark a bean as an alternative, annotate it with the `javax.enterprise.inject.Altertative` annotation, and then specify it within an alternative element in the `beans.xml` file. For example, in this scenario, the human resources department would like to implement a standard employee hiring process, as well as an alternative testing implementation. All of the processes that must be initiated for hiring an employee are defined within an interface named `Hire`, as follows.

```
package org.javaee7.chapter07;

/**
 * This is the definition of an employee hiring process.  This interface
 * declares the processes that must be initiated when an employee is hired.
 * @author Juneau
 */
public interface Hire {
    public String badgeEmployee();
    public String trainEmployee();

}
```

The employee hiring implementation class must then implement `Hire`. In this case, both the standard class and the testing class must implement the `Hire` interface, but each can have its own implementation of the declared methods. For brevity, lets take a look at the test implementation, assuming that the standard implementation looks exactly the same, but includes a different implementation for each of the methods. Note that the test implementation class is annotated with `@Alternative`, meaning that it can be specified as an alternative for the standard implementation class at deployment time. The following class, `EmployeeProcessorTestImpl`, is the test implementation for the employee hiring process.

```
package org.javaee7.chapter07;

import javax.enterprise.inject.Alternative;

/**
 * This bean would be a test implementation for the employee hiring process.
 * To make this bean active, it must be specified within the beans.xml as an
 * alternative implementation for EmployeeProcessor.
 * @author Juneau
 */
@Alternative
public class EmployeeProcessorTestImpl implements Hire {

    @Override
    public String badgeEmployee() {
        String result = null;
        // Perform a test implementation for badging an employee
        return result;
    }

    @Override
    public String trainEmployee() {
        String result = null;
        // Perform a test implementation for training an employee
        return result;
    }

}
```

To make use of the alternative implementation, the alternative class must be specified within the beans.xml, which can be changed at deployment time.

```
<beans ... >
    <alternatives>
         <class>org.javaee7.chapter07.EmployeeProcessorTestImpl</class>
     </alternatives>
 </beans>
```

■ **Note** In order to use the standard implementation rather than the alternative, simply comment out the `<alternatives>` elements along with all enclosing alternative class specifications.

In CDI 1.1, the `@Priority` annotation can be used to indicate that an alternative is to be used for an entire application. For instance, in the following code, the `EmployeeProcessorTestImpl` alternative contains a priority of `APPLICATION`:

```
@Alternative
@Priority(APPLICATION)
public class EmployeeProcessorTestImpl implements Hire {
...
}
```

For more information on alternatives, please see the online documentation in the Java EE 7 tutorial.

Deprecations

The @New annotation was previously used to allow the application to obtain a new instance of a bean, which is not bound to the declared scope but has had dependency injection performed. The CDI 1.1 update deprecates the use of the @New qualifier and injects @Dependent-scoped beans instead. Let's take a look at how the @New qualifier used to work, and then you will learn how to utilize the `@Dependent` scope instead.

In the following example, the @New qualifier is specified at an injection point to obtain a new instance of a bean that is not bound to the declared scope.

```
@Produces @ConversationScoped
Order getOrder(@New(Order.class) Order order){
  ...
}
```

This same type of result can be achieved by declaring a bean as `@Dependent`. When a bean is declared to have `@Dependent` scope, the following are all true:

- It is not possible to share an injected instance of that bean between any other injection points.
- Any instance of the bean that has been injected into an object that is created by the container is bound to the same life cycle as the newly created object.
- At most one instance of the bean is instantiated if referred to within JSF or JSP EL.

- Any instance of the bean that utilizes a producer method or field, disposer method or field, or observer method invocation can service only that invocation.
- Any injections of the bean into method parameters of disposer or observer methods exist to service that method invocation only.

Going back to the example that was previously demonstrated using the @New qualifier, the same results can be achieved using the following code:

```
@Dependent
public class Order (){
    ...
    @Produces @ConversationScoped
    Order getOrder(Order order){
        ...
    }
    ...
}
```

Summary

The CDI specification contains a plethora of beneficial information, and that is because this technology encompasses a plethora of capability. Utilizing what CDI has to offer can increase developer productivity and make an application more robust. CDI is a complex API that can take some time to get your head around, but once you take the time to learn it, the benefits will pay off.

CDI 1.0 was full of new concepts and techniques that had been brought forward from the Weld project into Java EE. It changed the way that Java EE developers create enterprise applications. The first release of CDI was revolutionary for Java EE. .The latest release continues to build upon the groundbreaking features that were introduced in Java EE 6. This chapter covered only the tip of the iceberg, so please do not stop here if this chapter introduced you to CDI; embrace it and empower your applications.

CHAPTER 8

Building RESTful Web Services

The Java EE 6 platform introduced the Java API for RESTful Web Services (JAX-RS), enabling developers to easily develop powerful web services. RESTful web services are those that support the Representational State Transfer (REST) architectural style, which is an architecture for producing web services that focus on a system's resources, specifically on how states are transferred over HTTP. JAX-RS web services are stateless, and they utilize HTTP methods explicitly by mapping methods of web service classes to HTTP protocols (`GET`, `POST`, `PUT`, `DELETE`) via annotations. A RESTful web service provides custom URIs for access to web service resources, allowing web service methods to be invoked and passing zero or more parameters via a simple URI call from a web service client. RESTful web services can send responses that are in XML, JavaScript Object Notation (JSON), or other formats. The JAX-RS stack provides an annotation-rich architecture for designing web services, which makes it much easier for developers to produce powerful web services without XML configuration.

Although JAX-RS was first introduced in the Java EE platform with the release of EE 6, the concept of RESTful web services has been around for a number of years. The reference implementation for JAX-RS is a project named Jersey, which is hosted on Java.net (`http://jersey.java.net`). As such, new features for the development of RESTful web services are first available in the reference implementation, so those who want to be on the bleeding edge of REST for Java enterprise applications can utilize the Jersey project within their applications.

Java EE 7 introduces the next evolution in JAX-RS, which is the release of JAX-RS 2.0. This release is considered a major release, because it greatly enhances the functionality of JAX-RS in a number of areas. For instance, in Java EE 6, there was no standard way to produce a JAX-RS client. Developers had to utilize different means for testing web services, provide nonstandard implementations for reading and processing web service data, and so on. With the release of JAX-RS 2.0, a new client API is being introduced to fill the gap in this area. The new release also provides asynchronous processing capabilities, the ability to filter and/or intercept requests, and many more enhancements to make JAX-RS even more attractive for web service development.

This chapter will first provide a brief overview of how to utilize JAX-RS, demonstrating how to produce a web service to produce and consume data. It will then delve into coverage of each new feature, providing examples of each. Although you are expected to be familiar with the Java EE concepts, this chapter will appeal to those who are new to JAX-RS as well, since the brief overview should be enough information to get started utilizing the API.

Overview of JAX-RS

For years, some developers have cringed over the idea of developing web services because they entailed lots of XML configuration and coding. However, even though web services were historically time-consuming to create, they have proven to be a major benefit to enterprise technology. The Java EE 6 platform introduced JAX-RS for the development of web service resources, which makes it much easier to develop such resources using annotations and little or no XML configuration. JAX-RS provides the ability to create web services that have the capability of producing or consuming content by annotating Plain Old Java Object (POJO) classes with a special set of annotations according to the service you want to provide. In this section, you'll take a brief look at how to develop web services using JAX-RS, along with an overview of the different concepts. If you are new to JAX-RS, this section will provide you with enough information to get started using the technology. For those who are familiar with the API, feel free to move onto the next section of the chapter to begin learning the new features that JAX-RS 2.0 has to offer.

Utilizing the JAX-RS API

A JAX-RS application consists of one or more resources and zero or more providers that are configured via an application-supplied subclass of Application. A Java class that uses JAX-RS annotations to implement a corresponding web resource is also known as a *resource class*. A provider class implements one or more JAX-RS interfaces. As such, JAX-RS resources, and JAX-RS providers contain a myriad of annotations. JAX-RS resources must contain a constructor that can accept zero or more arguments. Public constructors may include parameters that are annotated with: @Context, @CookieParam, @HeaderParam, @PathParam, @MatrixParam, or @QueryParam. Let's begin by taking a look at an example of a JAX-RS web service resource class. The following JAX-RS service can be invoked to return a list of Jobs entities to be displayed in a String format:

```
@Path("/jobsService")
public class JobsService {

    @EJB
    JobsSession jobsSession;

    public JobsService(){

    }

    @GET
    @Produces("text/html")
    public String getAsHtml() {
        List<Jobs> jobList = jobsSession.retrieveJobsSynchronously();
        StringBuilder sb = new StringBuilder();
        sb.append("<p>");
        for (Jobs job:jobList){
            sb.append(job.getJobId() + " - " + job.getTitle());
        }
        sb.append("<p>");
        return sb.toString();
    }
}
```

As mentioned previously, JAX-RS applications must be configured via an application subclass of javax.ws.rs.core.Application. Therefore, if no Application subclass has been provided, then a servlet must be configured within web.xml to make use of Application. The following servlet resources should be added to the web.xml file of any Java EE application that will use JAX-RS, and does not already contain a servlet that handles the application accordingly:

```
<servlet>
        <servlet-name>javax.ws.rs.core.Application</servlet-name>
        <load-on-startup>1</load-on-startup>
    </servlet>
    <servlet-mapping>
        <servlet-name>javax.ws.rs.core.Application</servlet-name>
        <url-pattern>/rest/*</url-pattern>
    </servlet-mapping>
```

If however, an application contains a servlet that contains an initialization parameter of `javax.ws.rs.core.Application`, and whose value is the fully qualified name of the `Application` subclass, then no additional configuration is necessary.

Once an application has been configured to use JAX-RS or contains a servlet that handles the application, resource classes and providers can be implemented. To invoke the JobsService REST service that was implemented in the example, deploy the application that has been configured to accordingly, and load the appropriate URL (`http://localhost:8080/IntroToJavaEE7/rest/jobsService`) into a web browser. In this case, the application is named `IntroToJavaEE7`, since you are working with the book sources. Table 8-1 describes the possible annotations that can be used to create a REST service.

Table 8-1. *REST Service Annotations*

Annotation	Description
`@POST`	Request method designator that processes HTTP `POST` requests.
`@GET`	Request method designator that processes HTTP `GET` requests.
`@PUT`	Request method designator that processes HTTP `PUT` requests.
`@DELETE`	Request method designator that processes HTTP `DELETE` requests.
`@HEAD`	Request method designator that corresponds to the HTTP `HEAD` method. It processes HTTP `HEAD` requests.
`@Path`	The value of this annotation should correlate to the relative URI path that indicates where the Java class will be hosted. Variables can be embedded in the URIs to make a URI path template.
`@Context`	Injects an instance of a supported resource.
`@MatrixParam`	A type of parameter that can be extracted for use in the resource class. Matrix parameters are extracted from the request.
`@CookieParam`	Extracts the value of a cookie.
`@HeaderParam`	Extracts the value of a header.
`@PathParam`	A type of parameter that can be extracted for use in the resource class. URI path parameters are extracted from the request URI, and the parameter names correspond to the URI path template variable names specified in the `@Path` class-level annotation.
`@QueryParam`	A type of parameter that can be extracted for use in the resource class. Query parameters are extracted from the request.
`@Consumes`	Used to specify the MIME media types of representations that a resource can consume.
`@Produces`	Used to specify the MIME media types of representations that a resource can produce.
`@Provider`	Used to specify a provider class for automatic discovery.

To designate a class a REST service, the `@Path` annotation must be placed prior to the class or before at least one of the class method signatures. The `@Path` annotation is responsible for constructing the URI that will be used for accessing the web resource. To learn more detail regarding `@Path`, please see the following section, "Constructing Meaningful URIs."

Designate methods with the `@GET`, `@POST`, `@PUT`, or `@DELETE` designator to process the type of web service request that is desired. Methods annotated as such are also known as resource methods. Adding resource methods to a resource class generates web service functionality. If more than one resource method exists within a REST web service implementation and `@Path` is specified only at the class level and not at the method level, then the method that returns the MIME type the client requires will be invoked. If you want your method to display content, designate a method with @GET. If you want to create a method for updating or inserting an object or data, designate the method as @POST. If you are creating a method for inserting new objects only, then designate it with @PUT. Finally, if you are creating a method for removing objects, then designate it with @DELETE.

REST services can become fairly complex if they constitute many different methods and paths. Entire applications exist based upon REST services, where all Create, Retrieve, Update, Delete (CRUD) manipulations are invoked via web service calls. This example provides only the foundation for developing with JAX-RS, but it should be enough to get you started using the API.

Constructing Meaningful URIs

To use a web service, a client must make a call to a URI that will, in turn, invoke the service. Therefore, URIs map to resource methods, which in turn invoke web service content production or consummation. The URI of a web service makes a resource method accessible to a web URI. Therefore, it is important to ensure that the URL makes logical sense with regard to the data that the web resource is consuming or producing. The @Path annotation is used to indicate the URI that should correspond to the service. The full URI includes the host name, port number, application name, and REST servlet name, followed by the path designated with the @Path annotation. The following example demonstrates a simple REST service implementation named SimpleRest.

```
package org.javaee7.services;

import javax.ws.rs.Consumes;
import javax.ws.rs.GET;
import javax.ws.rs.POST;
import javax.ws.rs.Produces;
import javax.ws.rs.Path;
import javax.ws.rs.QueryParam;

// Set the PATH to http://host:port/application/rest/simplerest/
@Path("/simplerest")
public class SimpleRest {

    private String message = "Hello from a simple REST Service";
    private String htmlMessage = "<p><b>" + message + "</b></p>";

    @GET
    // Produces plain text message
    @Produces("text/plain")
    public String getPlainMessage() {
        return message;
    }

    @GET
    // Produces plain text message
    @Produces("text/html")
    public String getHTMLMessage() {
        return htmlMessage;
    }

    @POST
    @Path("add")
    @Consumes("text/plain")
```

```
    public String add(@QueryParam("text") String text){
        this.message = text;
        return message;
    }
}
```

In the example, the @Path annotation specifies /simplerest as the service path, so the URL http://localhost:8080/IntroToJavaEE7/rest/simplerest will invoke the web service. It is possible to include variables within a URL by enclosing them in the @Path annotation, within brackets using the syntax {var}. For example, if each user had his or her own profile for a particular site, the @Path designation could be as follows:

```
...
@Path("/simplerest/{user}")
...
```

In such a case, the URL could look like the following: http://localhost:8080/IntroToJavaEE7/rest/simplerest/juneau.

In addition to specifying the @Path annotation at the class level, it can also be specified before any methods that are marked with @GET, @POST, @PUT, or @DELETE in order to specify a URI for invoking the denoted method. Moreover, variables can be placed within the path in order to accept a more dynamic URL. For instance, suppose a method was added to the class in Solution #1 that would return a greeting for the user specified as a parameter within the URL. You can do something like the following in order to make the URL unique:

```
@Path("{user}")
@GET
@Produces("text/html")
public String getUserMessage(@PathParam("user") String user){
  return "Greetings " + "<b>" + user + "</b>";
}
```

In this case, the getUserMessage method would be invoked if a URL such as the following were placed into the browser: http://localhost:8080/IntroToJavaEE7/rest/simplerest/josh. If this URL were specified, then the method would be invoked, passing josh as the user variable value, and the message would be displayed as follows:

```
Greetings josh
```

Producing Content

To produce content via a web resource, create a Java class and annotate it with the @Path annotation, specifying a path you want to use for publishing the resource. Use the @Produces annotation to specify the MIME type for content you want to produce from a decorated method. The following excerpt demonstrates the use of @Produces:

```
...
    @GET
    @Path("/get")
    // Produces an XML message
    @Produces(MediaType.APPLICATION_XML)
    public String getProducts() {
        List<Product> productList = productSession.findAll();
        StringBuilder xmlstring= new StringBuilder();
```

```
        for(Product product:productList){
            xmlstring.append("<product>");
            xmlstring.append("<id>" + product.getId() + "</id>");
            xmlstring.append("<name>" + product.getName() + "</name>");
            xmlstring.append("<description>" + product.getDescription() + "</description>");
            xmlstring.append("</product>");

        }
        return xmlstring.toString();
    }
```

The @GET annotation designates this as a resource method that will be utilized for obtaining data. When the specified URI that is designated within the @Path annotation is visited, this method will be invoked, producing XML content.

Consuming Content

Annotate resource methods within a JAX-RS class with @POST or @PUT to indicate that some content is being passed to the method. The following briefly summarizes the different HTTP methods that can be used for consuming content:

- POST updates an existing resource or creates a new resource.
- PUT creates a new idempotent resource.

To specify the type of content being passed, annotate the same method with @Consumes(content-type). The following excerpt demonstrates the use of @Consumes:

```
@Path("simplerest")
public class SimpleRest {
...
@PUT
    @Path("add")
    @Consumes("text/plain")
    public String add(@QueryParam("text") String text){
        this.message = text;
        return message;
    }
...
}
```

Note that the add method specifies the @Path annotation, so it becomes accessible by appending the add string to the URI that was specified in the class's @Path. To input a new message stating Java, you would visit a URL using the following format in your browser, which would pass the new message to the text variable:

```
http://your-host:port/ApplicationName/rest/simplerest/add?text=Java
```

■ **Note** For the list of different content types that can be produced or consumed, please refer to Table 8-2.

Client API

Historically, it has involved many lines of code to invoke REST services. That is because in order to access a REST service, clients using HttpUrlConnection had to be created. In the JAX-RS 2.0 release, a client API has been included, allowing developers to follow a standard API for developing clients.

To use the client API, obtain an instance of javax.ws.rs.client.Client by calling the javax.ws.rs.client.ClientBuilder newClient method. Once a Client instance is obtained, it can be configured by setting properties or registering Provider and/or Feature classes. Properties are simply name-value pairs that can be passed to the client via the setProperty method. Features are Providers that implement the Feature interface. A Feature can be used for grouping related properties and Providers into a single unit, making configuration even easier.

Let's take a look at a simple client that will call upon a target URI for the simplerest service that was created in one of this chapter's earlier examples. In the following example, a Client instance is obtained, and then a URI target is set. The client goes on to request a response of type application/xml and then makes the call to get the request.

```
public class RestClientJava {

    public static void main(String[] args){
        // Obtain an instance of the client
        Client client = ClientBuilder.newClient();

        WebTarget webTarget = client.target("http://localhost:8080/IntroToJavaEE7/rest/simplerest");
        Response res = webTarget.request("text/plain").get();

        System.out.println(res.readEntity(String.class));
    }
}
```

As a result of running this client class, the output of the web service call will be written to the server log. Although this client simply prints the result, a real client could be created using the same technique, and then it could process the data into a more useful format. If one wished to create a web client, rather than a standard Java client, the same JAX-RS client API can be used within a web application. For instance, the following JSF managed bean can be used to implement the same tests as RestClientJava that was demonstrated above.

```
import javax.faces.application.FacesMessage;
import javax.faces.bean.ManagedBean;
import javax.faces.context.FacesContext;
import javax.ws.rs.client.Client;
import javax.ws.rs.client.WebTarget;
import javax.ws.rs.core.Response;

@ManagedBean(name="restClientOne")
public class RestClientOne {

    private String clientOutput;

    // May be able to do @Inject before final release
    public void testServiceOne(){
        // Obtain an instance of the client
        Client client = javax.ws.rs.client.ClientBuilder.newClient();
```

```
        WebTarget webTarget =  client.target("http://localhost:8080/IntroToJavaEE7/rest/simplerest");
        Response res = webTarget.request("text/plain").get();

        FacesContext.getCurrentInstance().addMessage(null, new FacesMessage(
                FacesMessage.SEVERITY_INFO, "Invoked test client",
                "Invoked test client"));
        setClientOutput(res.toString());

    }

    /**
     * @return the clientOutput
     */
    public String getClientOutput() {
        return clientOutput;
    }

    /**
     * @param clientOutput the clientOutput to set
     */
    public void setClientOutput(String clientOutput) {
        this.clientOutput = clientOutput;
    }

}
```

Web Resource Targets

The first step toward invoking a web resource is to make a call to a target. This can be done in a couple of ways. The previous example demonstrated the use of the `Client` target method, which accepts a URI and returns a `WebTarget`.

```
WebTarget myTarget = client.target("http://somehost.com/service");
```

Once the target has been obtained, a number of things can be done with it. A request can be made against it, as in the `RestClientOne` example, by invoking the target's request method. A target can also be further qualified by calling its path method and passing the next sequence in a URI path.

```
WebTarget myTarget =
    client.target("http://somehost.com/service").path("one");
```

A path can also contain dynamic content in the form of `URI` template parameters. To include a template parameter, wrap the dynamic portion of the path in curly brackets, as in { }, and then chain a call to the `pathParam` method, passing the name-value pair of the parameter.

```
WebTarget myTarget =
  client.target("http://somehost.com/service").path("one").path("{code}")
  .pathParam("code","100375");
```

WebTarget objects are immutable, in that methods for altering WebTargets, such as path, return new instances of WebTarget. This pattern is very similar to the Builder pattern, although there is no build() method call. WebTargets can also be configured by registering features or providers via a call to the target's register method, passing either type of class.

```
client.register(Feature.class)
client.register(Provider.class)
```

An example of a basic provider class that implements MessageBodyWriter is as follows:

```
@Provider
public class MyProvider implements WriterInterceptor {

    @Override
    public void aroundWriteTo(WriterInterceptorContext ctx) throws IOException,
WebApplicationException {
        String customMessage = "This is a custom message";
        OutputStream os = ctx.getOutputStream();
        ctx.proceed();
        os.write(customMessage.getBytes());
    }

}
```

■ **Note** WriterInterceptor wraps calls to MessageBodyWriter.writeTo(). That wrapping makes it easy to develop a MessageBodyWriter solution by simply implementing the aroundWriteTo method.

Now let's take a look at how this provider class is registered to a web service client. In the following client, the MyProvider interceptor is applied to the client for testing.

```
public static void main(String[] args){
        // Obtain an instance of the client
        Client client = ClientBuilder.newClient();
        client.register(MyProvider.class);
        WebTarget webTarget =  client.target("http://localhost:8080/IntroToJavaEE7/rest/simplerest");
        Response res = webTarget.request("text/plain").get();

        System.out.println(res.readEntity(String.class));
    }
```

Obtaining a Response

The example at the beginning of this section demonstrated a simple client that returns an XML response. However, it is possible to return different response types by passing different Strings or MediaType fields to the client target request method. Table 8-2 lists the different MediaType fields that can be used. All fields listed within the table that contain a _TYPE suffix are of type MediaType, whereas the others are static String types.

Table 8-2. *MediaType Fields*

Field	String
APPLICATION_ATOM_XML	"application/atom+xml"
APPLICATION_ATOM_XML_TYPE	
APPLICATION_FORM_URLENCODED	"application/x-www-form-urlencoded"
APPLICATION_FORM_URLENCODED_TYPE	
APPLICATION_JSON	"application/json"
APPLICATION_JSON_TYPE	
APPLICATION_OCTET_STREAM	"application/octet-stream"
APPLICATION_OCTET_STREAM_TYPE	
APPILCATION_SVG_XML	"application/svg+xml"
APPLICATION_SVG_XML_TYPE	
APPLICATION_XHTML_XML	"application/xhtml+xml"
APPLICATION_XHTML_XML_TYPE	
APPLICATION_XML	"application/xml"
APPLICATION_XML_TYPE	
MEDIA_TYPE_WILDCARD	"*"
MULTIPART_FORM_DATA	"multipart/form-data"
MULTIPART_FORM_DATA_TYPE	
TEXT_HTML	"text/html"
TEXT_HTML_TYPE	
TEXT_PLAIN	"text/plain"
TEXT_PLAIN_TYPE	
TEXT_XML	"text/xml"
TEXT_XML_TYPE	
WILDCARD	"*/*"
WILDCARD_TYPE	

To obtain a requested resource, call the `WebTarget.request().get()` method, which will return a `javax.ws.rs.core.Response` object. The returned `Response` can be used to process the results accordingly, depending upon the results you are trying to achieve within the client. In the example, the `Response` object's `readEntity` method is called, which simply returns the results in the requested format. In the example, a `String.class` is passed to the `readEntity` method, implying that a response should be returned in `String` format. To see a complete list of methods that can be called against a `Response` object, please refer to the online documentation (`http://docs.oracle.com/javaee/7/api/javax/ws/rs/core/Response.html`) because the list is quite lengthy.

It is possible to filter a response by chaining methods, as needed, to specify headers, cookies, and so on, off of the `request` method. Each of these chained method calls returns a `Builder` object, which can be further built upon. The methods that can be chained to further build the request are cookie(Cookie); cookie(String, String); header(String, Object); headers(MultivaluedMap<String, Object>); and register.

Returning Entities

Sometimes there is a requirement to return a type other than Response from a web resource. In these cases, it is possible to obtain an entity type by passing the entity class to the get call. The following lines of code demonstrate how to return a Jobs entity, rather than a standard Response object:

```
Client client = ClientBuilder.newClient();

Jobs jobs = client.target("http://localhost:8080/IntroToJavaEE7/rest/jobsSearch")
.request("application/xml").get(Jobs.class);

System.out.println(jobs.getJobId() + " - " + jobs.getTitle());
```

In cases where entities are being returned, the request type is required to be application/xml or APPLICATION_XML_TYPE.

Invoking at a Later Time

There are cases when it makes sense to obtain a request and prepare it for execution but not invoke that request until a later time. In such cases, you can prepare an Invocation that can be executed at a later time. In the following lines of code, an Invocation is created by making a request to a WebTarget and then calling the buildGet method.

```
Invocation inv1 = client.target("http://localhost:8080/IntroToJavaEE7/rest/simplerest")
                .request("text/plain").buildGet();
// Sometime later...
Response res = inv1.invoke();
```

If you were posting a response, the buildPost method could be called against the WebTarget instead, as shown here:

```
Invocation inv1 = client.target("http://localhost:8080/IntroToJavaEE7/rest/makeithappen")
                .request("text/plain").buildPost(order);
 Response res = inv1.invoke();
```

■ **Note** To asynchronously execute an Invocation, call the invocation submit method, rather than the invoke method.

Invocation objects can be configured similarly to WebTarget and Client objects. Filters, interceptors, properties, features, and providers can be configured on an Invocation by calling the register method and passing the appropriate configuration instance, as demonstrated here:

```
// Assume that inv1 is an Invocation instance
String result = inv1.register(MyInterceptor.class).invoke(String.class);
```

■ **Note** To learn more about filters and interceptors, read the "Filters and Interceptors" section in this chapter.

WebTarget Injection

A WebTarget can be injected into any JAX-RS managed resource by specifying the @Uri annotation and passing the WebTarget URI. In following example, where a WebTarget resource is injected into a JAX-RS resource to demonstrate this concept:

```
@Path("/orderservice")
public class OrderService {
    @Uri("order/{id}")
    WebTarget orderId;

    //...
}
```

Filters and Interceptors

The concept of filters and interceptors is analogous to the post office processing your mail before it comes to your address. Rather than a message being delivered directly from point A to point B, it is first routed to one or more postal offices where it is further processed before reaching point B. Web resource filters and interceptors apply that same concept to requests or responses that are being processed via a web service. If a filter or interceptor is bound to a web resource, then it will be invoked at some point in the life cycle of a request or response to that web resource. The type of filter or interceptor determines at what point in the life cycle it is applied. Interceptors (otherwise known as *entity interceptors*) wrap around a method invocation at a specified extension point. Filters, on the other hand, execute code at a specified extension point, but they are not wrapped around methods. In the next few sections, you will take a closer look at each and how they are used.

Filters

An extension point is an interface that includes a method, which is responsible for filtering or intercepting the request or response. Filters have four such extension point interfaces: ClientRequestFilter, ClientResponseFilter, ContainerRequestFilter, and ContainerResponseFilter. The name of the extension point helps describe to what a filter is applied and at what point. ClientRequestFilter and ClientResponseFilter are for use with the JAX-RS Client API. A ClientRequestFilter is applied before an HTTP request is delivered to the network, and a ClientResponseFilter is applied when a server response is received and before control is returned to the application. ContainerRequestFilter and ContainerResponseFilter classes are for use with the JAX-RS Server API. Similar to the client-side filters, a ContainerRequestFilter is applied upon receiving a request from a client, and a ContainerResponseFilter is applied before the HTTP response is delivered.

Before going any further, let's take a look at an example of a client filter, as well as an example of a server filter. The client filter will be used to print a message to the server log when a request is received or before a response is sent.

```
import java.io.BufferedReader;
import java.io.IOException;
import java.io.InputStream;
import java.io.InputStreamReader;
import javax.ws.rs.container.ContainerRequestContext;
import javax.ws.rs.container.ContainerRequestFilter;
import javax.ws.rs.container.ContainerResponseContext;
import javax.ws.rs.container.ContainerResponseFilter;
import javax.ws.rs.ext.Provider;
```

```
@Provider
class AlertFilter implements ContainerRequestFilter,
        ContainerResponseFilter {

    @Override
    public void filter(ContainerRequestContext requestContext)
            throws IOException {
        alert(requestContext);
    }

    @Override
    public void filter(ContainerRequestContext crc, ContainerResponseContext crc1) throws
IOException {
        alert(crc);
    }

    public void alert(ContainerRequestContext context) {

        try(InputStream in = context.getEntityStream();) {
            if (in != null) {
                InputStreamReader inreader = new InputStreamReader(in);
                BufferedReader reader = new BufferedReader(inreader);
                String text = "";

                while ((text = reader.readLine()) != null) {
                    System.out.println(text);

                }

            }
        } catch (IOException ex) {
            // Error handling
        }
    }
}
```

■ **Note** Both filter methods in the implementation are required because each accepts different parameters, and implementing the `ContainerRequestFilter` and `ContainerResponseFilter` require it.

Note that the `AlertFilter` class is decorated with the `@Provider` annotation. That is because all filters and interceptors are provider classes and must be annotated as such. The filter must implement `ContainerRequestFilter` and `ContainerResponseFilter` since it is a server-side filter implementation. These two classes provide information regarding the filter, such as URIs, headers, and so on.

Filters are grouped into chains, and each of the extension points contains their own filter chain. The filters in the chain are executed in order of precedence via priority. To learn more about setting the priority, please refer to the "Filter and Interceptor Priorities" section. If a request filter needs to be executed upon receiving a request but before a resource is matched, then the `@PreMatching` annotation can be placed on that filter.

■ **Note** The `abortWith(Response)` method of a `ClientRequestFilter` or `ContainerResponseFilter` can stop execution of the filter chain.

Entity Interceptors

As mentioned in the previous section, an extension point is an interface that includes a method, which is responsible for filtering or intercepting the request or response. Entity interceptors have two such extension points: `ReaderInterceptor` and `WriterInterceptor`. An entity interceptor class must implement one or both of these extension points. Also mentioned previously, entity interceptors wrap calls to methods. More specifically, `MessageBodyWriter` implementations wrap calls to the `writeTo` method, whereas `MessageBodyReader` implementations wrap calls to the `readFrom` method.

Let's take a look at an interceptor so that you can more easily visualize how they are coded. In the following example, the `aroundWriteTo` method converts an `OutputStream` to a `ZipOutputStream`:

```
@Provider
public class ZipEncoder implements WriterInterceptor {

    public void aroundWriteTo(WriterInterceptorContext ctx) throws IOException,
WebApplicationException {
        ZipOutputStream zip = new ZipOutputStream(ctx.getOutputStream());

        try {
            zip.putNextEntry(new ZipEntry("Test));
            ctx.setOutputStream(zip);
            ctx.proceed();
        } catch (ZipException ex){
            System.out.println("ZipEncoder ERROR: " + ex);
        } finally {
            zip.finish();
        }
    }
}
```

As you can see in the example, a `aroundWriteTo` method must accept a `WriteInterceptorContext` argument, whereas a `readFrom` method must accept a `ReaderInterceptorContext` argument. These arguments provide read and write access to any parameters that are passed into the wrapped methods. Entity interceptors can be chained, just like filters. To proceed to the next interceptor in the chain, an interceptor must call its `proceed` method.

Binding Filters and Interceptors

Filters and interceptors must be associated to application classes or methods, and this process is also known as *binding*. The default type of binding is global binding, and any filter or interceptor that does not include annotations is bound globally. Global binding associates the filter or interceptor with all resource methods (those annotated with `@GET`, `@POST`, and so on) in an application. That said, any time a resource method is invoked, all globally bound filters and interceptors are processed as well.

Filters and interceptors can be registered manually via `Application` or `Configuration`, or they can be registered dynamically. To indicate that a filter or interceptor should be registered dynamically, it can be annotated with `@Provider`. If a filter or interceptor is not annotated as such, it must be registered manually.

To manually bind a filter or interceptor to a resource method, the filter or interceptor class must be denoted with an @NameBinding annotation. An @NameBinding annotation can be coded just like a standard annotation, but the annotation implementation should also include the @NameBinding annotation in its interface. The following annotation code could be used to create an @NameBinding annotation that might be placed on a filter that is responsible for firing alerts:

```
@NameBinding
@Target({ ElementType.TYPE, ElementType.METHOD })
@Retention(value = RetentionPolicy.RUNTIME)
public @interface Alerter { }
```

To associate the @NameBinding with a filter or interceptor, simply annotate the filter or interceptor class with it. The following AlertFilter class is a filter implementation that is denoted with the @Alerter annotation:

```
@Provider
@Alerter
class AlertFilter implements ContainerRequestFilter,
        ContainerResponseFilter {

...

}
```

That filter can now be bound to a resource method by annotating the resource method with the same @ NameBinding as the filter class, as demonstrated here:

```
@GET
@Produces("text/html")
@Alerter
public String  getJobs(){
    ...
}
```

■ **Note** This same concept can be applied to Application subclasses in order to globally bind the filter or interceptor.

Setting Priorities

As mentioned in the previous sections, filters and interceptors can be chained. Chains of filters or interceptors invoke individual filters or interceptors based upon a given priority. To assign priority to a filter or interceptor, denote the implementation class with the @Priority annotation. The Priorities class in JAX-RS is used to specify the type of priority that needs to be set. There are built-in priorities for security, header decorators, decoders, and encoders. In the following example, the priority of a filter, the AlertFilter that was introduced in the previous section, is set to a priority of Priorities.USER:

```
@Provider
@Alerter
@Priority(Priorities.USER)
```

```
class AlertFilter implements ContainerRequestFilter,
        ContainerResponseFilter {

    @Override
    public void filter(ContainerRequestContext requestContext)
            throws IOException {
        alert(requestContext);
    }
...
```

Table 8-3 lists the different priorities that are available by default, along with their priority number.

Table 8-3. *Priority Values*

Priority	Number
`Priorities.AUTHENTICATION`	1000
`Priorities.AUTHORIZATION`	2000
`Priorities.HEADER_DECORATOR`	3000
`Priorities.ENTITY_CODER`	4000
`Priorities.USER`	5000

The default priority, if nothing is specified, is `Priorities.USER`.

Asynchronous Processing

Asynchronous processing with JAX-RS is available for both the Client API and Server API. On the server side, it is possible for a resource method to suspend a client connection and then resume it at some point in the future when the response becomes available. To make this occur, the method that is responsible for receiving requests within the web resource must accept an `@Suspended final AsyncResponse` argument. It is assumed that this method will be performing some long-running task, and hence it will be made asynchronous in order to achieve better performance. The `AsyncResponse` argument will be called at some point in the future when the long-running task has completed, and its resume method will be invoked.

Asynchronous tasks usually involve the spawning of a thread, which will be used to run a process in the background. JAX-RS asynchronous processing is no different; the long-running operation should occur within a `Runnable` instance, and the `AsyncResponse resume` method should be called at the end of the task within the `Runnable`. The `ManagedExecutorService`, part of the new Java EE Concurrency API (covered in Chapter 11), can be used to submit the `Runnable` for processing. The following example demonstrates this process:

```
@Path("/async/longRunningservice")
public class LongRunningService {

    @Resource(name = "concurrent/BatchExecutor")
    ManagedExecutorService mes;
```

```
    @GET
    public void longRunningOp(@Suspended final AsyncResponse ar) {
        mes.submit(
                new Runnable() {
            public void run() {
                // Long running operation
                ar.resume("Return asynchronously!");
            }
        });
    }
}
```

An EJB resource can also be utilized in an asynchronous manner, although coded a bit differently. A web resource method within an EJB can denoted with the @Asynchronous annotation to signify that the method contents are to be processed asynchronously. The method should accept the same @Suspended AsyncResponse argument, and that argument's resume method should be invoked at the end of the long-running process. There is no need to create a Runnable or work with an Executor in an EJB web resource because the @Asynchronous annotation takes care of that detail. The EJB container automatically allocates the resources necessary to handle the asynchronous operation. The following example demonstrates the coding of an asynchronous method within an EJB:

```
...
@GET @Asynchronous
public void longRunningOp(@Suspended AsyncResponse ar){
    // Long running operation
    ar.resume("Return asynchronously");
}
```

Note that there is no special treatment that needs to be done, with regard to threading or utilization of Runnable. Everything just works because the EJB container takes care of the concurrency.

Resource Context

The JAX-RS API provides contexts that can be used to obtain metadata information about the application deployment context and/or the context of individual requests. To obtain metadata regarding context, the required metadata can be injected into a web resource by specifying the @Context annotation along with the context type you want to inject. For instance, if there is a requirement to obtain metadata regarding an application's configuration, an instance of the application-supplied Application subclass can be injected into a web resource class field or method parameter by specifying the @Context annotation.

```
@Context Application app;
```

Other contexts are made available via the @Context annotation as well. Table 8-4 describes the different context types.

Table 8-4. Context Types

Context Type	Description
`Application`	Provides information regarding application configuration
`UriInfo`	Provides static or dynamic information regarding a request URI
`HttpHeaders`	Provides access to request header information, either in a map format or via convenience methods
`Request`	Provides support for content negotiation and preconditions
`SecurityContext`	Provides information about the security of a request
`Providers`	Allows for a lookup of provider instances
`ResourceContext`	Provides access to the instantiation and initialization of resource or subresource classes in the per-request scope

Summary

The JAX-RS API has been re-worked to enable more customization of REST services. Along with an expanded API for creating services, a client API has been included with JAX-RS 2.0, providing another standard means for which to create stand-alone or web clients. Features such as asynchronous processing and filters will increase the capability of services, while making them more useable via rich clients such as those written in HTML5.

CHAPTER 9

WebSockets and JSON-P

The Java EE 7 platform aims to provide a common ground for developing Java Enterprise solutions that incorporate HTML5 technology. As such, there are a few core features that have been added to Java EE 7, allowing for better bi-directional support of HTML5.

This chapter will focus on examples that demonstrate these HTML5 application programming interfaces (APIs). You will learn how to make use of WebSockets and JSON-P so that your application's client-server communication can become seamless, whether the user interface is written with HTML5, JSF, or another markup language.

WebSockets

The Java EE 7 platform eases communication between the client and the server via a technology named WebSockets, enabling more parity with the HTML5 standard. WebSockets are full-duplex communication mechanisms that allow for both text and binary messages to be sent between clients and servers, without the HTTP request/response lifecycle. WebSockets allow either the client or the server to send a message at any time, providing an asynchronous solution for delivering data while the user is performing a task, most often a browser task or event.

To get started, it is useful to familiarize yourself with a few of the most common terms that you may come across when reading about WebSockets. Here are some terms to know:

> *Connection*: Networking connection between two endpoints that are utilizing the WebSocket protocol.
>
> *Endpoint*: A Java component that is stationed at one end of a communication between two peers.
>
> *Client Endpoint*: Initiates connections to a peer, but may not accept connections.
>
> *Server Endpoint*: Accepts WebSocket connections from peers, but cannot initiate connections.
>
> *Peer*: Represents the opposite participant from an endpoint in a WebSocket communication.
>
> *Session*: Represents a sequence of WebSocket connections between endpoint and a single peer.

A WebSocket application consists of endpoints that can be created in a couple of different ways. The first way to create an endpoint is to implement the WebSocket API interfaces, also referred to as a programmatic endpoint. The second is to utilize annotations from the WebSocket API to decorate a "Plain Old Java Object," or POJO, also referred to as an annotated endpoint. If using the second means, the implementation creates the appropriate objects to deploy the POJO as a WebSocket endpoint at runtime. Endpoints that are designed to listen for incoming requests are known as `ServerEndpoints`. Likewise, endpoints that are designed to initate requests and not to listen are known as `ClientEndpoints`. To see the complete Javadoc for WebSockets, please refer to it online at: `http://docs.oracle.com/javaee/7/tutorial/doc/websocket.htm#GKJIQ5`.

…ming Messages

…er-side class can accept messages from clients by configuring it as a WebSocket endpoint. To develop a …oSocket endpoint, you can utilize an annotation-based approach or an interface implementation approach. …o use annotations for creating a WebSocket server endpoint, create a Java "Plain Old Java Object" POJO, and annotate it with `@ServerEndpoint` (`javax.websocket.server.ServerEndpoint`). The `@ServerEndpoint` annotation accepts a String-based path attribute, which is used to indicate the URI path at which the server is available to accept client messages. Therefore, when the server is started, the specified path would be appended to the end of the context path and application name in which the WebSocket resides. Additionally, a path may include one or more string-based parameters after the server endpoint to pass additional parameters to subsequent method calls. By initiating a call to that URL, a method annotated with `@OnMessage` (`javax.websocket.OnMessage`), will be invoked to process the message that is sent, and any additional parameters may be accepted via the inclusion of the `@PathParam` annotation within the list of parameters for that method's signature. There are two other important methods within a WebSocket server endpoint, and those are the methods that are invoked when a connection is established and when it is closed. The method that is to be invoked when the connection has been established should be annotated with `@OnOpen`, whereas the method that is to be invoked when the connection is closed should be annotated with `@OnClose`.

Let's dive a bit deeper into the three important methods for implementing a WebSocket endpoint. Each of the three methods can accept a number of optional parameters. To begin, it should be noted that each of the methods accepts zero or more strings annotated with `@PathParam`. As mentioned previously, these parameters refer to strings that have been appended to the WebService endpoint URI.

The `@OnMessage` method can accept the following three types of parameters:

- `javax.websocket.Session`
- any number of strings annotated with `@PathParam`
- the message itself

The `@OnOpen` method can accept the following three types of parameters:

- `javax.websocket.Session`
- an `EndpointConfig` instance (Contains metadata regarding the endpoint configuration)
- any number of strings annotated with `@PathParam`

Lastly, the `@OnClose` method can accept any of the following three types of parameters:

- `javax.websocket.Session` (Not accessible after the connection is closed)
- `javax.websocket.CloseReason` (Contains the reason why connection was closed)
- any number of strings annotated with `@PathParam`

In the example below, a class named `AcmeChatEndpoint` is annotated as a WebSocket, so it is accessible to clients as an endpoint for receiving messages, and returning a response. When initiating communication with the WebSocket endpoint, the client must utilize the URL that contains a scheme of "ws", rather than "http" (e.g., `ws://localhost:8080/AppName/ServerEndpoint`). The "ws" URI scheme was introduced by the WebSocket protocol, and as such, indicates that the URI is used for communication with a WebSocket. In this example, a client can send a message to the server via the `AcmeChatEndpoint` WebSocket, and the server can send a message back at the same time, because WebSockets allow for full-duplex communication, as opposed to half-duplex communication, which is offered by HTTP. Full-duplex communication is an HTML5 standard, accomplishing similar functionality to Asynchronous JavaScript and XML (AJAX), which utilizes a request-response communication.

In the following example, a simple POJO class, named `org.javaee7.chapter09.AcmeChatEndpoint`, is annotated to indicate that it should be accessible via the web as a WebSocket endpoint. The class contains a method named `messageReceiver`, which is annotated with `@OnMessage` to make it accessible to a client as a callable message consumer.

```
@ServerEndpoint("/acmechat")
public class AcmeChatEndpoint {

    /**
     * Message receiver method
     *
     * @param message
     * @return
     */
    @OnMessage
    public String messageReceiver(String message) {
        System.out.println("Received message:" + message);
        // Do something with message
        return message;
    }

    @OnOpen
    public void onOpen(Session session) {
        System.out.println("onOpen: " + session.getId());
        // Do something with session object
    }

    @OnClose
    public void onClose(Session session) {
        System.out.println(session.getId());
        // Do something with session object
    }
}
```

The WebSocket endpoint will be accessible to clients at the URL `ws://localhost:8080/IntroToEE7/acmechat`. When a message is sent from a client to the endpoint, it is sent to the `messageReceiver` method, where is processed accordingly. In this case, a simple `String` message is returned to the client. Note that the `messageReceiver` method could have accepted a number of string-based parameters, as mentioned previously. For instance, to send a `messageId` parameter to the endpoint, path of `/acmechat/{messageId}` could have been used, and the method would then look as follows:

```
@OnMessage
public String messageReceiver(String message,
                              @PathParam("messageId") String messageId) {
    System.out.println("Received message:" + message + messageId);
    // Do something with message
    return message;
}
```

To learn more regarding `@PathParam`, please see the online documeantation at `http://docs.oracle.com/javaee/7/api/javax/websocket/server/PathParam.html`.

To implement a WebSocket endpoint without using annotations, extend `javax.websocket.Endpoint`. In such a case, the endpoint implementation must override the `onMessage` method, and can optionally override `onOpen` and `onError`. The following example class demonstrates a WebSocket endpoint using the interface implementation approach.

```
public class AcmeChatEndpointIf extends javax.websocket.Endpoint {

    @Override
    public void onOpen(Session session, EndpointConfig config) {
        // Implementation here
    }

    public void onClose(Session session){
        // Implementation here
    }

    public void onError(Session session){
        // Implementation here
    }

}
```

Creating WebSocket Clients

A POJO class can be made a WebSocket client by annotating it with `@ClientEndpoint`. Any POJO that is annotated as such can be used to initiate, but will not listen for incoming requests and therefore contains on path specification. The following code demonstrates an example of such a client.

```
@ClientEndpoint
public class AcmeChatClient {

    @OnOpen
    public void onOpen(Session session) {
        System.out.println("Connected to endpoint: " + session.getAsyncRemote());

        String name = "Message from the Acme Chat Client";

        session.getAsyncRemote().sendText(name);

    }

    @OnMessage
    public void processMessage(String message) {
        System.out.println("Received message in client: " + message);
    }
}
```

Utilizing a Simple Client

To test a WebSocket without creating the associated browser client page, make use of the `ContainerProvider.getWebSocketContainer()` method. This method returns a `WebSocketContainer` object, which can then be used to connect to an existing web socket endpoint. The following class demonstrates how to test a connection to a WebSocket endpoint using a simple client.

```
public class WebSocketClient {

    public static void main(String[] args) {
        try {
            WebSocketContainer container = ContainerProvider.getWebSocketContainer();
            String uri = "ws://localhost:8080/IntroToEE7/acmechat/";
            System.out.println("Connecting to " + uri);
            container.connectToServer(AcmeChatEndpoint.class, URI.create(uri));
            // send and receive messages
        } catch (DeploymentException | IOException ex) {
            Logger.getLogger(Client.class.getName()).log(Level.SEVERE, null, ex);
        }
    }
}
```

Sending Messages

The ability to asynchronously send messages (text or binary) from a browser client to a server defines the foundation of AJAX and WebSocket (in HTML5) capability. The WebSockets API allows browser clients to send messages asynchronously to the server via JavaScript calls to a WebSocket endpoint. Conversely, the API allows clients to asynchronously receive messages and process them accordingly via a series of JavaScript functions. The following example demonstrates how to send a message to a WebSocket endpoint by clicking on a button in a web page. When the button is clicked, a JavaScript function named `acmeChatRelay` is invoked, which embodies the processing implementation.

To send a message to a WebSocket endpoint via a JavaScript function, the first task is to confirm whether the user's browser is capable of working with WebSockets (HTML5 compliant). This confirmation can be done by using a conditional statement to verify if the "WebSocket" object is available within the client by using the following if-statement, written in JavaScript.

```
if("WebSocket" in window){
...
} else {
...
}
```

If the client browser is capable of working with WebSockets, then the implementation inside of the `if` block is invoked, otherwise, the implementation within the `else` block is invoked. To process the WebSocket message, a new WebSocket object must be instantiated to establish the server connection, which is done by passing the URL to the WebSocket endpoint to a new WebSocket object.

```
var ws = new WebSocket("ws://localhost:8080/IntroToEE7/acmechat");
```

The constructor for creating a browser client JavaScript WebSocket takes either one or two parameters. The first parameter is the URL of the server to which the WebSocket will connect, and the second optional parameter is a `String` of protocols that can be used for message transmission. The WebSocket object contains a handful of events that are utilized to help implement message processing. Table 9-1 lists the different events that can occur in the lifecycle of a WebSocket object, along with a description of what they do.

Table 9-1. JavaScript WebSocket Object Events

Event	Handler Method	Description
open	onOpen	occurs when the WebSocket connection is established
close	onClose	occurs when the WebSocket connection is closed
error	onError	occurs when there is a communication error
message	onMessage	occurs when data is received from the server

After the WebSocket object has been instantiated successfully, a connection to the server will be established, which will cause the open event to occur. To process this event, assign a function to the onOpen handler, and process events accordingly within that function. Messages can be sent to the server when the open event occurs, and this is demonstrated within the example.

```
ws.onopen = function()
{
   // Web Socket is connected, send data using send()
   ws.send("Message to send");
   alert("Message is sent...");
};
```

Similarly, we can listen for any other events to occur, and then process tasks accordingly when they do. In the example, when a message is received from the server, it is printed within an `alert` dialog. Also, in the example shown below when the WebSocket is closed, an `alert` dialog is presented to the user.

The example does not demonstrate all of the possible ways that the WebSocket object in JavaScript can be utilized. For instance, we could send messages to the server by invoking the `send()` method, and passing the data that we wish to send as a parameter. The `close()` method can be called on a WebSocket to manually terminate the existing connection. WebSocket objects also contain the helpful attributes, `readyState` and `bufferedAmount`, that can be used for obtaining information about a connection. The `readyState` attribute will advise the current state of the WebSocket connection via a returned number, and the `bufferedAmount` attribute value represents the number of bytes of UTF-8 text that have been queued using the `send()` method. Table 9-2 displays the different possible values for the `readyState` attribute, along with a description of each.

Table 9-2. JavaScript WebSocket readyState Values

Value	Description
0	connection not yet established
1	connection established, and communication is possible
2	connection going through closing handshake
3	connection is closed and cannot be opened

Ready to dig into the code? In the following example, a JavaScript solution is engineered that can be used to send messages from a client browser to a WebSocket endpoint. Invoke the JavaScript function via an action event that is bound to an HTML input tag within the view. In the following example, a button contains an `onclick` attribute that will invoke a JavaScript function named `acmeChatRelay`. The `acmeChatRelay` function is responsible for opening a session with a WebSocket endpoint so that messages can be sent. The listing below is an excerpt from the `<head>` section of the `/layout/custom_template.xhtml` JSF view, which is located within the `web` directory of the IntroToEE7 project.

```
...
<h:head>
<script type="text/javascript">
            function acmeChatRelay()
            {
                alert("working");
                if ("WebSocket" in window)
                {
                    alert("WebSocket is supported by your Browser!");
                    // Let us open a web socket
                    var ws = new WebSocket("ws://localhost:8080/IntroToEE7/acmechat");
                    ws.onopen = function()
                    {
                        // Web Socket is connected, send data using send()
                        ws.send("Message to send");
                        alert("Message is sent...");
                    };
                    ws.onmessage = function(evt)
                    {
                        var received_msg = evt.data;
                        alert("Message from server: " + received_msg);
                    };
                    ws.onclose = function()
                    {
                        // websocket is closed.
                        alert("Connection is closed...");
                    };
                }
                else
                {
                    // The browser doesn't support WebSocket
                    alert("WebSocket NOT supported by your Browser!");
                }
            }
        </script>
</h:head>
```

The following excerpt is taken from web/chapter09/acmeChatClient.xhtml, and it demonstrates how to invoke the WebSocket call.

```
...
<h:body>
        <ui:composition template="../layout/custom_template.xhtml">
            <ui:define name="content">
                <h:form>
                    <p>
                        Welcome to the Acme Chat Client.  Use the
                    </p>
                    <h:inputTextarea id="messageText" cols="30" rows="10"/>
                    <br/>
```

```
                <input id="wsRelay" type="button" value="Send Message"
                       onclick="acmeChatRelay();"/>

            </h:form>
        </ui:define>
    </ui:composition>
</h:body>
...
```

When the button is pressed, the message will be sent from the browser client to the WebSocket endpoint, and a message will be returned from the endpoint to the client. Alerts will be displayed as the asynchronous events occur.

Message Types

As noted before, WebSockets can be very useful for sending different types of messages. In fact, just about any Java object can be sent as a WebSocket message. Classes known as encoders and decoders can be utilized to facilitate different message types. A message can be encoded in to any Java object type by implementing a custom encoder class, and similarly, an object can be decoded back into a message by implementing a custom decoder class. Encoders and Decoders can be created for the processing of the following types of messages:

- Text Messages
- Binary Messages
- Pong Messages (Messages containing metadata regarding the WebSocket connection)

Let's take a look at a simple example to demonstrate how to encode a String based message into a Java object, and then decode it back into a message later. The class below, `AjaxChatObj`, is a simple Java object that can be used to hold String based messages.

```
public class AcmeChatObj {
    private String message;

    /**
     * @return the message
     */
    public String getMessage() {
        return message;
    }

    /**
     * @param message the message to set
     */
    public void setMessage(String message) {
        this.message = message;
    }

}
```

To encode a string-based message into an object of type AcmeChatObj, an encoder can be registered with a WebSocket endpoint by specifying a value for the @ServerEndpoint annotation encoders attribute. In this example, an encoder named AcmeChatEncoder will be used to encode string-based messages into objects of type AcmeChatObj. The example code is as follows:

```
public class AcmeChatTextEncoder implements javax.websocket.Encoder.Text<AcmeChatObj> {

    @Override
    public String encode(AcmeChatObj object) throws EncodeException {
        return object.getMessage();
    }

    @Override
    public void init(EndpointConfig config) {
        throw new UnsupportedOperationException("Not supported yet.");
    }

    @Override
    public void destroy() {
        throw new UnsupportedOperationException("Not supported yet.");
    }

}
```

Similarly, a decoder class can be implementd to convert the AcmeChatObj back into a string. To register a decoder with a WebSocket endpoint, specify a value for the @ServerEndpoint annotation decoders attribute. In this example, a decoder named AcmeChatDecoder will be used to decode an AcmeChatObj into a String. The example code is as follows:

```
public class AcmeChatTextDecoder implements javax.websocket.Decoder.Text<AcmeChatObj> {

    @Override
    public AcmeChatObj decode(String s) throws DecodeException {
        AcmeChatObj obj = new AcmeChatObj();
        obj.setMessage(s);
        return obj;
    }

    @Override
    public boolean willDecode(String s) {
        if (s != null) {
            return true;
        } else {
            return false;
        }
    }

    @Override
    public void init(EndpointConfig config) {
        throw new UnsupportedOperationException("Not supported yet.");
        //To change body of generated methods, choose Tools | Templates.
    }
```

```
    @Override
    public void destroy() {
        throw new UnsupportedOperationException("Not supported yet.");
        //To change body of generated methods, choose Tools | Templates.
    }
}
```

As mentioned previously, the encoder and decoder classes can be registered with a WebSocket endpoint by specifying the encoders and decoders attributes, respectively. The following example demonstrates how to do so for registering the example classes to the AcmeChatEndpoint WebSocket endpoint:

```
...
@ServerEndpoint(value="/acmechat", encoders=AcmeChatTextEncoder.class,
                decoders=AcmeChatTextDecoder.class)
...
```

JavaScript Object Notation—JSON

The universally supported JSON (JavaScript Object Notation) object has become a widely adopted solution for sending data between web communication endpoints. HTML5-based web applications can utilize JSON to transport data, using WebSockets, Ajax, or other transport technologies. The Java EE 7 platform provides the JSON-P API, which introduces utilities that make it easier to build and work with JSON objects within the Java language. JSON-P, also referred to as "JSON with padding," has become the standard way to build JSON objects using Java.

This section will delve into the JSON-P API, which is part of the Java EE 7 platform. You will learn how to build a JSON file using the API, read JSON, and parse JSON. These are barebones steps to producing data sets with JSON, and they should get you on your way to building applications with JSON and HTML5! To see the complete Javadoc for JSON, please refer to the online documentation at: http://docs.oracle.com/javaee/7/api/javax/json/package-frame.html.

Building JSON

The JSON-P API includes a helper class that can be used to create JSON objects using the builder pattern. Using the JsonBuilder class, JSON objects can be built using a series of method calls, each building upon each other, hence, the builder pattern. Once the JSON object has been built, the JsonBuilder build method can be called to return a JsonObject.

In the example in this section, we construct a JSON object that provides details regarding a book. The JsonBuilder.add() method can be called to return a JsonObjectBuilder, which is a building block of a JSON object. The add method is used to build components to the object, including name/value properties, much like that of a Map. Therefore, the following line adds a property named title with a value of Intro to Java EE 7:

```
.add("title", "Intro to Java EE 7")
```

Objects can be embedded inside of one another, creating a hierarchy of different sections within one JsonObject. In the example that follows, the first call to add initiates the build of an embedded JsonObjectBuilder, 'jsonJob', within the JsonObjectBuilder in the example, providing an object name for the embedded structure, jsonJob. Subsequent calls to add build sub-objects inside of the initial JsonObject by calling, passing the name/value of the embedded object. Embedded objects can also contain properties, so to add properties to the embedded object, call the add() method within the embedded object, nesting to as many levels as needed. JsonObjects can embody as many embedded objects as needed. The following lines of code demonstrate the beginning and end of an embedded object definition:

```
JsonObjectBuilder builder = Json.createObjectBuilder();
builder.add("jsonJob", Json.createObjectBuilder()
    .add("jobId", job.getJobId())
    .add("division", job.getDivision())
    .add("title", job.getTitle())
    .add("salary", job.getSalary()));
```

It is also possible that a `JsonObject` may have an array of related sub-objects. Arrays can consist of objects, and even hierarchies of objects, arrays, etc. In the example that follows, the "`jsonJob`" object consists of a single array. Once a `JsonObject` has been created, it can be passed to a client. WebSockets work well for passing `JsonObjects` back to a client, but there are a bevy of different technologies available for communicating with JSON. The following example class utilizes an EJB call to obtain `Jobs` entities, which are then used to build a JSON object.

```
import java.io.StringWriter;
import java.util.List;
import javax.ejb.EJB;
import javax.inject.Named;
import javax.json.Json;
import javax.json.JsonObject;
import javax.json.JsonObjectBuilder;
import javax.json.JsonWriter;
import org.javaee7.entity.Jobs;
import org.javaee7.jpa.session.JobsSession;

@Named
public class JsonController {

   @EJB
    JobsSession jobsFacade;

    public String buildJobs() {
        List<Jobs> jobs = jobsFacade.findAll();
        JsonObjectBuilder builder = Json.createObjectBuilder();
        StringBuilder json = new StringBuilder();
        for (Jobs job : jobs) {
            builder.add("jsonJob", Json.createObjectBuilder()
                    .add("jobId", job.getJobId())
                    .add("division", job.getDivision())
                    .add("title", job.getTitle())
                    .add("salary", job.getSalary()));
            JsonObject result = builder.build();
            StringWriter sw = new StringWriter();
            try (JsonWriter writer = Json.createWriter(sw)) {
                writer.writeObject(result);
            }
            json.append(sw.toString());
        }
        return json.toString();
    }
}
```

Once created, the `JsonObject` can be passed to a client for processing. In this example, the object sections are printed to the server log, and the output looks similar to the following:

```
{"jsonJob":{"jobId":1,"division":"IT","title":"IT TITLE A","salary":60000}}
```

Persisting JSON

The `JsonWriter` class can be utilized to write a `JsonObject` to a Java writer object. A `JsonWriter` is instantiated by passing a `Writer` object as an argument. Instantiating a `JsonWriter` will prepare the Writer object that had been passed as an argument to write JSON format. After that `Writer` has been created, the `JsonWriter writeObject()` method can be invoked, passing the `JsonObject` that is to be written. Once the `JsonObject` has been written, the `JsonWriter` can be closed by calling its `close()` method. These are the only steps that are necessary for writing a JSON object to a Java `Writer` class type.

The example below goes one step further and writes the JSON object to disk. In this case, a `StringWriter` encapsulates the `JsonWriter`. To do so, a new `FileWriter` is instantiated, passing the name of the file that we wish to create. Next, a `BufferedWriter` is created, passing the `FileWriter` that was previously instantiated. Lastly, the contents of the `StringWriter` that contains the JSON object is written to the `BufferedWriter` by calling `out.write()`. Doing so writes the content to the File that was created. When this process is complete, a new JSON object will have been written to disk.

The following example utilizes the JSON-P API to build a JSON object, and then store it to the file system. The `JsonWriter` class makes it possible to create a file on disk and then write the JSON to that file.

```
public void writeJson() {
        try {
            JsonObject jsonObject = jsonController.buildJobsJson();
            StringWriter writer = new StringWriter();
            JsonWriter jsonWriter = Json.createWriter(writer);
            jsonWriter.writeObject(jsonObject);
            jsonWriter.close();
            writer.close();
            // Write file
            FileWriter fstream = new FileWriter("Jobs.json");
            BufferedWriter out = new BufferedWriter(fstream);
            out.write(writer.toString());
            out.close();
            FacesContext.getCurrentInstance().addMessage(null, new FacesMessage(
                FacesMessage.SEVERITY_INFO, "JSON Built",
                "JSON Built"));
        } catch (IOException ex) {
            System.out.println(ex);
        }
    }
```

Parsing JSON

In order to perform some tasks, a JSON object must be searched to find only the content that is desired and useful for the current task. Utilizing a JSON parser can make jobs such as these easier, as a parser is able to break the object down into pieces so that each different name/value pair or attribute can be examined as needed to locate the desired result.

The `javax.json.Json` class contains a static factory method, `createParser()`, that accepts a bevy of input, and returns an `iterable JsonParser`. Table 9-3 lists the different possible input types that are accepted via the `createParser()` method.

Table 9-3. *createParser Method Input Types*

Input Type	Method Call
InputStream	createParser(InputStream in)
JsonArray	createParser(JsonArray arr)
JsonObject	createParser(JsonObject obj)
Reader	createParser(Reader reader)

Once a `JsonParser` has been created, it can be made into an `Iterator` of `Event` objects. Each Event correlates to a different structure within the JSON object. For instance, when the JSON object is created, a START_OBJECT event occurs, adding a name\value pair that will trigger both a KEY_NAME and VALUE_STRING event. These events can be utilized to obtain the desired information from a JSON object. In the example, the event names are merely printed to a server log. However, in a real-life application, a conditional would most likely test each iteration to find a particular event, and then perform some processing. Table 9-4 lists the different JSON events, along with a description of when each occurs.

Table 9-4. *JSON Object Events*

Event	Occurrence
START_OBJECT	start of an object
END_OBJECT	end of an object
START_ARRAY	start of an array
END_ARRAY	end of an array
KEY_NAME	name of a key
VALUE_STRING	value of a name\value pair in String format
VALUE_NUMBER	value of a name\value pair in numeric format
VALUE_TRUE	value of a name\value pair in Boolean format
VALUE_FALSE	value of a name\value pair in Boolean format
VALUE_NULL	value of a name\value pair as NULL

Obtain a JSON object that you would like to parse, and then parse it using the `javax.json.Json createParser` utility. In the following example, a JSON file is read from disk, and then parsed to determine the hierarchy of events within. Each of the events is printed to the server log as the JSON is being parsed.

```
public void parseObject() {
        Reader fileReader = new InputStreamReader(getClass().getResourceAsStream("BookObject.json"));
        JsonParser parser = Json.createParser(fileReader);
        Iterator<Event> it = parser.iterator();
```

```
        while (it.hasNext()) {
            Event ev = it.next();
            System.out.println(ev);
        }
    }
```

The resulting server log will look as follows:

```
START_OBJECT
KEY_NAME
VALUE_STRING
KEY_NAME
START_OBJECT
KEY_NAME
VALUE_STRING
KEY_NAME
VALUE_STRING
END_OBJECT
KEY_NAME
START_OBJECT
KEY_NAME
VALUE_STRING
KEY_NAME
VALUE_STRING
END_OBJECT
KEY_NAME
START_ARRAY
START_OBJECT
KEY_NAME
VALUE_STRING
KEY_NAME
VALUE_STRING
END_OBJECT
START_OBJECT
KEY_NAME
VALUE_STRING
KEY_NAME
VALUE_STRING
END_OBJECT
END_ARRAY
KEY_NAME
START_ARRAY
START_OBJECT
KEY_NAME
VALUE_STRING
KEY_NAME
VALUE_STRING
END_OBJECT
START_OBJECT
KEY_NAME
VALUE_STRING
```

```
KEY_NAME
VALUE_STRING
END_OBJECT
END_ARRAY
```

Utilizing APIs such as WebSockets and JSON-P can help to make applications more versatile and compliant with HTML5. Asynchronous communication, such as WebSockets solutions, is a must-have for modern web applications. Modern Java EE 7 applications that send and receive messages can now utilize standards by combining WebSockets and JSON-P to create robust solutions.

Summary

The release of Java EE 7 comes a long way in revolutionizing the way in which Java enterprise applications are built. HTML5 has changed the way that we interact with applications and/or websites via a browser. In order to make the best use of HTML5, technologies such as WebSockets and JSON must be used. The WebSockets and JSON-P APIs help to ensure that Java EE applications can be written to enable responsive and easy-to-use application interfaces. Although these APIs have been recently added to Java EE, they can also be used with older techonlogies to help clear the way for more advanced messaging and functionality.

CHAPTER 10

Java Message Service

The Java Message Service (JMS) is an API that allows software to create, edit, read, and send messages among other software applications or components. The API allows resources to be created within an application server that facilitate messaging capability in various contexts. The application server creates, houses, and maintains Connection Factory and Destination resources. That being said, different application server implementations may have minor differences in their JMS implementations.

In addition to the basic messaging facilities, JMS also provides the ability to send messages to destinations and publish messages to subscriptions. This chapter contains examples that focus on basic concepts of JMS, as well as some advanced techniques and new additions with Java EE 7. When following along with the examples, it should be noted that JMS could be used in various situations for creating many different types of messages. That being said, many of the examples in this chapter will be invoked using JSF view actions, although in real-life applications there are many different ways to implement the sending and receiving of messages. From internal message invocation, to scheduled tasks via an Enterprise JavaBean (EJB) timer, and even implementation of JMS messaging with EJB message-driven beans, JMS can be utilized in many different contexts. After reading through the examples, you should be able to apply the strategies utilized within the recipes in order to create the messaging system of your needs.

New to JMS 2.0 is a simplified API for sending and receiving messages. In this chapter, you will see the standard API in comparison with the simplified API. The updated API also includes enhancements to message subscriptions, delivery delay, and more. This chapter will touch upon these new features, providing examples to get you started for using them within your own applications.

Brief Overview

JMS provides a facility for applications to send and receive messages in a loosely coupled manner. Senders can publish messages to a JMS destination, and consumers can retrieve messages from those destinations via subscription. Utilizing this messaging model, the sender and receiver do not need to know about each other; they only need to know the types of messages being sent and consumed, along with the destination.

JMS offers a couple of different messaging domains that can be used, each providing different features so that an application can utilize the one that makes the most sense for the particular solution. The two types are Point-To-Point (PTP) and Publish/Subscribe (pub/sub). PTP messaging involves message queues, in which publishers can send messages to a specific queue, and receivers extract messages from a specific queue. Queues have the following characteristics:

- Messages sent to a queue can have only one consumer.
- Senders and receivers do not have to coordinate the sending/receiving process. The sender publishes the message and the receiver consumes it, when available.
- Receivers acknowledge a successful processing once they have consumed a message.

The other type of messaging domain, pub/sub, is facilitated by means of message topics. Publishers address messages to a specific topic, and subscribers can subscribe to a specific topic to consume messages. Topics differ from queues because they can contain multiple messages, and the messages can have more than one consumer. Messages sent to a topic are anonymous, meaning that publishers do not have to address to a specific consumer. Clients that subscribe to a topic can only consume messages that have been sent to the topic after the subscription time, and subscribers must remain active in order to continue consuming messages.

JMS Resources

The JMS API utilizes administrative resources in order to create and consume messages. We refer to these resources as JMS resources. There are a couple of different types of JMS resources that can be created: Connection Resources and Destination Resources. The Connection resources are used to create connections to a provider. There are three types of connection resources that can be created:

> `ConnectionFactory`: Instance of `javax.jms.ConnectionFactory` interface. Can be used to create JMS Topics and JMS Queue types.
>
> `TopicConnectionFactory`: Instance of `javax.jms.TopicConnectionFactory` interface
>
> `QueueConnectionFactory`: Instance of `javax.jms.QueueConnectionFactory` interface

JMS connection factory resources are very similar to JDBC connection factories in that they provide a pool of connections that an application can use in order to connect and produce a session. There are many attributes that can be provided when creating connection factory resources:

> **Initial and Minimum Pool Size**: The initial and minimum number of connections that will be created and maintained by the connection pool.
>
> **Maximum Pool Size**: The maximum number of connections that can be created within the pool.
>
> **Pool Resize Quantity**: The number of connections that will be removed when the pool idle timeout expires.
>
> **Idle Timeout**: The maximum amount of time that connections can remain in the pool if they are idle. (Seconds)
>
> **Max Wait Time**: The maximum amount of time that a caller will wait before a connection timeout is sent. (Milliseconds)
>
> **On Any Failure**: If set to true (checked), all connections will be closed and reconnected on failure.
>
> **Transaction Support**: The level of transaction support (`XATransaction`, `LocalTransaction`, `NoTransaction`. The default is empty.
>
> **Connection Validation**: If set to true, then connections will need to be validated.

Connection factory and destination resources are created and reside within an application server container. They can be created using an IDE, such as Netbeans, or by using the application server administrative tools. The most important piece of information to provide when creating a destination is the name. As with any JMS resource, the JNDI name should begin with the `jms/` prefix. When creating a destination resource, a unique name must also be provided for the Destination Resource Name, although other Java EE application servers may or may not make this a mandatory specification.

To get started with the examples in this book, we will briefly demonstrate how to create these resources using the Glassfish v4 administrative console. Let's take a look at how to create a `javax.jmx.Queue` resource. Follow the steps below in order to create the resource:

1. Log into the Glassfish Administrative Console, and Expand the Resources➤JMS Resources menu in the navigation tree to expose the "Destination Resources" menu option (Figure 10-1).

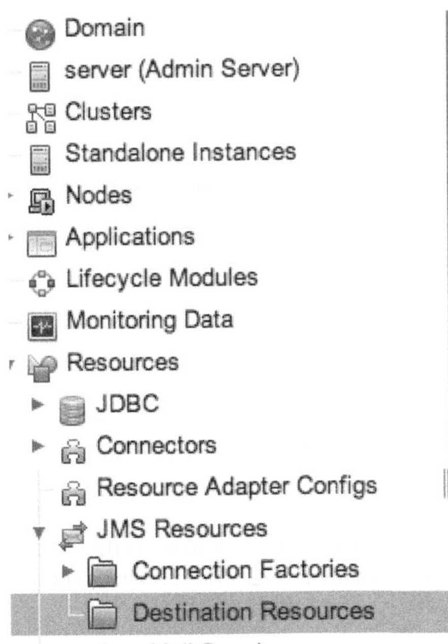

Figure 10-1. *Glassfish Administration Console Destination Resource Menu*

2. Click the "New" button within the "JMS Destination Resources" window (Figure10-2) to open the "New JMS Destination Resource" window. Enter a JNDI name (beginning with `jms/`), followed by providing a unique name for the "Physical Destination Name," and finally, choose the Resource Type that you wish to create.

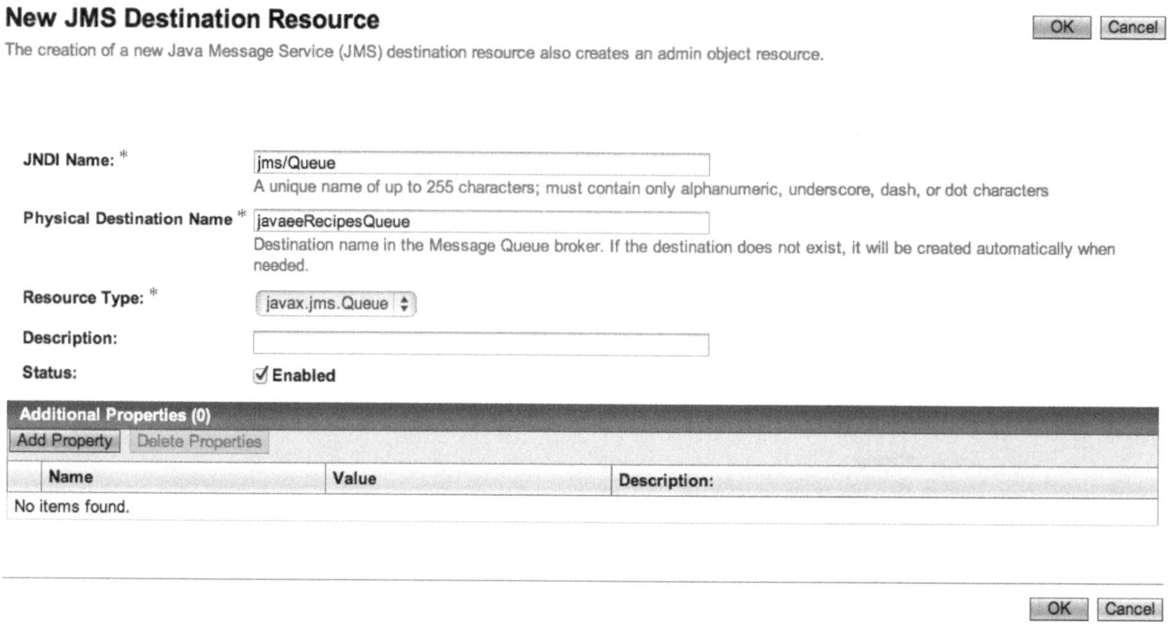

New JMS Destination Resource

OK Cancel

The creation of a new Java Message Service (JMS) destination resource also creates an admin object resource.

JNDI Name: * jms/Queue

A unique name of up to 255 characters; must contain only alphanumeric, underscore, dash, or dot characters

Physical Destination Name * javaeeRecipesQueue

Destination name in the Message Queue broker. If the destination does not exist, it will be created automatically when needed.

Resource Type: * javax.jms.Queue

Description:

Status: Enabled

Additional Properties (0)

Add Property Delete Properties

Name	Value	Description:
No items found.		

OK Cancel

Figure 10-2. *Glassfish Administration Console New JMS Destination Resource*

3. Click “OK” to create the destination.

Application server resources can also be generated via a command-line or terminal using the asadmin create-jms-resource command. The following demonstrates usage of the create-jms-resource command, although you can see the complete help by typing asadmin create-jms-resource -help.

```
create-jms-resource [--help]
        --restype type
        [--target target]
        [--enabled={true|false}]
        [--description text]
        [--property (name=value)[:name=value]*]
        [--force[={false|true}]]
        jndi_name
```

ConnectionFactory objects are registered automatically with JNDI once created, and they can then be injected into Java classes and used. The following lines of code demonstrate how to inject a ConnectionFactory resource into a class:

```
@Resource(name = "jms/MyConnectionFactory")
private static ConnectionFactory connectionFactory;
```

Destination resources can be injected into Java classes in the same manner as ConnectionFactory resources. The following lines of code demonstrate the injection of a Topic resource.

```
@Resource(name="jms/myTopic")
private Topic myTopic;
```

JMS Sessions

As mentioned previously, the JMS 2.0 release utilizes a newer simplified API. However, previous versions of the API may still need to be used for maintenance purposes and other reasons. For that reason, it is useful to understand the concept of JMS Sessions, which are abstracted away from the developer when using the newer simplified API.

When using the standard API, you must obtain a JMS connection so that you can start a session before you can begin to send or consume messages. A session can be used to create JMS resources such as Message Consumers, Message Producers, Messages, Queue Browsers, and Temporary Queues and Topics. A session can be created using a `Connection` object. The following line of code demonstrates how to obtain a `Connection` from an injected `ConnectionFactory`.

```
Connection connection = connectionFactory.createConnection();
```

To create a session, call a `Connection` object's `createSession` method, and pass the appropriate arguments depending upon your application's needs. The `createSession` syntax is as follows:

```
createSession(boolean isTransacted, int acknowledgementType)
```

The first argument to the `createSession` method is a `boolean` value to indicate if transactions should take place within the session. If a session is created as transacted (set `true` for the first argument to `createSession`), acknowledgement occurs once the entire transaction is successfully committed. If, for some reason, the transaction is not committed, the entire transaction is rolled back, and all messages are redelivered. However, if a session is not transacted, one must indicate which type of acknowledgment must be received to consider a message successfully sent. The second argument to the `createSession` method indicates the acknowledgment type. Table 10-1 lists the different acknowledgment types along with a description of each.

Table 10-1. *JMS Session Message Acknowledgment*

Acknowledgment Type	Description
`Session.AUTO_ACKNOWLEDGE`	The session automatically acknowledges a client's receipt of a message either when the client has successfully returned from a call to receive or when the `MessageListener` it has called to process the message returns successfully.
`Session.CLIENT_ACKNOWLEDGE`	The client acknowledges the receipt of a message by calling the message's acknowledge method.
`Session.DUPS_OK_ACKNOWLEDGE`	Lazy acknowledgement of messages . . . allowing duplicates to be received.

For example, session creation may look something like the following:

```
Session session = connection.createSession(false,
    Session.AUTO_ACKNOWLEDGE);
```

The session that is created above is non-transactional, and the receipt type is `Session.AUTO_ACKNOWLEDGE`. This is the most common type of JMS session that is created. Once the session has been created, then it can be used to create JMS resources.

JMS Messages

This section will give you a basic understanding of the standard (older) API for sending and receiving messages. In a later section entitled API Enhancements, you will see the newer simplified API. Let's begin by taking a look at a sample of code using the standard API for sending a message. This example demonstrates how to send a text message to a queue destination.

```
...
    public void sendMessage() {
        if (connection != null) {
            System.out.println("Creating Session");
            try(Session session = connection.createSession(false, Session.AUTO_ACKNOWLEDGE);) {
                myQueue = (Queue) getContext().lookup("jms/javaEERecipesQueue");
                MessageProducer producer = session.createProducer(myQueue);
                TextMessage message = session.createTextMessage();
                message.setText("Java EE 7 Is the Best!");

                producer.send(message);
                producer.close();
                setConnectionString("Message Successfully Sent to Queue");

            } catch (NamingException | JMSException ex) {
                System.out.println(ex);
                setConnectionString("Session not created and message not sent");
            }
        } else {
            setConnectionString("No connection available");
        }
    }
...
```

Now let's discuss the example. To send a JMS message using the standard API, you need to create a resource destination for your message, and obtain a connection as well as a JMS session, as mentioned previously. Once you have obtained a JMS session, the next step is to create a `MessageProducer` using the `Session createProducer` method, passing the destination as an argument. After this legwork has been completed, the message can be constructed. You can create a message by calling the `javax.jms.Session` method that corresponds to the type of message that you wish to create. To see all of the available methods, please refer to the online documentation at: `http://docs.oracle.com/javaee/6/api/javax/jms/Session.html`. In the example shown above, a text message is created by calling the `session.createTextMessage()` method. The text is then set by calling the `TextMessage` object's `setText` method.

Once a message has been created, a `MessageProducer` must be created in order to facilitate the sending of the message. Again, `javax.jms.Session` comes to the rescue here, as we can call its `createProducer` method, passing the destination resource for which we'd like to create the `MessageProducer`. Once created, the producer's `sendMessage` method can be invoked, passing the message that you wish to send.

As mentioned previously, the `javax.jms.Session` can be used to generate different message types. Table 10-2 lists the different message types that can be created, along with a description.

Table 10-2. JMS Message Types

Message Type	Creation Method
StreamMessage	The message body contains a stream of primitive values in the Java programming language. Filled and read sequentially.
MapMessage	Message body contains a set of name/value pairs that are formed from Strings objects and Java primitives. May be accessed sequentially or randomly by name, and the order of entries is undefined.
TextMessage	Message body contains a String object. Able to be used for plain text as well as XML messages.
ObjectMessage	Message body contains a Serializable Java object.
BytesMessage	Message body contains a stream of uninterpreted bytes.

The receiving client of a message is also known as the message consumer. Message consumers can be created using the standard or the simplified JMS API. Using the standard API, a consumer is created from JMS `Session` objects in the same manner that producers are created, that is, by calling the `createConsumer` method of JMS `Session` and passing the destination object from which the consumer will listen for and accept messages. Message consumers have the ability to consume messages that are waiting within a queue, and they listen indefinitely for new incoming messages. Let's take a look at an example that uses the standard API for consuming messages. In this example, the method named `receiveMessage` is responsible for consuming messages from a specified destination point `Queue`.

```
...
public void receiveMessage() {
        boolean stopReceivingMessages = false;
        if(connection == null){
            createConnection();
        }
        try(Session session = connection.createSession(false, Session.AUTO_ACKNOWLEDGE);) {
            createConnection();
            myQueue = (Queue) getContext().lookup("jms/javaEERecipesQueue");
            try (MessageConsumer consumer = session.createConsumer(myQueue)) {
                connection.start();

                while (!stopReceivingMessages) {
                    Message inMessage = consumer.receive();
                    if (inMessage != null) {
                        if (inMessage instanceof TextMessage) {
                            String messageStr = ((TextMessage) inMessage).getText();
                            setDisplayMessage(messageStr);
                        } else {
                            setDisplayMessage("Message was of another type");
                        }
                    } else {
                        stopReceivingMessages = true;
                    }
                }
                connection.stop();
            }
        } catch (NamingException | JMSException ex) {
```

```
            // log errors
        } finally {
            if (connection != null){
                closeConnection();
            }
        }
    }
...
```

To set up a consumer, call the JMS Session object's `createConsumer` method, and pass the destination object that you wish to consume from. The next step is to call the JMS Connection start method. This will tell JMS that the consumer is ready to begin receiving messages. After invoking the `connection.start()` method, a consumer can receive a message by calling the `Consumer` object's `receive` method, optionally passing a time in milliseconds for the consumer to listen for messages. If no time limit is specified, the consumer will listen indefinitely.

As you can see from the example in this recipe, once the `receive` method is called, a `Message` object is retrieved. Once the message is received, the application can glean whatever it needs by calling the `Message` object's getter methods accordingly.

Additional Information

This has been a brief overview of the JMS messaging concepts, and the use of the standard API for working with messages. At this point, if you would like to delve deeper into these concepts, please refer to online documentation via the Java EE 7 tutorial, or a book that covers these topics in detail. The remainder of this chapter will focus on new features that JMS 2.0 has to offer.

API Enhancements

Prior to the release of Java EE 7, the JMS API had not been overhauled for a number of years. The newer features of the Java platform were not being utilized to the fullest potential, and working with JMS was more complex than it needed to be. The JMS 2.0 release brings the API up-to-date with the latest developments in Java EE, and makes it easier to use. This section will cover some of those enhancements, including the newer simplified API, and the ability to utilize try-with-resources, which gave the JMS API the facelift that it needed to become useful with Java 7 capabilities.

New Simple API

The reason that any application makes use of JMS is to incorporate the ability to send or receive messages. Therefore, it is no surprise that the JMS API has been developed to make these tasks very easy for the developer. In Java EE 7, things get even easier using the simplified JMS API.

Sending Messages

In the overview, we discussed the underlying concepts behind sending JMS messages. We also looked at how to send messages using the standard API. Now let's take a look at how we can do the same work using the new simplified API. To utilize the simplified API, create a `JMSContext` object, and then utilize it to create a `MessageProducer` and send the message to the appropriate destination. In the following example, a simple String-based message is sent to a `Queue` using the simplified API.

```
@Resource(name = "jms/acmeConnectionFactory")
    private ConnectionFactory connectionFactory;
    @Resource(lookup = "jms/Queue")
    Queue inboundQueue;
...
    public void sendMessage() {
        JMSContext context = connectionFactory.createContext();
        StringBuilder message = new StringBuilder();
        message.append("Java EE 7 Is the Best!");
        context.createProducer().send(inboundQueue, message.toString());
        FacesContext.getCurrentInstance().addMessage(null, new FacesMessage(
                FacesMessage.SEVERITY_INFO, "Message sent",
                "Message sent"));

    }
```

When utilizing the simplified API, there are a few shortcuts that can be made, as compared to the standard API, also known as "Classic." In comparing the "Classic" versus Simplified APIs, the simplified API enables developers to produce the same results as the standard API with much less code. A `JMSContext` object is obtained via a call to the `ConnectionFactory`'s `createContext` method, and it can be used to begin a chain of method invocations that will result in the sending of a message in just one line of code. To break it down a bit, after the `JMSContext` has been obtained, its `createProducer` method can be called, chaining a call to the `send` method, passing the `Queue` and the message to be sent.

JMS message implementations may vary between the different application server products. However, all JMS messages types share some common characteristics. For instance, all JMS messages implement the `javax.jms.Message` interface. Messages are composed of a header, properties, and a body. The header of a message contains values that are utilized by clients and providers for routing and identification purposes; properties provide message filtering; and the body portion of the message carries the actual message content. The message header is used for linking messages to one another, and a field named the `JMSCorrelationID` contains this content. Message objects contain the ability to support application-defined property values. The properties can be set via a construct known as message selectors, and they are responsible for filtering messages. For more detailed information regarding message properties, please see the online documentation that can be found at `http://docs.oracle.com/javaee/6/api/javax/jms/Message.html`. The body varies across the different message types, as listed in Table 10-2.

Another means of sending messages in JMS involves the creation of a `QueueSession` to produce a `QueueSender`. Although this technique does not utilize the simplified API, we'll show a brief example using JMS 2.0 to demonstrate how this is performed using resource injection, rather than `InitialContext` to gain access to server resources. The following example demonstrates the domain-specific API for point-to-point messaging, and the sending of a message to a `Queue` resource.

```
...
    @Resource(name = "jms/QueueConnFactory")
    private QueueConnectionFactory queueConnFactory;
    @Resource(lookup = "jms/Queue")
    Queue queue;

    /**
     * Create and send a message using QueueSession
     * @throws NamingException
     * @throws JMSException
     */
```

```
    public void sendMessage() throws NamingException, JMSException {

        try (QueueConnection queueConnection = queueConnFactory.createQueueConnection();) {
            queueConnection.start();
            QueueSession queueSession =
                queueConnection.createQueueSession(false, QueueSession.AUTO_ACKNOWLEDGE);
            queue = queueSession.createQueue("JavaEEQueue");

            // create the message to send
            TextMessage textMessage = queueSession.createTextMessage("This is a test message");

            QueueSender sender = queueSession.createSender(queue);
            sender.send(textMessage);
            queueSession.close();

        }
    }
...
```

With the aid of resource injection, a number of lines can be removed from previous JMS solutions, making code easier to read and maintain.

Similarly, the domain specific API for pub/sub messaging has been made simpler via updated technologies such as resource injection. Although the simplified API is not used for creation of `TopicPublisher` object from a `TopicSession`, the work involved has been reduced significantly in JMS 2.0. The following example demonstrates how to create a `TopicPublisher` and send messages to a `Topic`.

```
    ...
    @Resource(name = "jms/TopicConnFactory")
    private TopicConnectionFactory topicConnFactory;
    @Resource(lookup = "jms/Topic")
    Topic topic;

    public void publishMessage() throws NamingException, JMSException {

        try (TopicConnection topicConnection = topicConnFactory.createTopicConnection();
                TopicSession topicSession =
                topicConnection.createTopicSession(false, TopicSession.AUTO_ACKNOWLEDGE);) {
            topicConnection.start();
            Topic topic = topicSession.createTopic("JavaEE");

            // create the message to send
            TextMessage textMessage = topicSession.createTextMessage("This is a test message");

            javax.jms.TopicPublisher topicPublisher = topicSession.createPublisher(topic);
            topicPublisher.setDeliveryDelay(1000);
            topicPublisher.publish(textMessage);

        }
    }
...
```

Consuming Messages

Let's take a look at how to consume messages using the simplified API. Utilize a `JMSContext` object to create the `JMSConsumer` in an efficient and simplified manner. The following example method resides within a managed bean controller. The message consumer in this example will be created and set up to receive the message that was sent by the producer in the previous example.

```
public String receiveMessage() {
    JMSContext context = connectionFactory.createContext();
    JMSConsumer consumer = context.createConsumer(inboundQueue);
    return consumer.receiveBody(String.class);
}
```

A client that receives a message is also known as the message consumer. Message consumers can be created using the standard or the simplified JMS API. As you can see from the example above, there are very few lines of code needed to create a message consumer using the simplified API. The `JMSContext` object aids in producing less code by calling its `createConsumer` method and passing the resource from which the application will need to consume messages. This method call will return a `JMSConsumer`, which has a similar API to `MessageConsumer`, with the ability to receive a message both synchronously and asynchronously. In the example, a String message is consumed synchronously.

It is possible to create an asynchronous consumer by registering a `MessageListener` with the `MessageConsumer`. After a listener has been registered for the consumer, the listener's `onMessage()` method will be called each time a message has been delivered. The following code demonstrates how to create a simple message listener that will be used to display the received message in the server log.

```
public class AcmeMessageListener implements MessageListener {

    @Override
    public void onMessage(Message message) {
        try {
            System.out.println("Do something with this message: " + message.getBody(String.class));
        } catch (JMSException ex) {
            Logger.getLogger(AcmeMessageListener.class.getName()).log(Level.SEVERE, null, ex);
        }
    }

}
```

To register the message listener with a consumer, call the consumer `setMessageListener` method, passing the listener.

```
JMSContext context = connectionFactory.createContext();
JMSConsumer consumer = context.createConsumer(inboundQueue);
javax.jms.MessageListener acmeMessageListener = new AcmeMessageListener();
consumer.setMessageListener(acmeMessageListener);
messageReceived = consumer.receiveBody(String.class);
```

Autocloseable Resources

The JMS API has been completely re-worked to make use of the Java 7 autocloseable API. If you are familiar with `AutoCloseable`, then you know that it allows for better resource handing in a simpler manner. When combined with the multi-catch implementation that was introduced in Java SE 7, code can become terse, easier to read, and more robust. In the following example, a message browser is used to iterate through the messages that are contained in a queue using the standard API. Note that the `Connection`, `Session`, and `QueueBrowser` instances do not have to be closed since they are contained within the `try`-clause. Encapsulating `AutoCloseable` instances within the `try`-clause ensures that they will be closed when they are no longer needed.

```
public void browseMessages() {

    try(Connection connection = connectionFactory.createConnection();
        Session session = connection.createSession(false, Session.AUTO_ACKNOWLEDGE);
        QueueBrowser browser = session.createBrowser(inboundQueue);) {

        Enumeration msgs = browser.getEnumeration();

        if(!msgs.hasMoreElements()){
            System.out.println("No more messages within the queue...");
        } else {
            while(msgs.hasMoreElements()){
                Message currMsg = (Message)msgs.nextElement();
                System.out.println("Message ID: " + currMsg.getJMSMessageID());
          }
        }

    } catch (JMSException ex) {
        System.out.println(ex);
    }
}
```

Message Body

A new `getBody` method has been added to the `javax.jms.Message` object to allow for easier access to the body of a message. The `getBody` method accepts one parameter that is the class type of the message body. For instance, to obtain the body of a message that is of the String type, make a call to the method, as follows:

```
...
message.getBody(String.class)
...
```

New Messaging Features

The JMS 2.0 update includes some important new messaging features that extend upon the pre-2.0 functionality, and help bring JMS in alignment with more modern technologies. Two of the biggest messaging additions include delivery delay of messages, and the ability to send asynchronous messages. This section will briefly touch upon each of these new features.

Message Delivery Delay

The JMS API provides a method, `setDeliveryDelay`, which can be applied to producers. This method can be called, passing the delay time in milliseconds, prior to sending the message. Once the delay has been set, this will cause all subsequent message deliveries by that producer to be delayed by the specified time.

Set the time of delay in milliseconds by calling the producer's `setDeliveryDelay(long)` method. In the following example, the message sending will be delayed by 1,000 milliseconds.

```
@Resource(name = "jms/topicConnFactory")
private TopicConnectionFactory topicConnFactory;
@Resource(lookup = "jms/Topic")
Topic topic;

public void publishMessage() throws NamingException, JMSException {

    TopicConnection topicConnection = topicConnFactory.createTopicConnection();
    topicConnection.start();
    TopicSession topicSession =
            topicConnection.createTopicSession(false, QueueSession.AUTO_ACKNOWLEDGE);

    Topic topic = topicSession.createTopic("JavaEE");
    TextMessage textMessage = topicSession.createTextMessage("This is a test message");

    javax.jms.TopicPublisher topicPublisher = topicSession.createPublisher(topic);
    topicPublisher.setDeliveryDelay(1000);
    topicPublisher.publish(textMessage);

    topicSession.close();
        topicConnection.close();
}
```

New Send Methods for Asynchronous Sending

JMS clients have the ability to send messages synchronously and asynchronously via a JMS message producer. In JMS 2.0, new send methods have been added for asynchronous message sending. Sending a message asynchronously allows the sending of a task to be performed in a separate thread from other tasks that are being performed. When using the classic API, the following methods allow for asynchronous sending:

- `send(Message message, CompletionListener listener)`
- `send(Message message, int deliveryMode, int priority, long timeToLive, CompletionListener completionListener)`
- `send(Destination destination, Message message, CompletionListener completionListener)`
- `send(Destination destination, Message message, int deliveryMode, int priority, long timeToLive, CompletionListener completionListener)`

When using the simplified API, the following method can be called on the JMSProducer prior to invocation of the synchronous sending methods:

- setAsync(CompletionListener completionListener)

The asynchronous sending of a message results in a message being sent without waiting for an acknowledgment of receipt before returning. When an acknowledgment is eventually sent, the JMS provider notifies the application by invoking the onCompletion method of the CompletionListener object that resides within the application. Conversely, if no receipt is sent, then the onException method of the CompletionListener is invoked.

Although JMS 2.0 offers asynchronous message sending, messages cannot be sent in an asynchronous manner from within a Java EE EJB or web container. As a result, violating applications will trigger a JMSException or JMSRuntimeException. Since this book focuses on Java EE 7 new features, this section will not delve any deeper into the asynchronous sending of messages. However, if you plan to use this feature in a different environment, please see more information at http://jms-spec.java.net/.

Multiple Consumers on the Same Subscription

Prior to JMS 2.0, a durable or non-durable topic subscription was only permitted to have one consumer at a time. This limited scalability since the processing work could not be distributed. In the 2.0 release, multiple consumers were allowed on the same subscription. With regards to non-durable subscriptions, otherwise known as "shared non-durable subscriptions," this type of subscription is useful for those cases where the work of receiving messages from a non-durable topic subscription needs to be shared amongst multiple consumers in order to distribute the payload. It should be noted that each message from the subscription is only delivered to one of the consumers on that subscription.

To facilitate this enhancement for non-durable subscriptions, each of the APIs for creating consumers has been updated as follows:

- If using the classic API, Session has been updated to include several createSharedConsumer methods, which return a MessageConsumer object. The createSharedConsumer message that is used depends upon the criteria specified.
- If using the simplified API, JMSContext contains several createSharedConsumer methods, which return a JMSConsumer object. The createSharedConsumer message that is used depends upon the criteria specified.
- If using the legacy domain-specific API for pub/sub, TopicSession has been updated to include several createSharedConsumer methods, which return a MessageConsumer object. The createSharedConsumer message that is used depends upon the criteria specified.

The following example demonstrates the creation of a subscription that accepts more than one consumer, using the simplified API.

```
  ...
    @Resource(name = "jms/connectionFactory")
    private ConnectionFactory connectionFactory;
    @Resource(lookup = "jms/Topic")
    Topic topic;
...
public void createSharedNonDurable(){
        String topicName = "JavaEE";
        JMSContext context = connectionFactory.createContext();
        JMSConsumer consumer = context.createSharedConsumer(topic, topicName);
```

```
        consumer.receive();
        //do something
    }
...
```

If you require the use of shared durable subscriptions, you will be happy to know that they received the same treatment as non-durable subscriptions in the JMS 2.0 release. As background, a durable subscription is useful for applications that need to receive all messages published on a topic, even those that have no consumer assigned. A shared, non-durable subscription is used by clients that need the ability to share the task of receiving messages from a durable subscription among multiple different consumers. Much like shared non-durable subscriptions; it is possible for shared-durable subscriptions to have multiple consumers. Again, each message from the subscription will only be sent to one of the consumers, not each of them.

To facilitate this enhancement for shared durable subscriptions, each of the APIs for creating consumers has been updated, as follows:

- If using the classic API, Session has been updated to include several `createSharedDurableConsumer` methods, each returning a `MessageConsumer` object. The `createSharedDurableConsumer` method that is used depends upon the specified criteria.
- If using the simplified API, `JMSContext` contains several `createSharedDurableConsumer` methods, each returning a `JMSConsumer` object. The `createSharedDurableConsumer` method that is used depends upon the specified criteria.
- If using the legacy domain-specific API for pub/sub, the `JMSContext` includes several `createSharedDurableConsumer` methods, each returning a `JMSConsumer` object. The `createSharedDurableConsumer` method that is used depends upon the specified criteria.

The following example demonstrates how to create a shared durable subscription using the simplified API.

```
...
    @Resource(name = "jms/connectionFactory")
    private ConnectionFactory connectionFactory;
    @Resource(lookup = "jms/Topic")
    Topic topic;
    ...
    public void createSharedDurable(){
        String topicName = "JavaEE";
        JMSContext context = connectionFactory.createContext();
        JMSConsumer consumer = context.createSharedConsumer(topic, topicName);
        consumer.receive();
      // do something
    }
...
```

Summary

JMS 2.0 is a completely overhauled release of the API, which applies modern programming techniques to make the use of JMS even easier. Using the simplified API, dozens of code lines can be cut from JMS applications, making code development and maintainability even easier. Going along with the Java 7 simplifications, JMS resources are now autocloseable, making the API more efficient. Additionally, features such as the ability to easily access message body content and set the delay on message sending help to provide developers with more fine-grained control. Although it has been a number of years since the API has been updated, this is one update that is certainly welcome since it modernizes the API, and adds simplification and more ability throughout.

CHAPTER 11

Concurrency and Batch Applications

The Java Enterprise platform has been missing a few key features since its inception. Those features include standard techniques for processing tasks concurrently, and standardization for batch application processing. In the release of Java EE 7, these two missing features have been addressed with the addition of the Java Concurrency Utilities and Batch Processing APIs.

The scope of these additional APIs is very large, and this chapter will not attempt to cover each feature. However, the examples contained within this chapter should provide enough information to get a developer up and running using some of the most frequently required pieces of each API. For more in-depth information regarding the details of the Concurrency Utilities for Java EE, please refer to the JavaDoc located at `http://concurrency-ee-spec.java.net/javadoc/`. The Batch Applications for the Java Platform API are immense, with a plethora of options available. This chapter will barely scratch the surface of the API; for more information, please refer to the specification at `https://java.net/projects/jbatch/pages/Home`.

Concurrency

Using Java SE concurrency utilities such as `java.util.concurrent` and `java.lang.Thread` in Java EE applications has been problematic in the past, since the application server container has no knowledge of such resources. Extensions of the `java.util.concurrent` API allows application servers and other EE containers to become aware of these concurrency resources. The extensions allow enterprise applications to appropriately utilize asynchronous operations via the use of `java.util.concurrent.ExecutorService` resources that are made available within the EE environment.

Understanding the Contextual Objects and Tasks

The Concurrency Utilities for Java EE API makes use of the following different types of managed objects:

- ManagedExecutorService
- ManagedScheduledExecutorService
- ContextService
- ManagedThreadFactory

In this section of the chapter, you will learn how to make use of these managed objects from within an application server container, such as GlassFish v4. You will then learn about using each of these managed objects to provide concurrency to your applications, and you will see examples of each.

■ **Note** As an option, task classes can implement the `javax.enterprise.concurrent.ManagedTask` interface. Task classes that implement this interface provide identity information and execution properties. Implementations of the ManagedTask interface can also register a `javax.enterprise.concurrent.ManagedTaskListener` instance to receive lifecycle events notifications.

Creating Application Server Concurrent Resources

In Java EE 7, the `ManagedExecutorService` was introduced, adding the ability to produce asynchronous tasks that are managed by an application server. Application server administrators can create `ManagedExecutorService` resources within an application server that can be utilized by one or more applications, much like a Java Message Service (JMS) `Topic` or `Queue`. There are a couple of ways to create application server concurrent resources. You can utilize the GlassFish command line `asadmin` utility. Alternatively, the GlassFish administration console has been enhanced with new forms for concurrent resource management for those who prefer working in a GUI. First, let's take a look at how to utilize the `asadmin` utility for creation of the resources.

To create a service, issue `the asadmin create-managed-executor-service` command at the command prompt, passing the name that you would like to use to identify the service. There are a bevy of options that can be used to customize the service in different ways. For instance, the service can be configured to let tasks run for a specified amount of time, thread pools can be configured, etc., allowing one to generate a `ManagedExecutorService` that will best suit the application requirements. To utilize concurrent utilities such as reporter tasks, the application server must be configured to utilize a `ManagedExecutorService`. To create a `ManagedExecutor` Service in GlassFish, run the following command at the command prompt:

```
<path-to-glassfish>/bin/asadmin create-managed-executor-service concurrent/BatchExecutor
```

In the preceding command-line action, the name of the `ManagedExecutorService` that is being created is `concurrent/BatchExecutor`. However, this could be changed to better suit the application; the service can be named with any valid String. To see all of the options available for the `create-managed-executor-service command`, issue the `--help` flag. The following shows the results of doing so:

```
bin/asadmin create-managed-executor-service --help
NAME
     create-managed-executor-service

SYNOPSIS
     Usage: create-managed-executor-service [--enabled=true] [--c
     ontextinfo=contextinfo] [--threadpriority=5] [--longrunningt
     asks=false] [--hungafterseconds=hungafterseconds] [--corepoo
     lsize=0] [--maximumpoolsize=2147483647] [--keepaliveseconds=
     60] [--threadlifetimeseconds=0] [--taskqueuecapacity=2147483
     647] [--description=description] [--property=property] [--ta
     rget=target] jndi_name
```

```
OPTIONS
     --enabled

     --contextinfo

     --threadpriority

     --longrunningtasks

     --hungafterseconds

     --corepoolsize

     --maximumpoolsize

     --keepaliveseconds

     --threadlifetimeseconds

     --taskqueuecapacity

     --description

     --property

     --target

OPERANDS
     jndi_name
```

For those who would prefer to work within the GlassFish administration console, there have been a few new administration panels added to make creation and management of concurrent resources easier. The new “Managed Executor Service” panel can be used to create new application server `ManagedExecutorService` resources, as well as manage those that already exist. To do so, authenticate successfully into the administrative console, and navigate to the “Concurrent Resources” ➤“Managed Executor Services” administration panel using the left-hand tree menu (Figure 11-1).

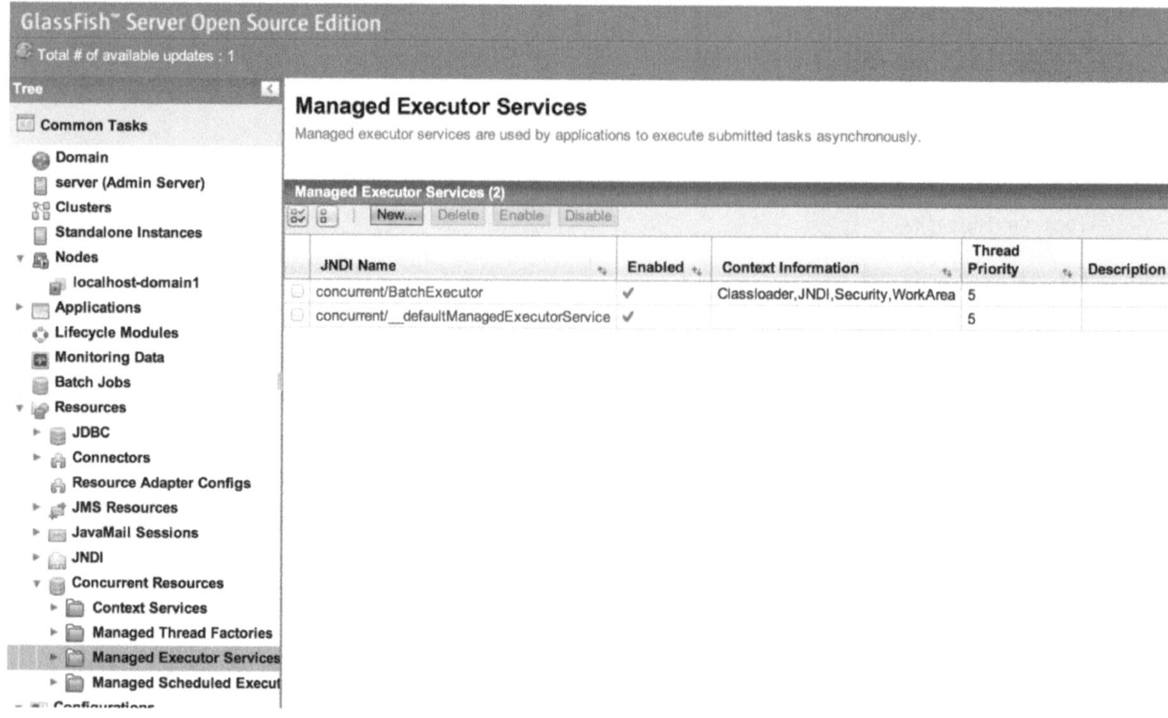

Figure 11-1. *GlassFish Managed Executor Services Panel*

Once you've opened the panel, click on the "New" button to create a new service. This will open the "New Managed Executor Service" panel, in which you will be required to populate a "JNDI Name" for your new service (Figure 11-2).

New Managed Executor Service

OK Cancel

Create a new managed executor service that will be used by application components such as servlets and EJBs.

JNDI Name: *

Context Information: ✓ Enabled

Classloader
JNDI
Security
WorkArea

Shift key for multiple selection.

Container contexts to propagate to other threads. If Disabled, selected context-info will be ignored.

Status: ✓ Enabled

Thread Priority: 5
Priority to assign to created threads

Long-running Tasks: Enabled

Hung After: 0 Seconds
Number of seconds tasks can execute before they are considered unresponsive

Description:

Pool Settings

Core Size: 0
Number of threads to keep in a thread pool

Maximum Pool Size: 2147483647
Maximum number of threads a thread pool can contain

Keep Alive: 60 Seconds
Number of seconds threads can remain idle when the number of threads is greater than core size

Figure 11-2. *New Managed Executor Service Panel*

This panel offers quite a few options for creation of the service. However, the only option that is required is the JNDI Name, as all others are populated with default values. The JNDI name that is specified should follow the format of `concurrent/YourExecutorServiceName`, where `YourExecutorServiceName` is a custom name of your choice.

Running the Reporter Task

After the `ManagedExecutorService` has been created, it can be utilized by one or more applications to perform concurrent operations. An application must be either configured via XML to allow access to the `ManagedExecutorService` resource in the application server container, or the resource can be injected via the use of the `@Resource` annotation. In the example, each of these options is demonstrated. For the purposes of the example, it is assumed that the `@Resource` annotation is utilized to inject the service into the servlet.

To run a task concurrently using the service, you must create the task in a separate class that implements `java.util.Runnable`, so that it can be invoked as a separate process, much like a standard Java `Thread`. In the example, a class named `ReporterTask` implements `Runnable`, and within the run method the reporter task performs the tasks that we wish to run in an asynchronous manner. In the case of this example, a couple of methods are invoked from within the run method. The `Runnable` class that has been generated can then be passed to the `ManagedExecutorService` to be executed concurrently while other tasks are being performed by the application.

To make use of the ManagedExecutorService, register it with the application via XML or by resource injection. In the example, resource injection is utilized, making the ManagedExecutorService available from within the Java servlet. To inject the resource, specify the name of it to the @Resource annotation.

```
@Resource(name = "concurrent/BatchExecutor")
ManagedExecutorService mes;
```

The ManagedExecutorService can then be invoked by calling the submit method, and passing an instance of the Runnable task that we'd like to submit for processing. In this case, the ReporterTask class is instantiated, and an instance of it is then passed to the service, returning a java.util.concurrent.Future object.

```
ReporterTask reporterTask = new ReporterTask("BookReport");
Future reportFuture = mes.submit(reporterTask);
```

Once submitted, the Future object that was returned can be periodically queried to see if it is still running, or if it has been completed by calling its isDone method. It can be cancelled by calling the cancel method, and a canceled task can be checked by calling its isCanceled method.

Example of ReporterTask

Once the application server has been configured and the ManagedExecutorService has been created, an application can be written to utilize the newly created service. Within an application, one can choose to configure the application to make use of the ManagedExecutorService via XML, or a @Resource annotation can be used to inject the resource. To configure via XML, add a <resource-env-ref> element to the web.xml deployment descriptor. In this case, you need to configure a resource of type javax.enterprise.concurrent.ManagedExecutorService, as shown in the excerpt from the web.xml below:

```
<resource-env-ref>
 <description>
This executor is used for the application's reporter task. This executor has the following
requirements:
Run Location: NA
Context Info: Local Namespace
 </description>
    <resource-env-ref-name>
        concurrent/BatchExecutor
    </resource-env-ref-name>
    <resource-env-ref-type>
        javax.enterprise.concurrent.ManagedExecutorService
    </resource-env-ref-type>
</resource-env-ref>
```

In the XML configuration, the resource has been assigned to a reference name of concurrent/BatchExecutor, but you could name the reference to best suit your application. If you would rather utilize an annotation, then the following @Resource annotation can be specified to inject a ManagedExecutorService into a class for use. You will see an example of this in use later on.

```
@Resource(name = "concurrent/BatchExecutor")
ManagedExecutorService mes;
```

Once the configuration is complete, you can create a report task class, which is a class that implements `Runnable` and is responsible for running the actual reports. The following class, `org.javaee7.chapter11.ReporterTask`, is an example of such as class.

```
package org.javaee7.chapter11;

import java.io.BufferedWriter;
import java.io.IOException;
import java.nio.charset.Charset;
import java.nio.file.Files;
import java.nio.file.Path;
import java.nio.file.Paths;
import java.util.List;
import javax.ejb.EJB;
import org.javaee7.entity.Jobs;
import org.javaee7.entity.Product;
import org.javaee7.jpa.session.JobsSession;
import org.javaee7.jpa.session.ProductSession;

/**
 *
 * @author Juneau
 */
public class ReporterTask implements Runnable {

    String reportName;
    @EJB
    private JobsSession jobsFacade;
    @EJB
    private ProductSession productFacade;

    public ReporterTask(String reportName) {
        this.reportName = reportName;
    }

    public void run() {
// Run the named report
        if ("JobsReport".equals(reportName)) {
            runJobReport();


        } else if ("ProductReport".equals(reportName)) {
            runProductReport();
        }
    }
```

```
    /**
     * Prints a list of jobs to the system log.
     */
    public void runJobReport() {
        List<Jobs> jobs = jobsFacade.getJobList();
        System.out.println("Job Listing Report");
        System.out.println("====================");

        for (Jobs job : jobs) {
            System.out.println(job.getTitle() + " " + job.getDivision());
        }
    }

    /**
     * Prints a list of products
     */
    void runProductReport() {
        System.out.println("Querying the database");
        Path reportFile = Paths.get("ProductReport.txt");

        try (BufferedWriter writer = Files.newBufferedWriter(
                reportFile, Charset.defaultCharset())) {
            Files.deleteIfExists(reportFile);
            reportFile = Files.createFile(reportFile);
            writer.append("Product Listing Report");
            writer.newLine();
            writer.append("==================");
            writer.newLine();
            List<Product> products = productFacade.obtainProduct();
            for (Product product : products) {
                writer.append(product.getName());
                writer.newLine();
            }
            writer.flush();
        } catch (IOException exception) {
            System.out.println("Error writing to file");
        }

    }
}
```

Lastly, the report needs to be invoked by the `ManagedExecutorService` that was configured within the `web.xml`. In this example, the `ManagedExecutorService` is injected into a Servlet, which is then used to invoke the report, as seen in the following code:

```
import java.io.IOException;
import java.io.PrintWriter;
import java.util.concurrent.Future;
import javax.annotation.Resource;
import javax.enterprise.concurrent.ManagedExecutorService;
```

```
import javax.servlet.ServletException;
import javax.servlet.annotation.WebServlet;
import javax.servlet.http.HttpServlet;
import javax.servlet.http.HttpServletRequest;
import javax.servlet.http.HttpServletResponse;

/**
 *
 * @author Juneau
 */
@WebServlet(name = "ReporterServlet", urlPatterns = {"/ReporterServlet"})
public class ReporterServlet extends HttpServlet {

    @Resource(name = "concurrent/BatchExecutor")
    ManagedExecutorService mes;

    protected void processRequest(HttpServletRequest request, HttpServletResponse response)
            throws ServletException, IOException {
        response.setContentType("text/html;charset=UTF-8");
        PrintWriter out = response.getWriter();
        try {

            out.println("<html>");
            out.println("<head>");
            out.println("<title>Job Report Invoker</title>");
            out.println("</head>");
            out.println("<body>");
            out.println("<h2>This servlet initiates the job report task.  Please look "
                    + "in the server log to see the results.</h2> <br />" +
                    " This task is not run asynchronously, however, the " +
                    " task will process independently.");
            out.println("<br/><br/>");
            ReporterTask reporterTask = new ReporterTask("JobsReport");
            Future reportFuture = mes.submit(reporterTask);
            while( !reportFuture.isDone() )
                out.println("Running...<BR>");
            if (reportFuture.isDone()){
                out.println("Report Complete");
            }
            out.println("</body>");
            out.println("</html>");
        } finally {
            out.close();
        }
    }
...
}
```

When the servlet is visited, the reporter task will be initiated and it will begin to produce results.

Running Multiple Tasks at Once Asynchronously

To coordinate the processing of tasks in an asynchronous manner via a ManagedExecutorService, two or more tasks that need to be processed should be contained in separate classes or multiple instances of the same task class. Each of the task classes should implement the java.util.concurrent.Callable and javax.enterprise.concurrent.ManagedTask interfaces. A task class should include a constructor that enables a caller to pass arguments that are required to instantiate the object, and should implement a call method, which returns the information that is needed to construct the report to the client. Two or more such task classes can then be invoked via the ManagedExecutorService in order to orchestrate the execution and process all results into the required format.

To assemble the tasks for processing, create an ArrayList<Callable>, and add instances of each task to the array. In the example below, the array is named builderTasks, and instances of two different task types are added to that array.

```
ArrayList<Callable<AuthorInfo>> builderTasks = new ArrayList<Callable<AuthorInfo>>();
builderTasks.add(new AuthorTask(authorId));
builderTasks.add(new AuthorTaskTwo(authorId2);
```

Next, pass the array that has been constructed to the ManagedExecutorService, returning a List<Future<object>>, which can then be used to process the results.

```
List<Future<AuthorInfo>> results = mes.invokeAll(builderTasks);
AuthorInfo authorInfo = (AuthorInfo) results.get(0).get();
// Process the results
```

Suppose you are writing an application that needs the ability to connect a database and retrieve data from two or more tables to obtain results at the same time. You wish to have the results aggregated before returning them to the user. Create a builder task that can be used to run two different tasks in parallel. Each of the tasks can retrieve the data from the different sources, and in the end the data will be merged together and aggregated to formulate the result. In this case, you need to configure a resource of type javax.enterprise.concurrent.ManagedExecutorService, as shown in the excerpt from the web.xml below:

```
<resource-env-ref>
 <description>
This executor is used for the application's builder tasks. This executor has the following
requirements:
Run Location: Local
Context Info: Local Namespace, Security
 </description>
    <resource-env-ref-name>
        concurrent/BuilderExecutor
    </resource-env-ref-name>
    <resource-env-ref-type>
        javax.enterprise.concurrent.ManagedExecutorService
    </resource-env-ref-type>
</resource-env>
```

In this example, the ManagedExecutorService resource in the application is configured to work with a resource that has been registered with the application server container and identified by the JNDI name of concurrent/BuilderExecutor. If you would rather utilize an annotation, then the following @Resource annotation can be specified to inject a ManagedExecutorService into a class for use within the Runnable.

```
@Resource(name = "concurrent/BuilderExecutor")
ManagedExecutorService mes;
```

Once the application has been configured to work with the `ManagedExecutorService` resource, you can create task classes for each of the different tasks that you wish to run. Each task class must implement the `javax.enterprise.concurrent.ManagedTask` interfaces. The following code is from the file `org.javaee7.chapter11.EmployeeTask.java`, and it shows what a task class should look like.

```
import java.math.BigDecimal;
import java.util.HashMap;
import java.util.Locale;
import java.util.Map;
import java.util.concurrent.Callable;
import javax.enterprise.concurrent.ManagedTask;
import javax.enterprise.concurrent.ManagedTaskListener;

/**
 *
 * @author Juneau
 */

public class EmployeeTask implements Callable<EmployeeInfo>, ManagedTask {
    // The ID of the request to report on demand.
    BigDecimal employeeId;
    EmployeeInfo employeeInfo;
    Map<String, String> execProps;

    public EmployeeTask(BigDecimal id) {
        this.employeeId = id;
        execProps = new HashMap<>();

        execProps.put(ManagedTask.IDENTITY_NAME, getIdentityName());
    }

    public EmployeeInfo call() {
// Find the entity bean and return it to the client.
        return employeeInfo;
    }

    public String getIdentityName() {
        return "EmployeeTask: AuthorID=" + employeeId;
    }

    public Map<String, String> getExecutionProperties() {
        return execProps;
    }

    public String getIdentityDescription(Locale locale) {
        // Use a resource bundle...
        return "EmployeeTask asynchronous EJB invoker";
    }
```

```
    @Override
    public ManagedTaskListener getManagedTaskListener() {
        return new CustomManagedTaskListener();
    }
}
```

One or more such task classes can be implemented, and then they can be processed via the builder task using the ManagedExecutorService resource that has been registered with the application server container. The following servlet makes use of a ManagedExecutorService to coordinate the invocation of two task classes. In this case the task class names are EmployeeTask and EmployeeTaskTwo.

```
import java.io.IOException;
import java.io.PrintWriter;
import java.math.BigDecimal;
import java.util.concurrent.ExecutionException;
import java.util.concurrent.Future;
import java.util.logging.Level;
import java.util.logging.Logger;
import javax.annotation.Resource;
import javax.enterprise.concurrent.ManagedExecutorService;
import javax.servlet.Servlet;
import javax.servlet.ServletException;
import javax.servlet.annotation.WebServlet;
import javax.servlet.http.HttpServlet;
import javax.servlet.http.HttpServletRequest;
import javax.servlet.http.HttpServletResponse;

@WebServlet(name = "BuilderServlet", urlPatterns = {"/builderServlet"})
public class BuilderServlet extends HttpServlet implements Servlet {
    // Retrieve our executor instance.

    @Resource(name = "concurrent/BuilderExecutor")
    ManagedExecutorService mes;
    EmployeeInfo employeeInfo;

    protected void processRequest(HttpServletRequest req, HttpServletResponse resp) throws
ServletException, IOException {
        try {
            PrintWriter out = resp.getWriter();
            // Create the task instances
            Future<EmployeeInfo> empFuture = mes.submit(new EmployeeTask(new BigDecimal(1)));
            Future<EmployeeInfo> empFuture2 = mes.submit(new EmployeeTask(new BigDecimal(2)));

            // Wait for results
            EmployeeInfo empInfo = empFuture.get();
            EmployeeInfo empInfo2 = empFuture2.get();
            // Process Results
```

```
        } catch (InterruptedException|ExecutionException ex) {
            Logger.getLogger(BuilderServlet.class.getName()).log(Level.SEVERE, null, ex);
        }
    }
     ’’’
}
```

Utilizing this technique, a series of tasks can be concurrently processed, returning results that can be later used to formulate a response. In the case of this example, a report is constructed by calling two task classes and returning the results of queried information. This same technique can be applied to an array of different tasks, allowing an application to process the results of multiple task invocations in one central location.

Scheduled Tasks

To schedule a task to run at specific times, utilize the `javax.concurrent.ManagedScheduledExecutorService` interface. This interface extends the `java.util.concurrent.ScheduledExecutorService` and `javax.enterprise.concurrent.ManagedExecutorService` interfaces. The `ManagedScheduleExecutorService` can be used to execute a `Runnable` task according to a specified schedule.

The Executor Service

As mentioned previously, a `ManagedScheduleExecutorService` can be used to schedule `Runnable` tasks. That is, any class that implements `java.lang.Runnable` can be invoked via the service. The code that is contained within the task class's `run` method is invoked each time the task is initiated. In the example that follows, the `run` method executes another method within the class that is used to query an entity and perform some work against the results.

To make use of a `ManagedScheduledExecutorService`, one can be created within the application server container. Similarly to the `ManagedExecutorService`, this resource can be created by issuing the `asadmin create-managed-scheduled-executor-service` command. The GlassFish 4.0 application server also contains a panel within the administrative console for creation of such resources. To create the resource from within the administrative console, log in and navigate to the Resources ➤ Concurrent Resources ➤ Managed Scheduled Executor Services panel (Figure 11-3).

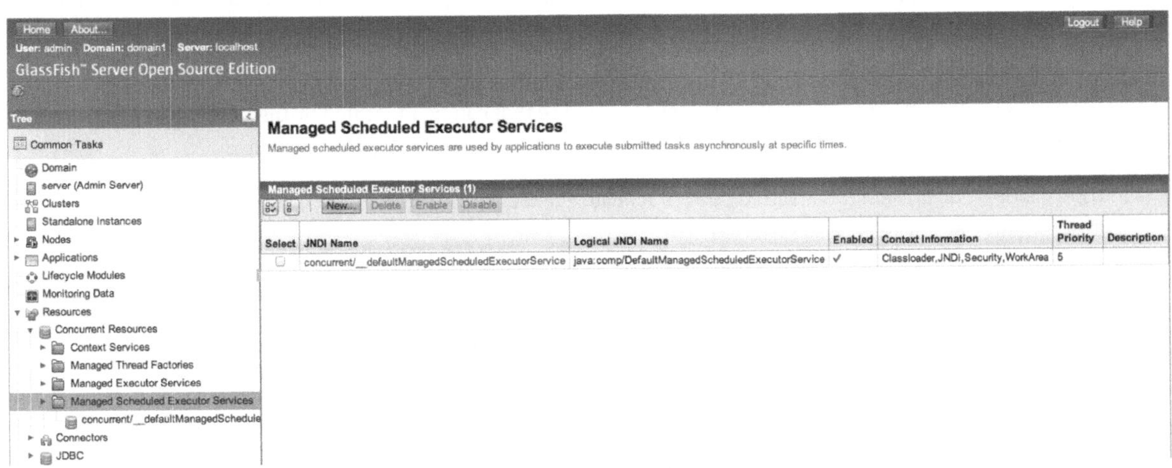

Figure 11-3. *Managed Scheduled Executor Services Panel*

Once you have successfully navigated to the panel, click on the "New" button to open the "New Managed Scheduled Executor Service" panel (Figure 11-4). Within this panel, you must specify a JNDI name for the resource, along with a number of optional parameters, including context settings, thread priority, and thread pool settings.

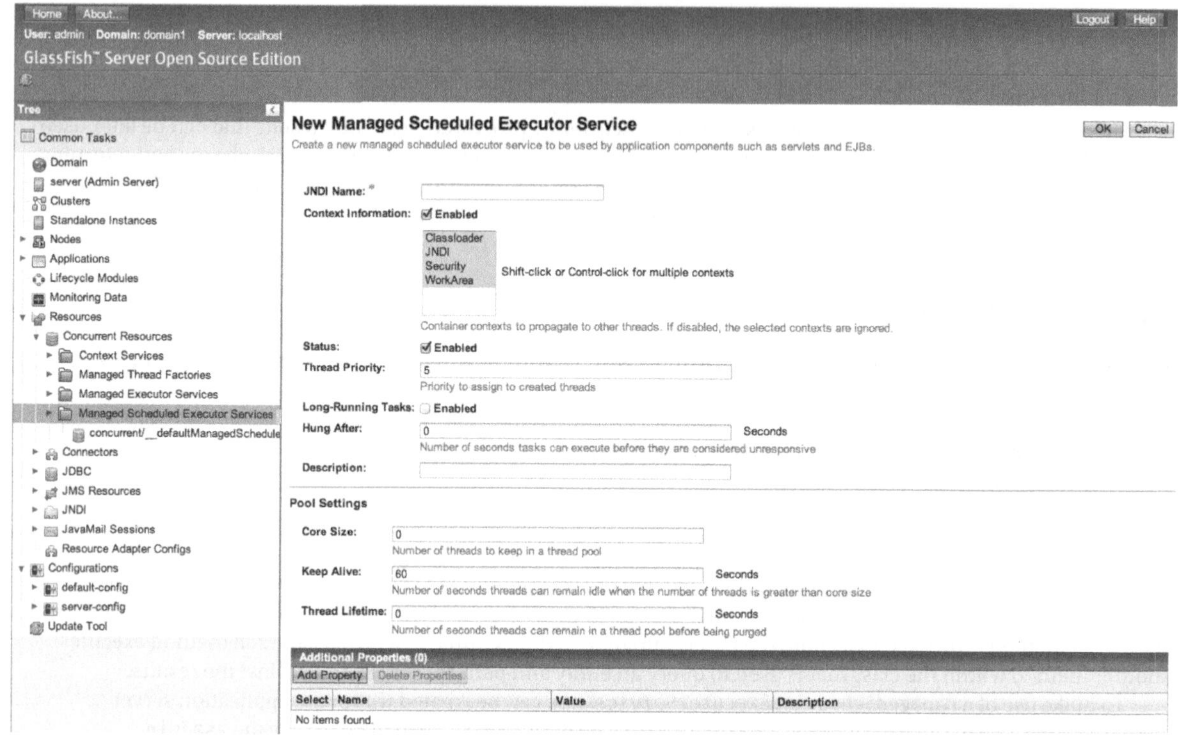

Figure 11-4. *New Managed Scheduled Executor Service Panel*

However, it is not necessary to generate your own `ManagedScheduledExecutorService` because GlassFish, and, any Java EE 7 compliant application server, should contain a default `ManagedScheduledExecutorService`. To enable an application to access the service, XML configuration within the `web.xml` deployment descriptor can be used, or a `@Resource` annotation can be used to inject the resource. In the example below, both techniques are demonstrated. However, in the class that is used to initiate the example task, the `@Resource` annotation is used to inject the application server's default `ManagedScheduledExecutorService` that can be identified by the name of `concurrent/__defaultManagedScheduledExecutorService`.

```
@Resource(name=" concurrent/__defaultManagedScheduledExecutorService ")
    ManagedScheduledExecutorService mes;
```

To schedule the task, create an instance of the task class, and then pass the instance to one of the `ManagedScheduledExecutorService` scheduler methods that are made available via the `ScheduleExecutorService` interface. The methods that can be used to schedule tasks are shown in Table 11-1.

Table 11-1. ScheduleExecutorService Methods

Method	Description
`schedule(Callable<V> callable, long delay, TimeUnit unit)`	Creates and executes a ScheduledFeature object. The object becomes available after the specified delay period.
`schedule(Runnable command, long delay, TimeUnit unit)`	Creates and executes a one-time task that becomes available after the specified delay.
`scheduleAtFixedRate(Runnable command, long initialDelay, long period, TimeUnit unit)`	Creates and executes a periodic tasks that becomes available after the initial specified delay period. Subsequent executions are then scheduled in increments of the specified period after the initial delay.
`scheduleWithFixedDelay(Runnable command, long initialDelay, long delay, TimeUnit unit)`	Creates and executes a periodic task that becomes available after the initial delay period. Subsequent executions are then scheduled with the specified delay period in between each execution.

In the example, the `scheduleAtFixedRate` method is called, passing the task class, along with the initial delay period of 5 minutes and then the task is executed every 5 minutes thereafter.

Example of Scheduled Task

Use the `ManagedScheduleExecutorService` to create a scheduled task within your application. As mentioned previously, before an application can use the service, it must be created within the application server container. To create a `ManagedScheduleExecutorService` instance within GlassFish, issue the following command from the command-line:

```
bin/asadmin create-managed-scheduled-executor-service concurrent/name-of-service
```

In the command above, name-of-service can be whatever name you choose. The `create-managed-scheduled-executor-service` command has many options that can be specified. To see and learn more about each option, invoke the command help by issuing the `--help` flag after the command, rather than providing the name of the service to create. Optionally, you could create the service using an application server resource, such as the GlassFish administration console.

Once the service has been created within the container, it can be utilized by an application. To utilize this type of service, the environment must be configured via XML or annotation. To utilize XML configuration, add a `<resource-env-ref>` element to the `web.xml` deployment descriptor. In this case, you need to configure a resource of type `javax.enterprise.concurrent.ManagedScheduledExecutorService`, as shown in the excerpt from the `web.xml` below:

```
<resource-env-ref>
 <description>Prints alerts to server log, if warranted, on a periodic basis</description>
<resource-env-ref-name>
concurrent/__defaultScheduledManagedExecutorService
</resource-env-ref-name>
 <resource-env-ref-type>
javax.enterprise.concurrent.ManagedScheduledExecutorService
 </resource-env-ref-type>
</resource-env-ref>
```

If you wish to use annotations rather than XML, the `@Resource` annotation can be used in client code to inject the `ManagedScheduledExecutorService`, as shown in the following lines. In this case, the injected resource references a ManagedScheduledExecutorService that is identified by the name concurrent/__defaultManagedScheduledExecutorService.

```
@Resource(name="concurrent/__defaultManagedScheduledExecutorService")
ManagedScheduledExecutorService mes;
```

To write the task that you wish to have scheduled, create a Java class that implements Runnable. As such, the class will contain a run method, which will be invoked each time the scheduled task is initiated. The following example demonstrates how to construct a task that can be used for logging. In this example, the Employee entity is queried on a periodic basis to determine if new employees have been added to the database.

```
import java.util.List;
import javax.persistence.EntityManager;
import javax.persistence.EntityManagerFactory;
import javax.persistence.EntityTransaction;
import javax.persistence.Persistence;
import javax.persistence.Query;
import org.javaee7.entity.Employee;

/**
 * Chapter 11 - Scheduled Logger
 * @author Juneau
 */
public class ScheduledEmployeeAlert implements Runnable {

    EntityManagerFactory emf = null;
    EntityManager em = null;

    @Override
    public void run() {
        emf = Persistence.createEntityManagerFactory("IntroToJavaEE7PU");
        em = emf.createEntityManager();
        queryEmployees();
    }

    public void queryEmployees(){
        EntityTransaction entr = em.getTransaction();
        entr.begin();
        String qry = "select object(o) from Employee o";
        Query query = em.createQuery(qry);
        List<Employee> emps = query.getResultList();
        for(Employee emp: emps){
            // if employee is new then alert
        }
    }
}
```

To periodically invoke the task, utilize the ManagedScheduledExecutorService resource. The following JSF managed bean class demonstrates how to invoke this type of service.

```
package org.javaee7.chapter11;

import java.util.concurrent.Future;
import java.util.concurrent.TimeUnit;
import javax.annotation.Resource;
import javax.enterprise.concurrent.ManagedScheduledExecutorService;
import javax.faces.application.FacesMessage;
import javax.faces.context.FacesContext;
import javax.inject.Named;

/**
 * Managed Bean for scheduling new employee alerts
 * @author Juneau
 */
@Named
public class ScheduledEmployeeAlerter {

    Future alertHandle = null;

    @Resource(name="concurrent/__defaultManagedScheduledExecutorService")
    ManagedScheduledExecutorService mes;

    public void alertScheduler() {

        ScheduledEmployeeAlert ae = new ScheduledEmployeeAlert();
        alertHandle = mes.scheduleAtFixedRate(
                ae, 5L, 5L, TimeUnit.MINUTES);
        FacesMessage facesMsg = new FacesMessage(FacesMessage.SEVERITY_INFO, "Task Scheduled",
"Task Scheduled");
                FacesContext.getCurrentInstance().addMessage(null, facesMsg);

    }

}
```

Thread Instances

Until the release of Java EE 7, multi-threaded enterprise applications were very customized. In fact, until the EE 7 release, there was no formal framework to utilize for spawning threads within an enterprise application. In this latest release that includes the Concurrency utilities, thread processing has been formalized. To utilize threading within an enterprise application, one should create `ManagedThreadFactory` resource(s) within the application server container, and utilize those resources within application(s), as needed.

Before an application can use the service, it must be created within the application server container. As with the other concurrent resources, there are a couple of different ways to create the `ManagedThreadFactory` within the GlassFish application server. To create a `ManagedThreadFactory` instance within GlassFish utilizing the command line utility, issue the following command from the command-line:

```
asadmin create-managed-thread-factory concurrent/name-of-service
```

In the command above, name-of-service can be whatever name you choose. The `create-managed-thread-factory` command has many options that can be specified. To see and learn more about each option, invoke the command help by issuing the `--help` flag after the command, rather than providing the name of the service to create. At a minimum, the desired name for the resource should be included with the invocation of the command. However, there are a number of different options that can be specified to customize the resource. To learn more about those options, please see the online documentation. One can also create a `ManagedThreadFactory` from within the GlassFish administrative console. To do so, log into the console, and navigate to the Resources ➤ Concurrent Resources ➤ Managed Thread Factories menu option from the left-hand tree menu (Figure 11-5).

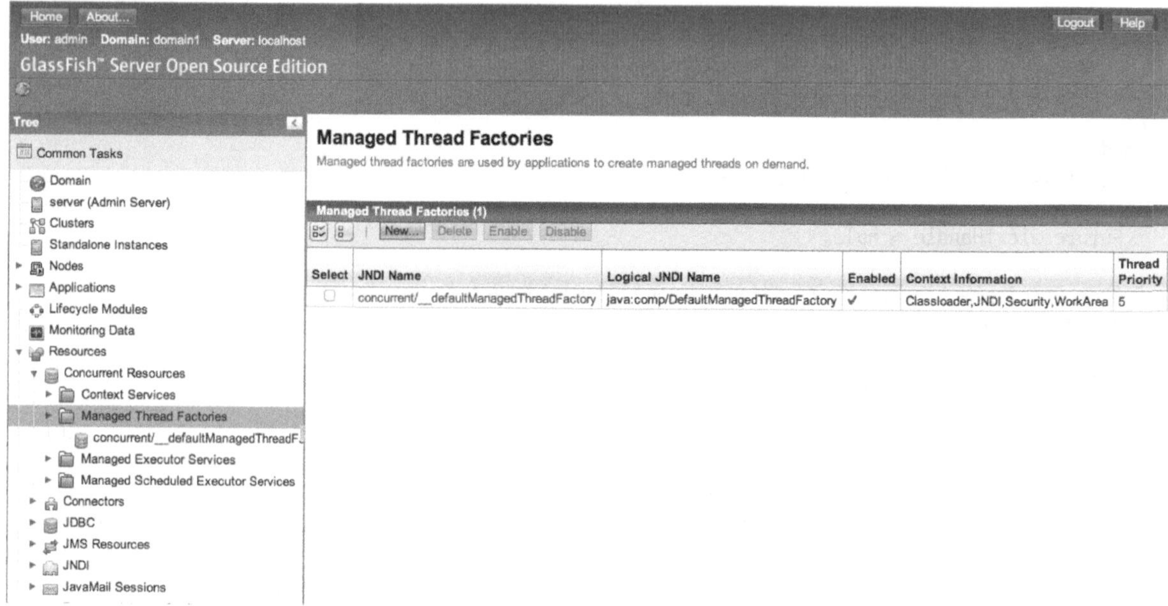

Figure 11-5. *Managed Thread Factories Panel*

Once you have navigated to the "Managed Thread Factories" panel, click on the "New" button to open the "New Managed Thread Factory" panel (Figure 11-6). Specify a JNDI name and, optionally, a thread priority. Lastly, click on "OK" to create the resource.

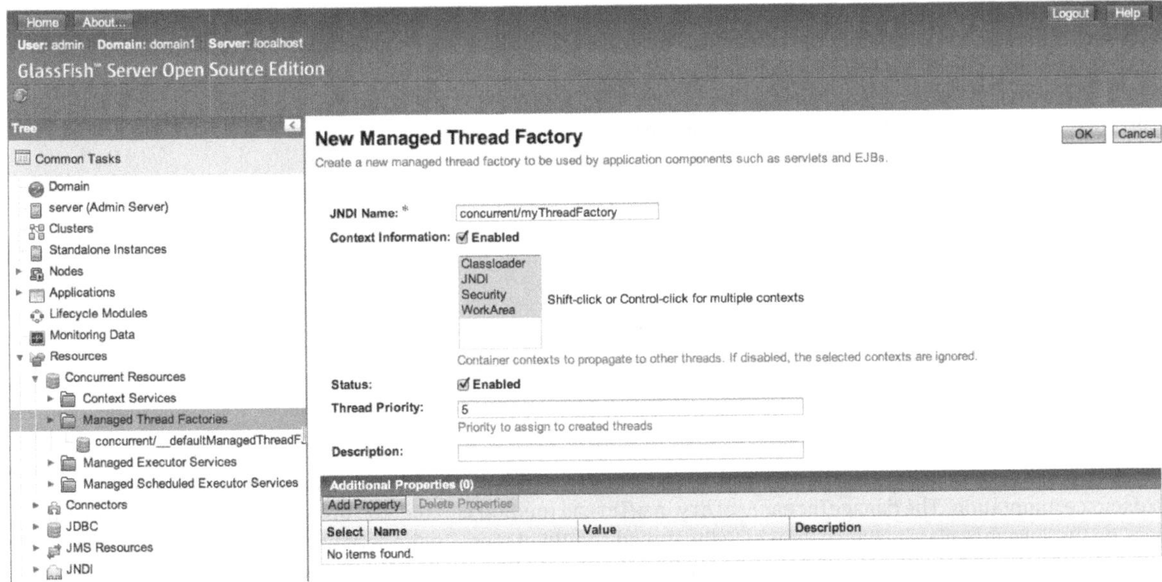

Figure 11-6. *New Managed Thread Factory panel*

As mentioned in the example, an application can make use of a `ManagedThreadFactory` resource by configuring XML within the `web.xml` deployment descriptor, or by injecting via the `@Resource` annotation within the classes that need to make use of the resource. Once that resource has been injected, calls can be made against it to spawn new threads using the `newThread` method. The `newThread` method returns a Thread instance, which can then be utilized by calling the `Thread` instance methods, as needed. In the example, the thread is started by calling the thread's `start` method, and when the context is destroyed, the thread's `interrupt` method is invoked.

To utilize a `ManagedThreadFactory`, the environment must be configured via XML or annotation. To utilize XML configuration, add a `<resource-env-ref>` element to the `web.xml` deployment descriptor. In this case, you need to configure a resource of type `javax.enterprise.concurrent.ManagedThreadFactory`, as shown in the excerpt from the `web.xml` below:

```
<resource-env-ref>
 <description>
</description>
<resource-env-ref-name>
concurrent/AcmeThreadFactory
</resource-env-ref-name>
 <resource-env-ref-type>
javax.enterprise.concurrent.ManagedThreadFactory
 </resource-env-ref-type>
</resource-env-ref>
```

To utilize annotations rather than XML configuration, the `ManagedThreadFactory` can be injected using an annotation such as the following:

```
@Resource(name="concurrent/AcmeThreadFactory");
ManagedThreadFactory threadFactory;
```

In this example, a ManagedThreadFactory will be injected into an EJB, so that a logging task can be used to print output to the server log when the EJB is created or destroyed. The following code demonstrates how to create a task that can be utilized by the ManagedThreadFactory:

```
public class MessagePrinter implements Runnable {

    @Override
    public void run() {
        printMessage();
    }

    public void printMessage(){
        System.out.println("Here we are performing some work...");
    }
}
```

To initiate the threading, call the ManagedThreadFactory, which can be injected into a using class via the @Resource annotation. The ManageThreadFactory newThread method can then be invoked to spawn a new thread, passing the Runnable class instance for which the thread should process. In the servlet context listener example below, when a thread context is initialized, then a Runnable class that was listed in the previous code listing, MessagePrinter, is instantiated and passed to the ManagedThreadFactory to spawn a new thread.

```
package org.javaee7.chapter11;

import javax.annotation.Resource;
import javax.enterprise.concurrent.ManagedThreadFactory;
import javax.servlet.ServletContextEvent;
import javax.servlet.ServletContextListener;

/**
 * Servlet Context Listener:  Prints message when context is initialized
 * @author Juneau
 */
public class ServletCtxListener implements ServletContextListener {
    Thread printerThread = null;

    @Resource(name ="concurrent/AcmeThreadFactory")
    ManagedThreadFactory threadFactory;

    @Override
    public void contextInitialized(ServletContextEvent scEvent) {

        MessagePrinter printer = new MessagePrinter();
        Thread loggerThread = threadFactory.newThread(printer);
        loggerThread.start();
    }
```

```
    public void contextDestroyed(ServletContextEvent scEvent) {
        synchronized (printerThread) {
            printerThread.interrupt();
        }
    }
}
```

The addition of a formal threading framework into Java EE is much welcomed. By adhering to the use of ManagedThreadFactory API, your enterprise applications can be made multi-threaded using an accepted standard solution.

Batch Applications for the Java Platform

The new API for batch processing provides a fine-grained experience for developers, which enables them to produce and process batch applications in a variety of different ways. Enterprise applications no longer need to utilize customized classes for performing batch processing, allowing enterprise applications to adhere to an adopted standard.

There are two different approaches to creating batch applications using the API, those being "item oriented" and "task-oriented." Item-oriented processing is useful for those applications that require many different processes to be combined together to formulate one job. This type of processing is also known as "chunk" processing, since the different processes are performed in chunks. The second approach is known as task-oriented, and this type of processing supports batch steps that are also known as batchlets.

Item-Oriented Processing

Prior to the inclusion of Batch Applications for Java EE, organizations and individuals had to write their own custom Java implementations for processing batch jobs. Utilizing the newly added API, developers can create batch jobs using a standard combination of XML for defining a job, and Java for programming the implementation. In the example below, a simple batch job reads text from a file, processes it using a comparison, and then writes out the processed text. The example batch program is simplistic, but it demonstrates how the API makes it easy to write very complex jobs.

Let's begin the explanation by taking a brief look at the API from a high level. A job consists of one or more steps, and each step has no more than one ItemReader, ItemWriter, and ItemProcessor. A JobOperator is responsible for launching a job, and a JobRepository is used to maintain metadata regarding the currently running job. Jobs are defined via XML, and the <Job> element is at the root of the job definition. Thus, a <Job> is the foundational element, which consists of one or more <step> elements, and also defines other specifics of the job such as the job name and if it is restartable or not. Each <step> of a job consists of one or more chunks or batchlets. In this example, which covers item-oriented processes, each step has just one chunk. To learn more about task-oriented jobs and batchlets, please see the specification or online documentation at https://java.net/projects/jbatch/pages/Home.

As expected, each chunk of a step is defined within the XML using a <chunk> element. A <chunk> element, which is a child of <step>, defines the reader, writer, processor pattern of a batch job. A chunk runs within the scope of a transaction, and it is restartable at a checkpoint if it does not complete. The <reader> element is a child element of <chunk>, and it is used to specify the reader for that chunk. The <reader> element can accept zero or more name/value pair properties using a <properties> element. The <processor> element is also a child element of <chunk>, which specifies the processor element for that chunk. Like a <reader> element, a <processor> element can accept zero or more name/value pair properties using a <properties> element. The <writer> element is a child element of <chunk> as well, which specifies the writer for the chunk step. Again, like the reader and processor, the <writer> element can accept zero or more name/value pair properties using a <properties> element.

The XML configuration for a job resides in an XML file that should be named similar to the batch job to which it belongs. This file should reside within a folder named batch-jobs, which in turn resides in the application META-INF folder. An XML file named batch.xml should also reside within the META-INF folder. This file contains the mapping for the item reader, writer, and processor elements using <ref> elements and mapping the item names to a Java implementation class.

```
<batch-artifacts xmlns="http://jcp.org.batch/jsl">
    <ref id="acmeReader" class="org.javaee7.chapter11.AcmeReader"/>
    <ref id="acmeProcessor" class="org.javaee7.chapter11.AcmeProcessor"/>
    <ref id="acmeWriter" class="org.javaee7.chapter11.AcmeWriter"/>
</batch-artifacts>
```

The implementation classes should either extend abstract classes (reader and writer), or implement an interface (processor). The ItemReader implementation class (AcmeReader in the example) extends the AbstractItemReader , and accepts an object into which the read items will be stored. In the example, that object class is named WidgetReportItem. As such, the class should implement the readItem method, which is responsible for performing the reading. The method should return the object to which the items are read, or return a null when there are no more items to read.

```
public class AcmeReader extends AbstractItemReader<WidgetReportItem> {
...
@Override
    public WidgetReportItem readItem() throws Exception {
        Path file = Paths.get("widgetFile.txt");
        List<String> fileLines;
        Charset charset = Charset.forName("US-ASCII");
        fileLines = Files.readAllLines(file, charset);
        for(String line:fileLines){
            return new WidgetReportItem(line);
        }
        return null;

    }
...
```

The ItemProcessor class implementation (AcmeProcessor in the example) is responsible for performing processing for the chunk, and it should implement the ItemProcessor interface, accepting both the object containing the read items, and an object to which the processed items will be stored. The ItemProcessor implementation class should implement a processItem method, which is responsible for performing the processing.

The ItemWriter class implementation (AcmeWriter in the example) is responsible for performing the writing for the chunk. The class implementation should extend the AbstractItemWriter class, and accept the object to which the processed items will be written. This implementation must contain the writeItems method, which is responsible for performing the writing.

Example of Item-Oriented Processing

In this example, a batch process is created to read text from a file, process that text accordingly, and then write out the processed text. To begin, construct an XML file to define the job. The XML file for this example will be called acmeFileProcessor.xml. Let's take a look at what a job process looks like. The lines below are from the acmeFileProcessor.xml file.

```
<?xml version="1.0" encoding="UTF-8"?>

<job id="acmeFileProcessor" xmlns="http://batch.jsr352/jsl">
    <step id="readingStep" >
        <chunk item-count="2">
            <reader ref="acmeReader"></reader>
```

```
            <processor ref="acmeProcessor"></processor>
        </chunk>
    </step>
    <step id="writingStep" >
        <chunk item-count="1">
            <writer ref="acmeWriter"></writer>
        </chunk>
    </step>
</job>
```

There are three tasks being performed in this particular job: acmeReader, acmeProcessor, and acmeWriter. These three tasks can be associated with Java class implementations within the batch.xml file, which is located within the META-INF directory. The following code shows what the batch.xml looks like.

```
<?xml version="1.0" encoding="UTF-8"?>
<batch-artifacts xmlns="http://jcp.org.batch/jsl">
    <ref id="acmeReader" class="org.javaee7.chapter11.AcmeReader"/>
    <ref id="acmeProcessor" class="org.javaee7.chapter11.AcmeProcessor"/>
    <ref id="acmeWriter" class="org.javaee7.chapter11.AcmeWriter"/>
</batch-artifacts>
```

Next, let's take a look at each of these class implementations. We will begin by looking at the AcmeReader class implementation below. This class is responsible for reading a file and creating a new WidgetReportItem object for each line of text.

```
package org.javaee7.chapter11;

import java.nio.charset.Charset;
import java.nio.file.Files;
import java.nio.file.Path;
import java.nio.file.Paths;
import java.util.List;
import javax.batch.api.AbstractItemReader;

/**
 * Example of a file reading task
 *
 * @author Juneau
 */
public class AcmeReader extends AbstractItemReader<WidgetReportItem> {

    public AcmeReader() {
    }

    /**
     * Read lines of report and store each into a WidgetReportItem object.  Once
     * all lines have been read then return null to trigger the end of file.
     * @return
     * @throws Exception
     */
    @Override
```

```
    public WidgetReportItem readItem() throws Exception {
        Path file = Paths.get("widgetFile.txt");
        List<String> fileLines;
        Charset charset = Charset.forName("US-ASCII");
        fileLines = Files.readAllLines(file, charset);
        for(String line:fileLines){
            return new WidgetReportItem(line);
        }
        return null;

    }
}
```

Next, let's take a look at the AcmeProcessor class. This class is responsible for processing each WidgetReportItem accordingly. In this case, if the line of text that is contained in the object has the text "Two" in it, then it will be added to a WidgetOutputItem object.

```
package org.javaee7.chapter11;

import javax.batch.api.ItemProcessor;

/**
 *
 * @author Juneau
 */
public class AcmeProcessor implements ItemProcessor<WidgetReportItem, WidgetOutputItem> {

    public AcmeProcessor(){}

    /**
     * Write out all lines that contain the text "Two"
     * @param item
     * @return
     * @throws Exception
     */
    @Override
    public WidgetOutputItem processItem(WidgetReportItem item) throws Exception {
        if(item.getLineText().contains("Two")){
            return new WidgetOutputItem(item.getLineText());
        } else {
            return null;
        }
    }

}
```

Lastly, let's see what the AcmeWriter class looks like. This class is responsible for writing the WidgetOutputItem objects that have been processed by AcmeProcessor.

```
package org.javaee7.chapter11;
```

```
import java.util.List;
import javax.batch.api.AbstractItemWriter;

/**
 *
 * @author Juneau
 */
public class AcmeWriter extends AbstractItemWriter<WidgetOutputItem> {

    @Override
    public void writeItems(List<WidgetOutputItem> list) throws Exception {
        for(WidgetOutputItem item:list){
            System.out.println("Write to file:" + item.getLineText());
        }
    }

}
```

The `WidgetReportItem` and `WidgetOutputItem` objects are merely containers that hold a String of text. Below is the implementation for `WidgetReportItem`, the `WidgetOutputItem` object is identical other than the name.

```
public class WidgetReportItem {
    private String lineText;

    public WidgetReportItem(String line){
        this.lineText = line;
    }

    /**
     * @return the lineText
     */
    public String getLineText() {
        return lineText;
    }

    /**
     * @param lineText the lineText to set
     */
    public void setLineText(String lineText) {
        this.lineText = lineText;
    }
}
```

When this batch job is executed, the text file is read, processed, and then specific lines of text are written to the system log. The read and process tasks are performed as part of the first step, and then the write is processed as the second step. To execute this batch job, the a `JobOperator` must be obtained by executing `BatchRuntime.geteJobOperator()`. Once the `JobOperator` has been obtained, its `start` method can be invoked, passing the name of the batch XML file for processing, along with the necessary Properties. In the example below, an EJB timer is used to schedule the batch job that we have created in the previous code examples.

```
package org.javaee7.chapter11;

import java.util.Properties;
import javax.annotation.Resource;
import javax.batch.operations.JobOperator;
import javax.batch.runtime.BatchRuntime;
import javax.ejb.Schedule;
import javax.ejb.Stateless;
import javax.ejb.TimerService;

@Stateless
public class BatchTimer {

    @Resource
    TimerService timerService;

    @Schedule(minute="*", hour="*")
    public void scheduledTimerExample(){
        System.out.println("Initiating the batch job...");
        JobOperator job = BatchRuntime.getJobOperator();
        job.start("acmeFileProcessor", new Properties());
    }
}
```

As mentioned in the introduction to this chapter, the Batch Applications for Java EE API is very detailed, and this example barely scratches the surface of how to write batch jobs. You are encouraged to learn more about the API by reading through the specification for JSR-352.

Summary

The Java Enterprise platform has been missing some commonly required APIs until the latest release of Java EE 7. Until the EE 7 release, there had not been a standard way to develop multi-threaded applications that are deployed in an application server environment. Moreover, there has never been a standard way to perform and/or schedule batch applications. The EE 7 release brings forth a handful of new APIs for enterprise development, and among those are the Concurrency Utilities for Java EE and Batch Applications.

This chapter reviewed some of the basic concepts for both the Concurrency and Batch APIs for Java EE. You learned how to configure application server resources that are used with these technologies, and also learned how to utilize the new APIs to integrate these techonlogies into your applications. Going forward, Java Enterprise developers can begin to utilize these new standards for developing applications that necessitate concurrency and/or batch solutions.

CHAPTER 12

NetBeans and Java EE 7

The NetBeans IDE has been completely overhauled for support of Java EE 7 and its APIs. For years, enterprise application development has been made easier by NetBeans and other IDEs because of their abstraction of tedious tasks. Capabilities such as auto-completion, syntax coloring, and compilation and CLASSPATH management make the use of IDEs a nearly essential ingredient for any developer's productivity. The latest releases of NetBeans aid in the development of Java EE 7 applications by providing mainstream support for the newer APIs, adding wizards to help configure applications for use with new features such as faces flows, and automatic bundling of newer libraries.

Configuring Application Servers

Before you can associate application projects with a server for deployment and testing, you need to configure one or more application servers for use within NetBeans. Please note that it is a good practice to only configure those application servers that are used for application development and testing purposes within NetBeans.

To add a local or remote server to NetBeans, perform the following tasks.

1. Navigate to the "Services" window, and right-click on the "Servers" menu selection. Click on "Add Server" as shown in Figure 12-1.

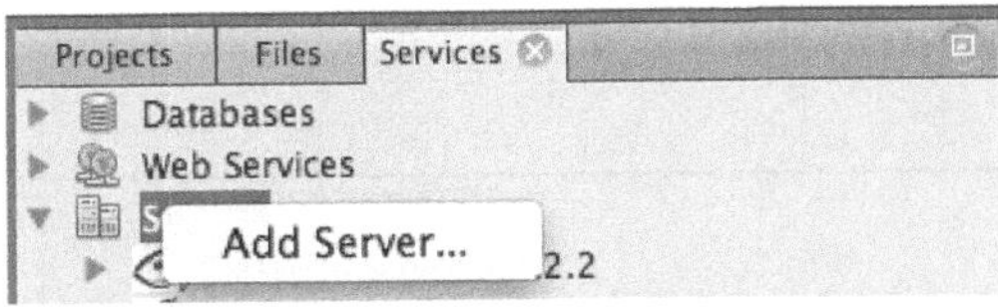

Figure 12-1. Add Server to NetBeans IDE

2. When the "Add Server Instance" dialog appears, choose the server type that you wish to add. (Figure 12-2)

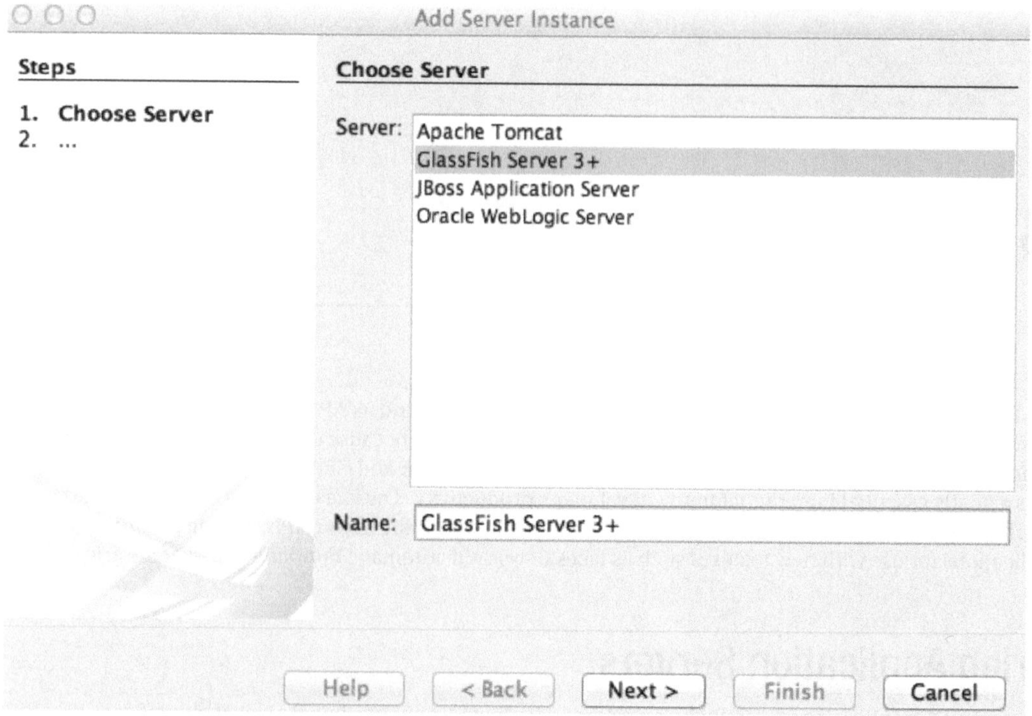

Figure 12-2. *Add Server Instance*

3. On the next screen, enter the path to the application server installation that you would like to configure within NetBeans (Figure 12-3). Once you have chosen the location, click the "Finish" button.

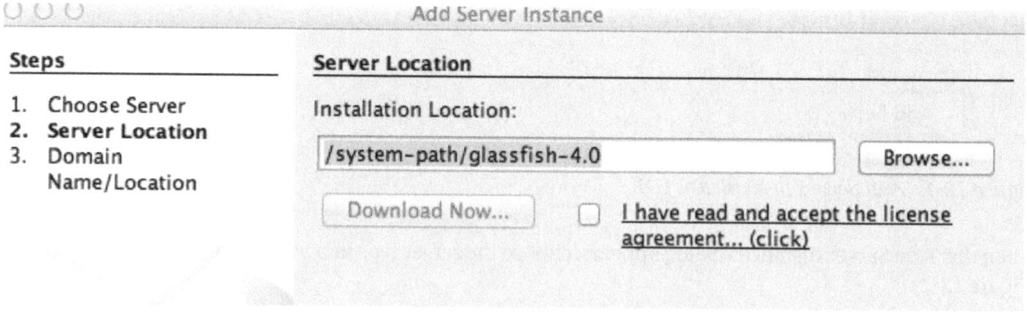

Figure 12-3. *Set Server Location*

4. You can now deploy applications to the server by registering them with a given project from within the project properties. Note that you can also perform some basic application server tasks by selecting the application server from within the "Services" window in NetBeans, as demonstrated in Figure 12-4.

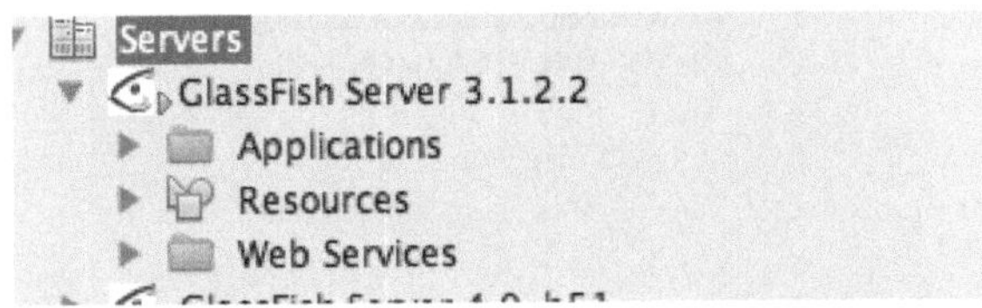

Figure 12-4. *Expand and Administer Server in NetBeans*

Developing Java Enterprise Applications

The NetBeans IDE really makes it easy to develop Java Enterprise Applications. To begin, you create a Java EE project within the IDE, and subsequently use the IDE to configure the project accordingly. NetBeans not only makes it easy to configure your application projects, but it also eases development with the aid of such features as auto-completion, syntax highlighting, auto-formatting, etc. This section will cover how NetBeans can help Java EE developers with some of the most commonly performed Java EE development tasks.

■ **Note** To make use of Java EE 7 specific wizards and features, the project type must be specified as Java EE 7 when it is created.

NetBeans Java Web Projects

There are a few different configurations to choose from for creation of a Java Enterprise project within NetBeans. This book covers the creation of "Java Web" application projects within NetBeans, which is the standard project selection for development of Java EE 6 and EE 7 applications.

To begin creation of a new project, open the "New Project" dialog by choosing "File" ➤ "New Project". In the "New Project" dialog, you will see all of the different Java project categories listed within the left-hand list box. Selecting one of the categories will display the project types for the selected category within the right-hand list box. To create a Java EE 6 or Java EE 7 project, select the "Java Web" category, and then "Web Application" as the project type (Figure 12-5).

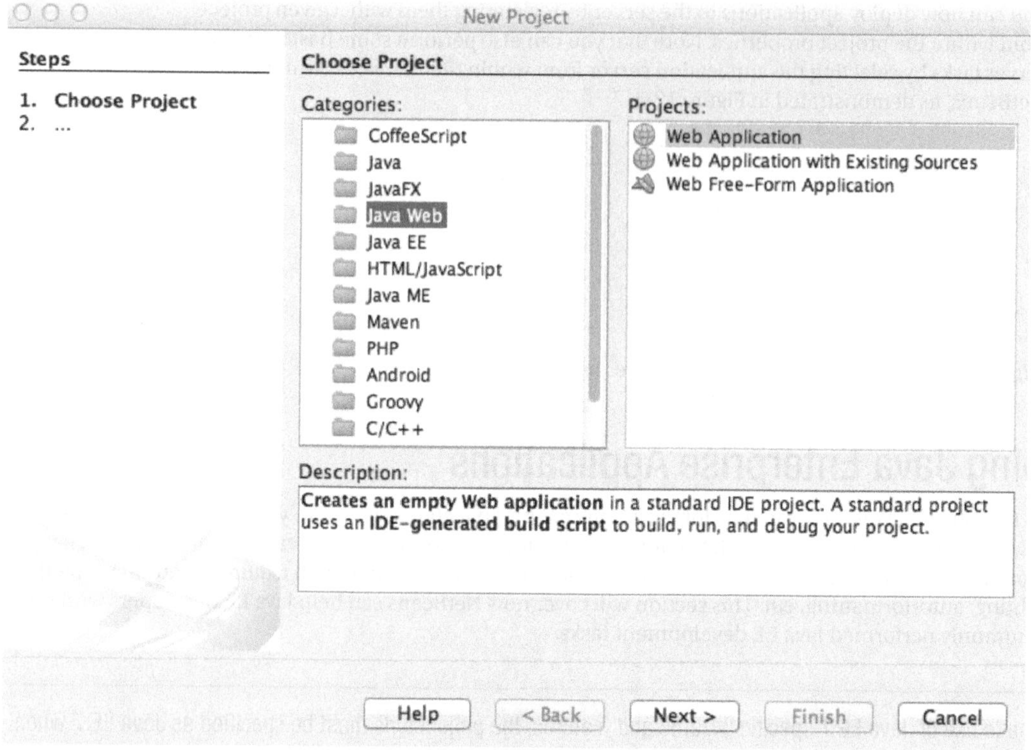

Figure 12-5. Creating a New Java EE Project in NetBeans

■ **Note** The "Java EE" category allows development of projects using the old-style Java EE configuration. That is, project types within the "Java EE" category adhere to standards for developing with Java EE 5 or earlier. In such projects, separate Web (WAR) and EJB (JAR) projects are created, rather than a single project that deploys to a single distributable WAR file.

After selecting the project type, the "New Web Application" dialog will open. Enter a project name and location, as shown in Figure 12-6. Once finished, choose "Next".

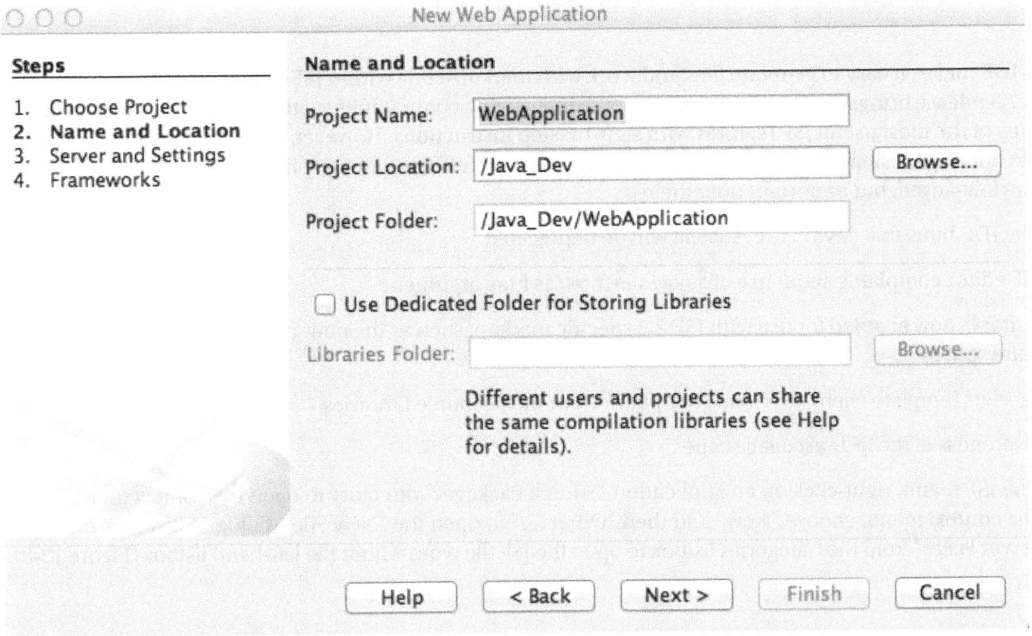

Figure 12-6. New Web Application

In the “Server and Settings” screen, choose the application server that you wish to use for deployment (see the preceding section “Configuring Application Servers”). Also choose the Java EE version that you wish to use. If you plan to make use of Contexts and Dependency Injection, then select the designated checkbox (Figure. 12-7).

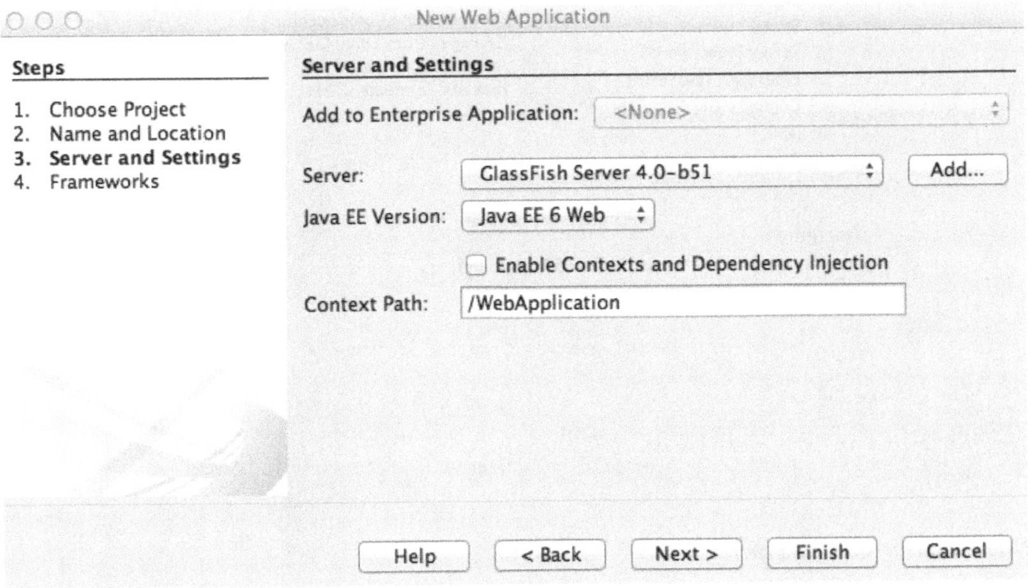

Figure 12-7. Server and Settings

JSF

The NetBeans IDE makes it easy to generate files and work with markup\code within JSF application projects. The NetBeans 7.3 release brings forth many enhancements that enable compatibility with Java EE 7. In this section, we'll cover many of the most useful JSF features with step-by-step instructions. However, there are many hidden features that do not require step-by-step instructions, but are very useful. The following list includes Java EE 7 specific updates that are low-keyed, but important nonetheless:

- The IDE hints that `javax.faces.bean` will be deprecated
- JSF editor complains about use of `java.sun.com/jsf` tag argument
- Editor is now enabled for use with JSF 2.2 specific markup, such as the new `jsf:` and `p:` namespaces
- Facelets template client now loads templates from the Resource Libraries
- Awareness of the `@FlowScoped` scope

To open the JSF menu, right-click on an application "Source Packages" directory to open the context menu. From within the context menu, choose "New" and then "Other..." to open the "New File" dialog. Within the dialog, choose "JavaServer Faces" from the Categories listbox to open the JSF file types within the left-hand listbox (Figure 12-8).

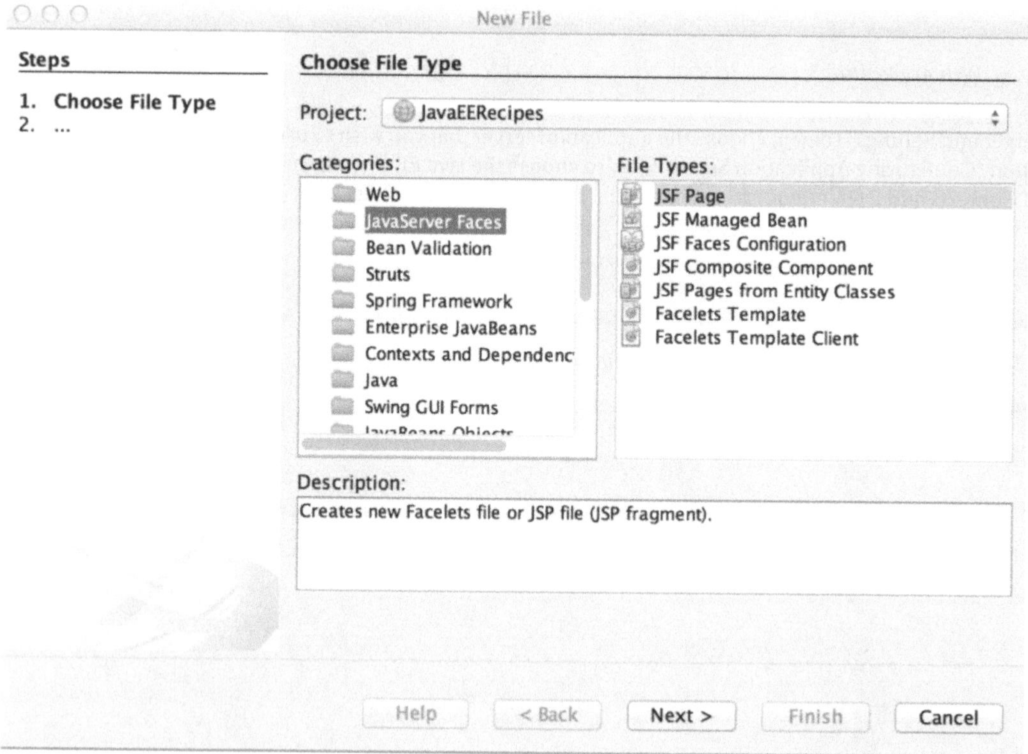

Figure 12-8. *New File Menu – JSF File Types*

The JSF file types include the following options:

- JSF Page
- JSF Managed Bean
- JSF Faces Configuration
- JSF Composite Component
- JSF Pages from Entity Classes
- Faces Template
- Faces Template Client

The JSF Page file selection opens a dialog that can be used to generate a new JSF page (Figure 12-9). The dialog allows one to choose a file location and name, and it also contains the ability to apply different options for the page type. The option choices for page type are Facelets (default), JSP File, or JSP Segment. The examples throughout this book feature the Facelets page type.

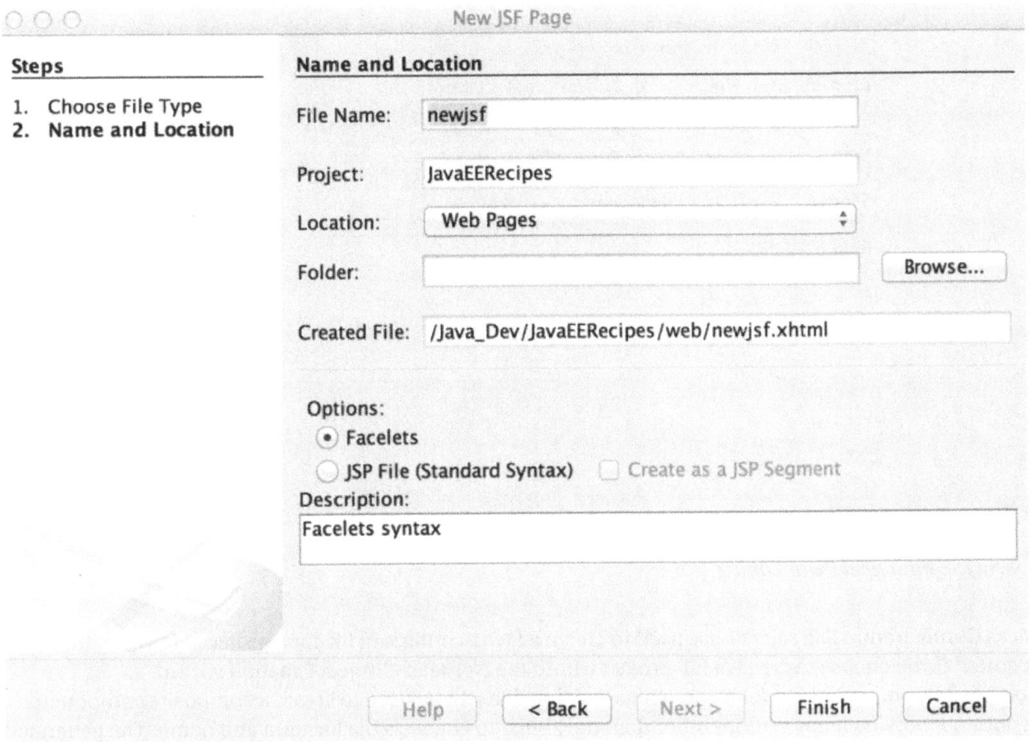

Figure 12-9. *New JSF Page Dialog*

The JSF Managed Bean file selection opens a dialog that allows one to generate a JSF Managed Bean controller class (Figure 12-10). The dialog provides the ability to choose to add the bean data to the faces-config file, as well as choose the scope of the bean.

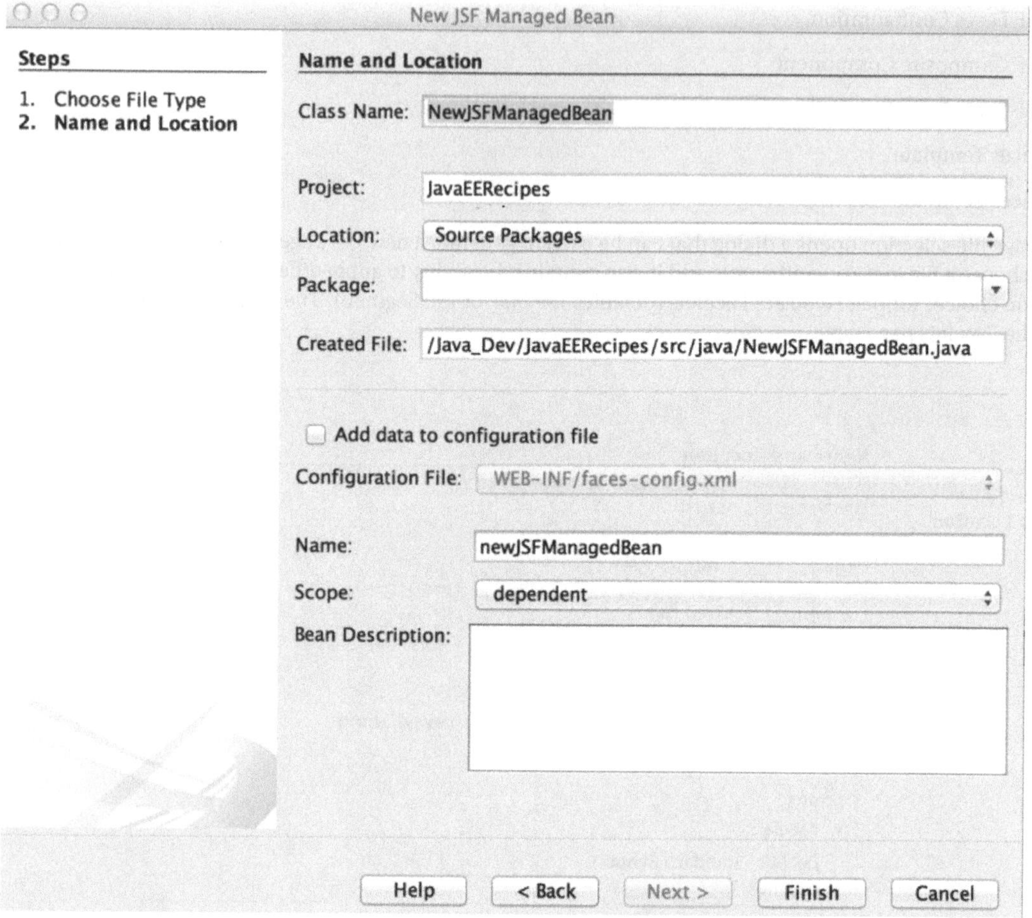

Figure 12-10. *New JSF Managed Bean Dialog*

The JSF Faces Configuration File selection is used to create a faces-config.xml file for a project. However, this option is not required if you choose to create a JSF project within the NetBeans Project Creation wizard.

The JSF Composite Component file selection opens a dialog that can be used to create a composite component file. The dialog does not provide many options other than the ability to choose a file location and name. The generated file contains the skeleton of a composite component, as listed in the following lines:

```
<?xml version='1.0' encoding='UTF-8' ?>
<!DOCTYPE html PUBLIC "-//W3C//DTD XHTML 1.0 Transitional//EN"
"http://www.w3.org/TR/xhtml1/DTD/xhtml1-transitional.dtd">
<html xmlns="http://www.w3.org/1999/xhtml"
      xmlns:cc="http://xmlns.jcp.org/jsf/composite">
```

```
    <!-- INTERFACE -->
    <cc:interface>
    </cc:interface>

    <!-- IMPLEMENTATION -->
    <cc:implementation>
    </cc:implementation>
</html>
```

The JSF Pages from Entity Classes file selection can be quite powerful, in that it allows one to choose an Entity Class from which to generate a JSF page, and then the resulting JSF page will be bound to the entity class upon generation. In order to use this option, the project must contain at least one entity class.

JPA

The NetBeans IDE provides excellent support for JPA, including schema generation support, code completion and annotation support, as well as facilities to help develop Entity Bean classes either manually, or based upon a selected database table. To access the entity class wizards, right-click on a project's "Source Packages" folder to open the context-menu, and then choose "New" ➤ "Other" to open the "New File" dialog. Once open, choose the "Persistence" category from the left-hand list box to display the file types in the right-hand list box (Figure 12-11).

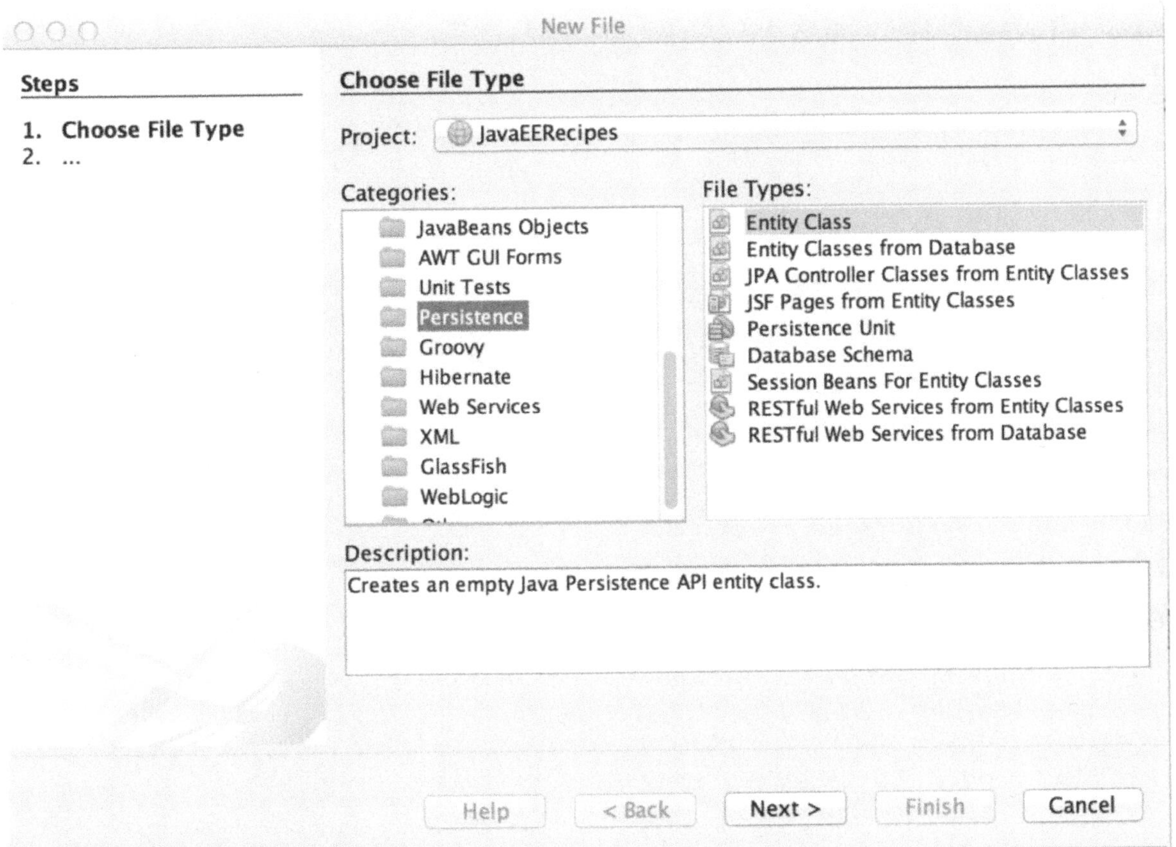

Figure 12-11. *New File - Persistence*

The option entitled "Entity Class" allows one to generate a blank entity class, and "Entity Classes from Database" allows one to generate an entity class from a selected database table. In doing so, all of the requisite code for mapping the entity class to the selected database table is automatically generated for you.

JPQL

NetBeans 7.3 and beyond include a new feature that allows one to query a database using JPQL syntax. This can be quite helpful for those who are using JPQL in their EJB session beans. To access the JPQL query tool, perform the following steps:

1. Expand a NetBeans Web Project that contains a persistence.xml configuration file in the project "Configuration Files" directory.
2. Right-click on the `persistence.xml` configuration file to open the context menu.
3. Click on "Run JPQL Query" to open the tool.
4. Type the JPQL query into the editor and click the run button to execute, as shown in Figure 12-12.

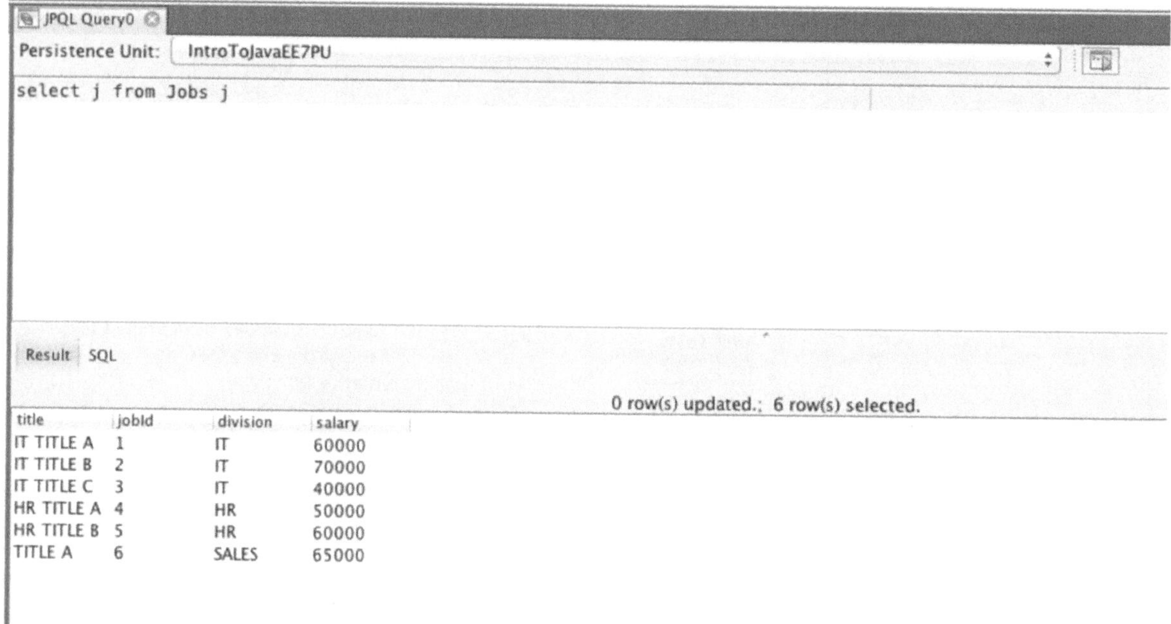

Figure 12-12. *JPQL Query*

JMS

The NetBeans IDE wizards help with the creation of JMS resources. To create a JMS resource from the IDE, perform the following steps:

1. Right-click on a project directory, or select File ➤ "New File" from the NetBeans File menu to open the "New File" dialog.
2. Select "Glassfish" from the "Categories" selection box of the "New File" dialog, and then choose "JMS Resource" from the "File Types" selection box. This will open the "New JMS Resource" dialog (Figure 12-13).

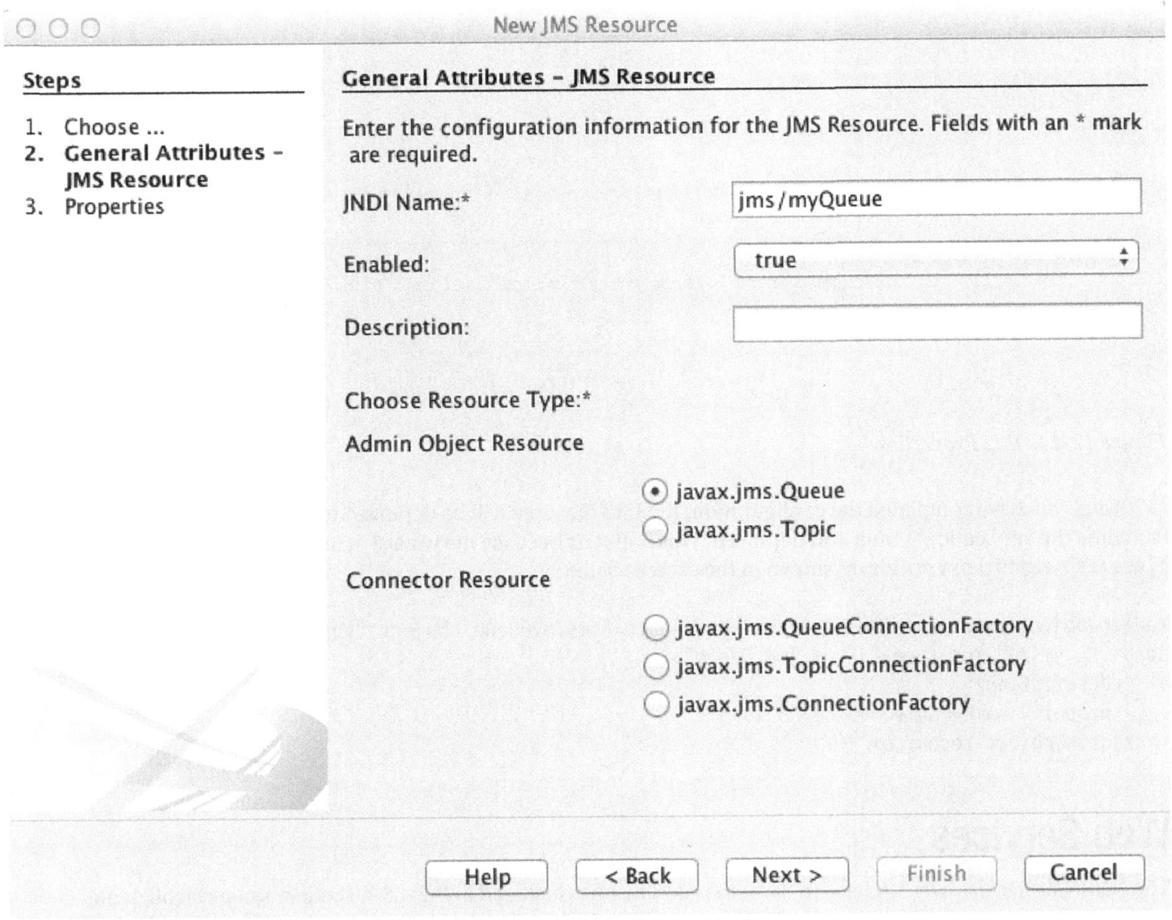

Figure 12-13. New JMS Resource

3. Type a JNDI name for the resource, and then choose the resource type from the given options. Once you've done this, press the "Next" button.
4. Add any properties to the JMS resource using the "JMS Properties" panel of the "New JMS Resource" dialog (Figure 12-14).

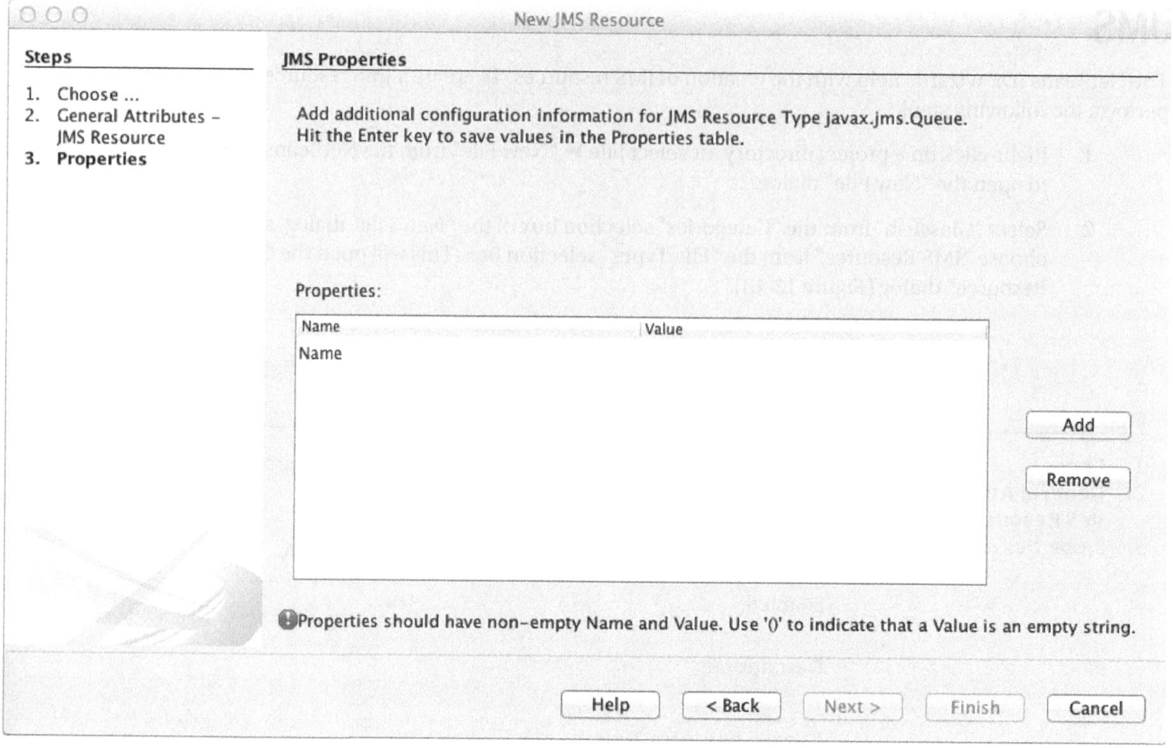

Figure 12-14. *JMS Properties*

Once you have completed the configuration, the JMS resource will be deployed to the Glassfish server the next time the application is built and deployed. This happens because the wizard actually generates XML into the `glassfish-resources.xml` file, as shown in the excerpt below:

```
<admin-object-resource enabled="true" jndi-name="jms/myQueue" object-type="user" res-
adapter="jmsra" res-type="javax.jms.Queue">
    <description/>
    <property name="Name" value="0"/>
  </admin-object-resource>
```

Web Services

The NetBeans IDE has been updated to cover the latest features included in JAX-RS. Of course, syntax highlighting and auto-completion are baked into the IDE for supporting the JAX-RS 2.0 API. NetBeans includes standard JAX-RS wizards for generation of JAX-RS web services from entity classes, databases, and patterns. The IDE also contains wizards for generation of SOAP web services and clients. Above and beyond the basic IDE support and web service wizards, NetBeans 7.3 includes wizards for generating JAX-RS 2.0 filters, interceptors and clients. In this section, we'll take a look at how to utilize these wizards to make filter and interceptor generation a breeze.

Filters

To create a JAX-RS 2.0 Filter, perform the following steps:

1. Right-click on a project directory, or select File ➤ "New File" from the NetBeans File menu to open the "New File" dialog.

2. Select "Web Services" from the Categories select box, and then select "JAX-RS 2.0 Filter" from the "File Types" select box, as shown in Figure 12-15.

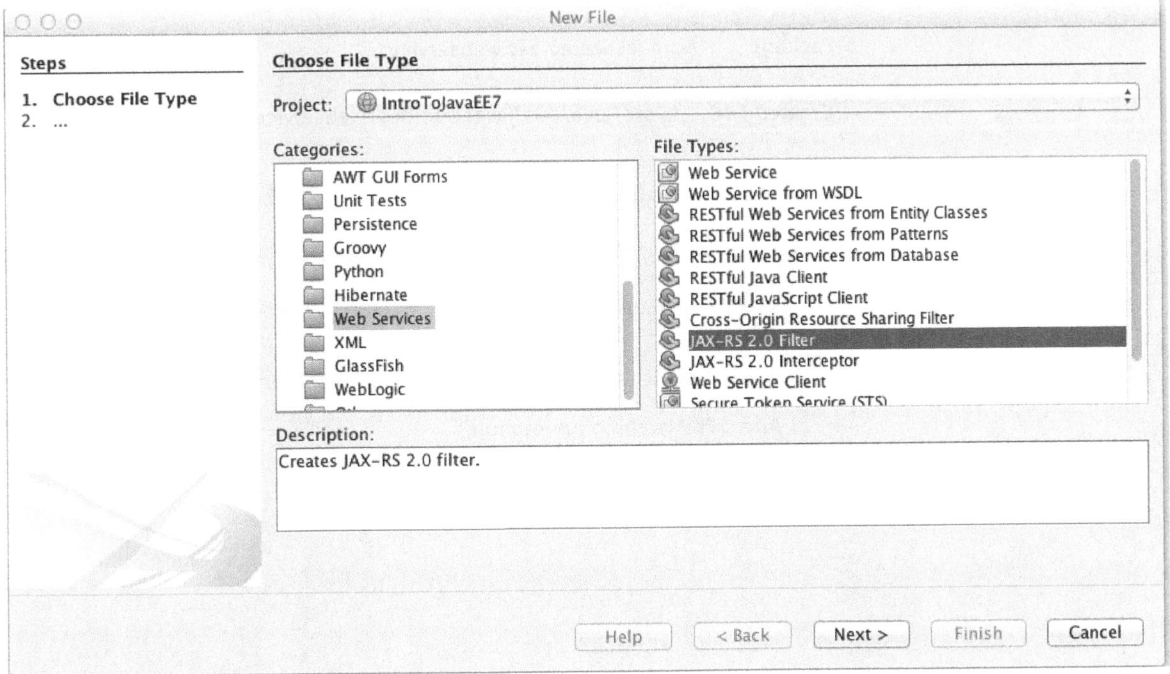

Figure 12-15. *Create JAX-RS 2.0 Filter*

3. Designate the type of filter you wish to create within the "New JAX-RS 2.0 Filter" dialog (Figure 12-16).

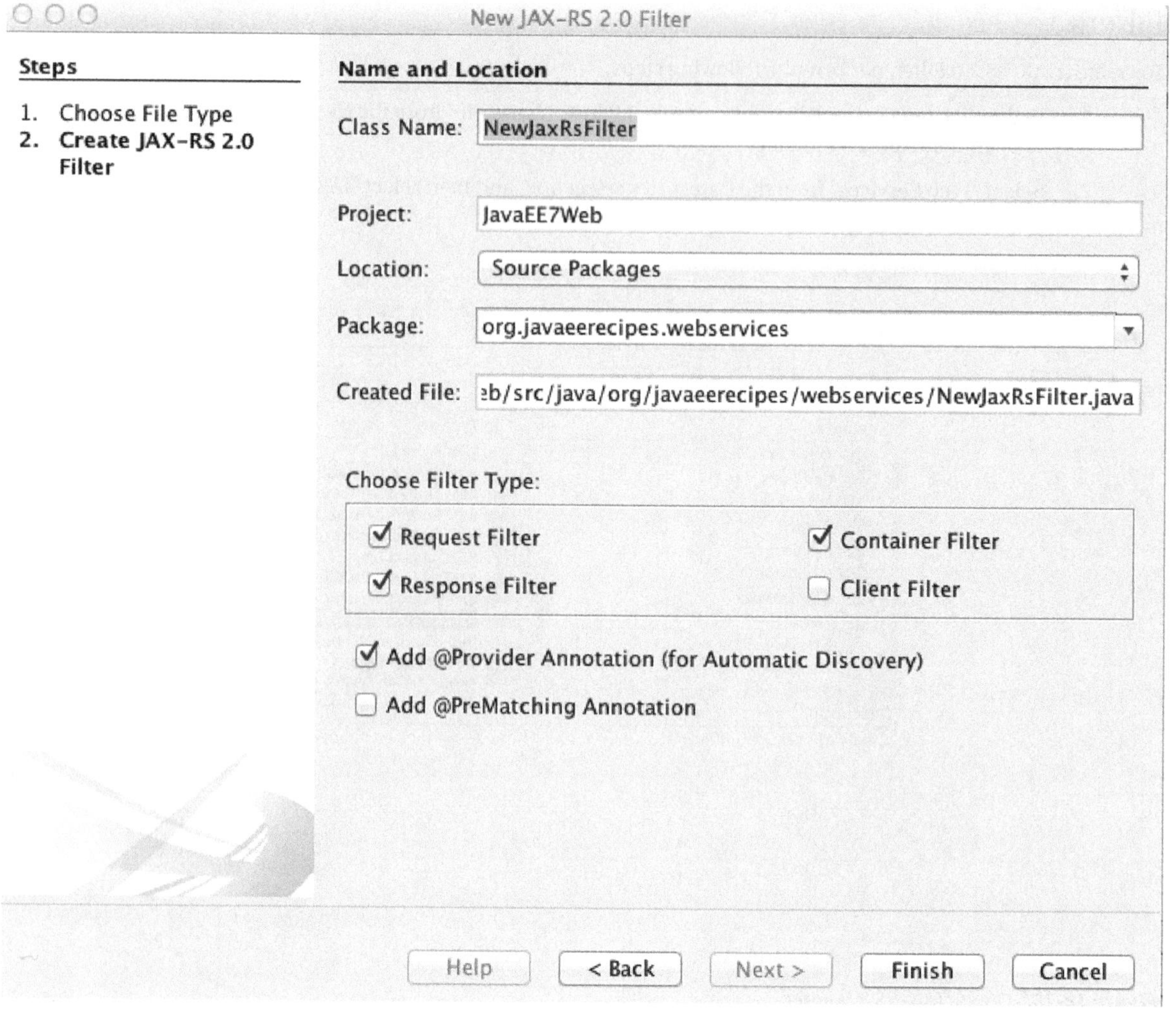

New JAX-RS 2.0 Filter

Steps

1. Choose File Type
2. **Create JAX-RS 2.0 Filter**

Name and Location

Class Name: NewJaxRsFilter

Project: JavaEE7Web

Location: Source Packages

Package: org.javaeerecipes.webservices

Created File: ɜb/src/java/org/javaeerecipes/webservices/NewJaxRsFilter.java

Choose Filter Type:

- [x] Request Filter
- [x] Container Filter
- [x] Response Filter
- [ ] Client Filter

- [x] Add @Provider Annotation (for Automatic Discovery)
- [ ] Add @PreMatching Annotation

Help | < Back | Next > | Finish | Cancel

Figure 12-16. *New JAX-RS 2.0 Filter Dialog*

4. Edit the generated JAX-RS 2.0 filter file accordingly (Figure 12-17).

```
/*
 * To change this template, choose Tools | Templates
 * and open the template in the editor.
 */
package org.javaeerecipes.webservices;

import javax.ws.rs.container.ContainerRequestContext;
import javax.ws.rs.container.ContainerRequestFilter;
import javax.ws.rs.container.ContainerResponseContext;
import javax.ws.rs.container.ContainerResponseFilter;
import javax.ws.rs.ext.Provider;

/**
 *
 * @author Juneau
 */
@Provider
public class NewJaxRsFilter implements ContainerRequestFilter, ContainerResponseFilter {

    @Override
    public void filter(ContainerRequestContext requestContext) {
    }

    @Override
    public void filter(ContainerRequestContext requestContext, ContainerResponseContext responseContex
    }

}
```

Figure 12-17. *Generated JAX-RS 2.0 Filter File*

Interceptors

To create a JAX-RS 2.0 Interceptor using the NetBeans wizard, follow these steps:

1. Right-click on a project directory, or select File ➤ "New File" from the NetBeans File menu to open the "New File" dialog.
2. Select "Web Services" from the Categories select box, and then select "JAX-RS 2.0 Interceptor" from the "File Types" select box.
3. When the "New JAX-RS 2.0 Interceptor" dialog opens, choose the type of interceptor you wish to create (ReaderInterceptor or WriterInterceptor), and specify file name and location, as seen in Figure 12-18.

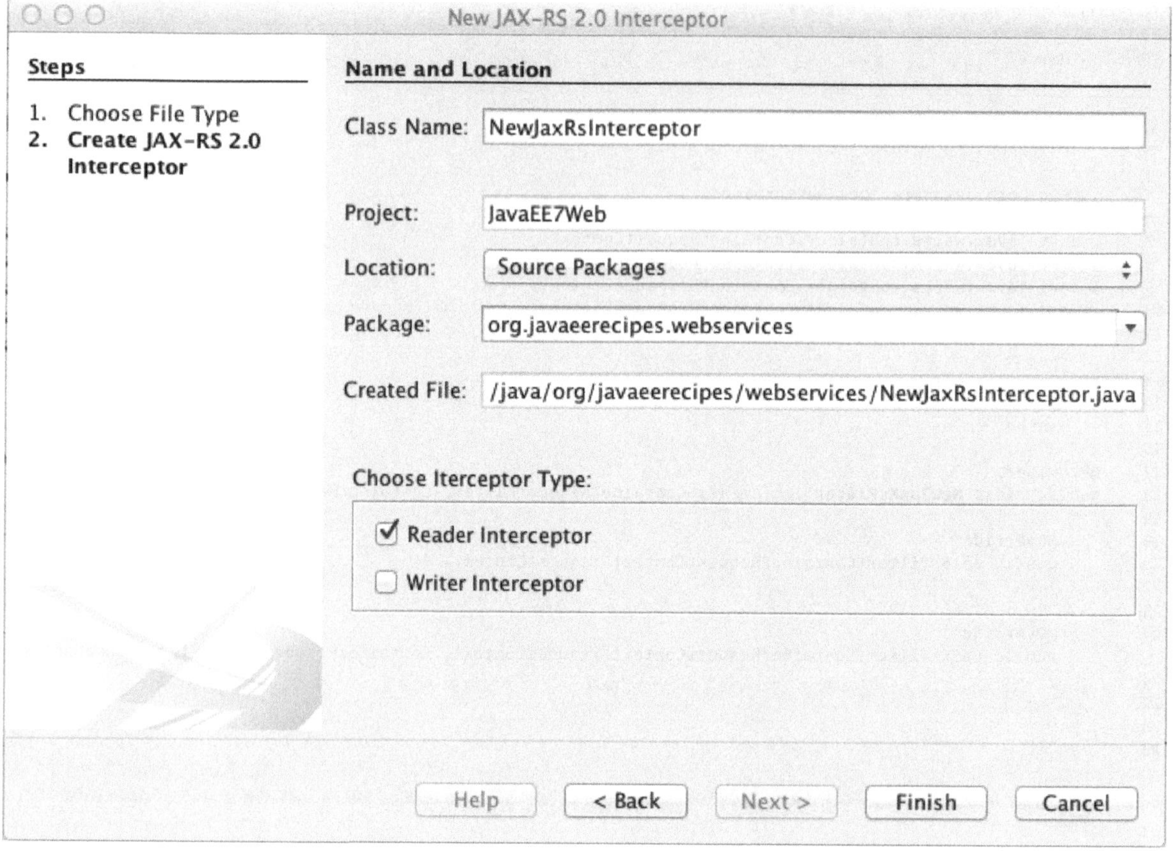

New JAX-RS 2.0 Interceptor

Steps

1. Choose File Type
2. **Create JAX-RS 2.0 Interceptor**

Name and Location

Class Name: NewJaxRsInterceptor

Project: JavaEE7Web

Location: Source Packages

Package: org.javaeerecipes.webservices

Created File: /java/org/javaeerecipes/webservices/NewJaxRsInterceptor.java

Choose Iterceptor Type:

☑ Reader Interceptor

☐ Writer Interceptor

Help | < Back | Next > | Finish | Cancel

Figure 12-18. *New JAX-RS 2.0 Interceptor Dialog*

4. Edit the generated interceptor file, accordingly (Figure 12-19).

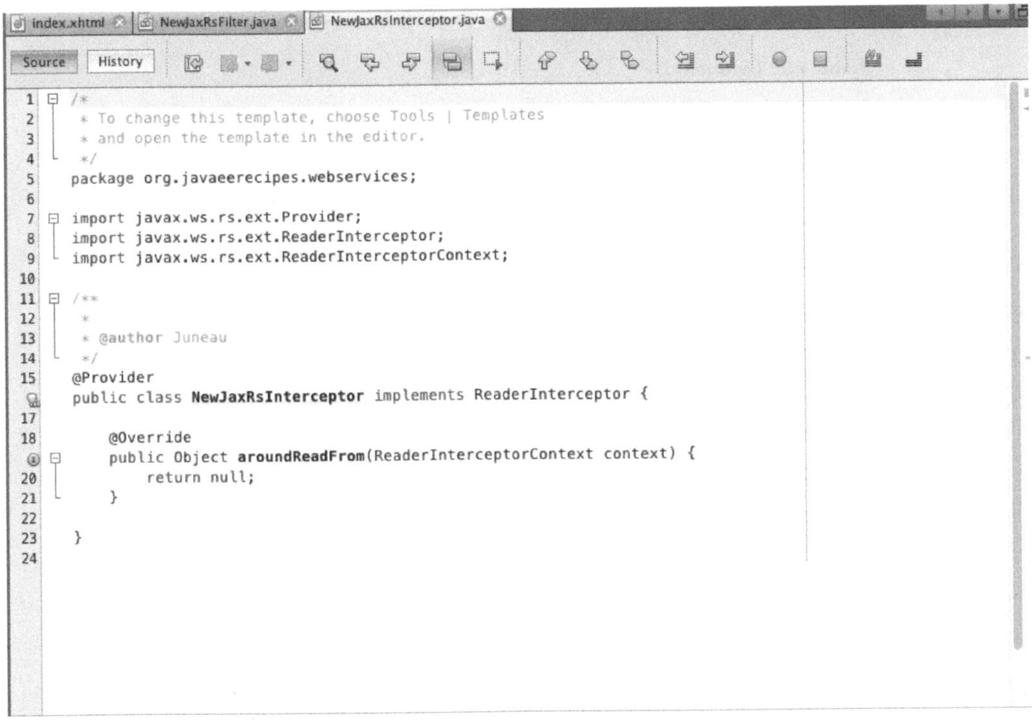

```
/*
 * To change this template, choose Tools | Templates
 * and open the template in the editor.
 */
package org.javaeerecipes.webservices;

import javax.ws.rs.ext.Provider;
import javax.ws.rs.ext.ReaderInterceptor;
import javax.ws.rs.ext.ReaderInterceptorContext;

/**
 *
 * @author Juneau
 */
@Provider
public class NewJaxRsInterceptor implements ReaderInterceptor {

    @Override
    public Object aroundReadFrom(ReaderInterceptorContext context) {
        return null;
    }

}
```

Figure 12-19. *JAX-RS 2.0 Interceptor Generated File*

Clients

One of the most useful additions to JAX-RS 2.0 is the ability to generate RESTful clients. NetBeans 7.3 accommodates this new feature by containing wizards for generation of RESTful Java clients and RESTful JavaScript clients. Let's begin by looking at the procedure to generate a RESTful Java client using the NetBeans wizard.

1. Right-click on a project directory or select "File" ➤ "New File" from the NetBeans File menu to open the "New File" dialog.

2. Select "Web Services" from the "Categories" select box, and then select "RESTful Java Client" from the "File Types" select box (Figure 12-20). Add a name for the client, along with the type of REST resource, whether it belongs to a project within the IDE, or if it has been registered as a cloud service with the IDE (such as Google or Amazon). Lastly, provide a type of authentication for the client.

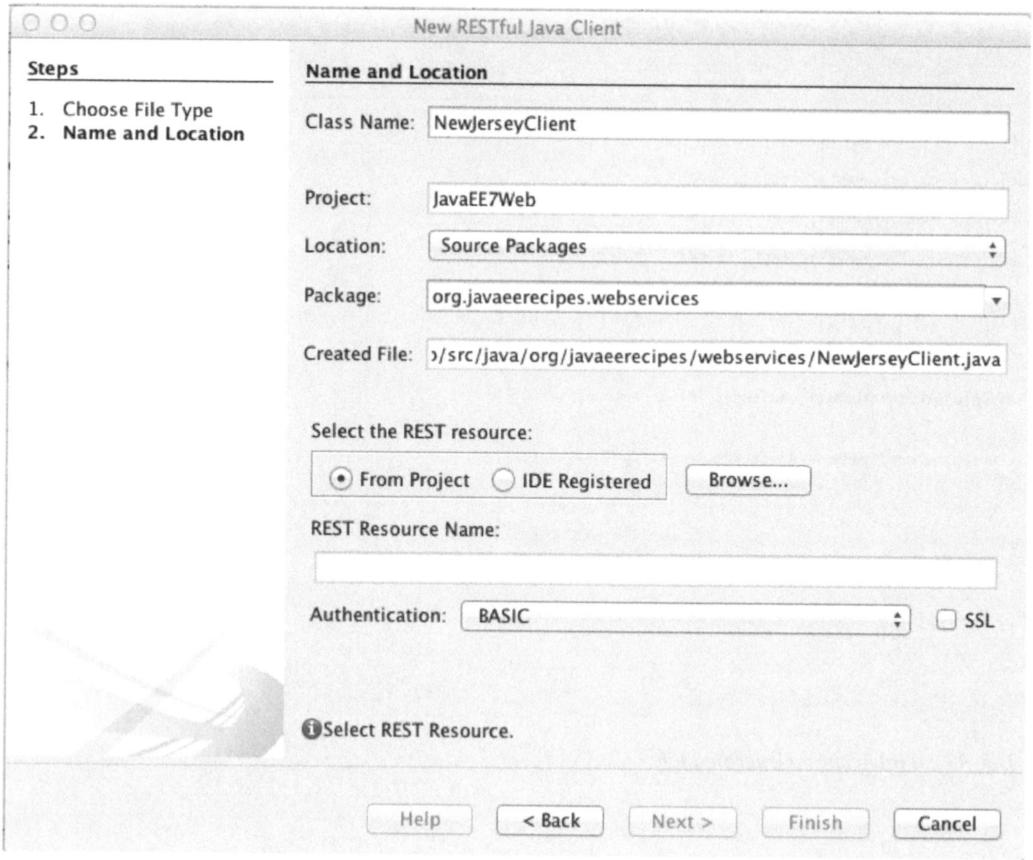

Figure 12-20. New RESTful Java Client Dialog

Once you've run though the wizard, a RESTful Java client will be generated for the REST resource that you had selected. If you would rather generate a JavaScript client, you can do that by performing the following steps:

3. Right-click on a project directory or select "File" ➤ "New File" from the NetBeans File menu to open the "New File" dialog.

4. Select "Web Services" from the "Categories" select box, and then select "RESTful JavaScript Client" from the "File Types" select box (Figure 12-21). After the dialog window opens, select a folder into which the JavaScript client should be generated. Also specify one or more projects for which you would like to have stubs generated. If you would rather specify a WADL to generate stubs, choose that option and select the file instead.

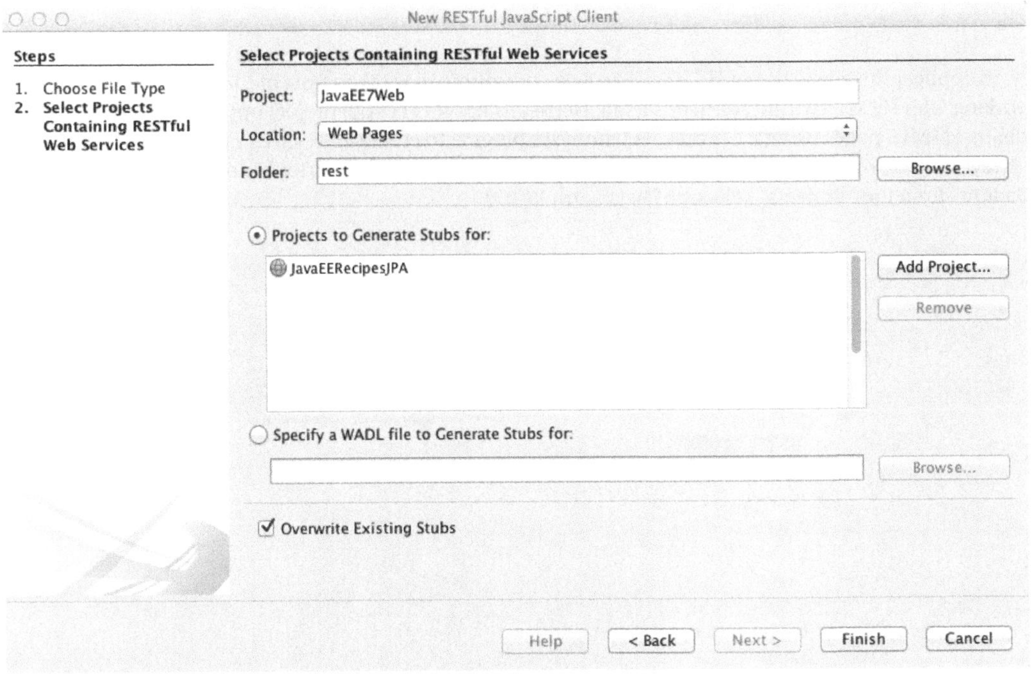

***Figure 12-21.** Creating New JAX-RS 2.0 JavaScript Client*

Once you have run the client, the necessary files for JavaScript client will be generated and placed into the folder that was designated from within the wizard. In Figure 12-22, you can see that the stubs for a project named `JavaEERecipesJPA` and `SimpleRest` have been placed inside of the `rest` folder.

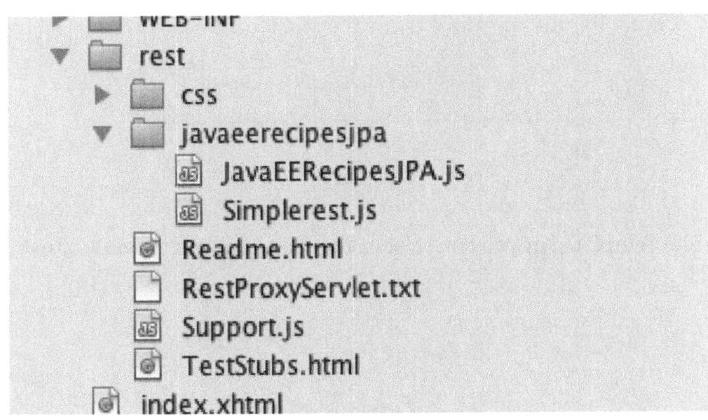

***Figure 12-22.** Generated JavaScript Client Stubs*

HTML5

Many modern web applications make use of HTML5. The Java community has taken note of that and has made it easy to begin working with HTML5 within NetBeans itself. NetBeans has an HTML5 project option, which enables developers to debug HTML5 pages using a Chrome web browser plugin. To create an HTML5 project from within the IDE, select the "New Project" option and then choose HTML/JavaScript in the "Categories" selection list, followed by "HTML5 Application" from the "Projects" selection list (Figure 12-23).

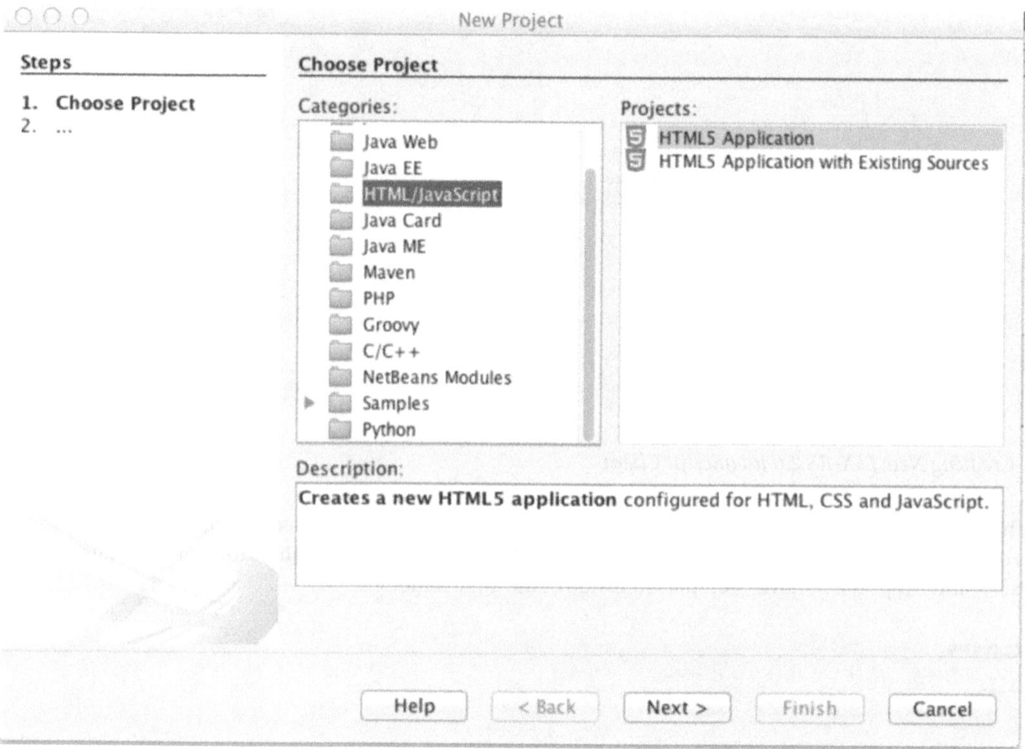

Figure 12-23. *Create New HTML5 Application*

Next, you are given the option to choose "No Site Template," or you can select a template that you provide, or use one that you can download, as seen in Figure 12-24.

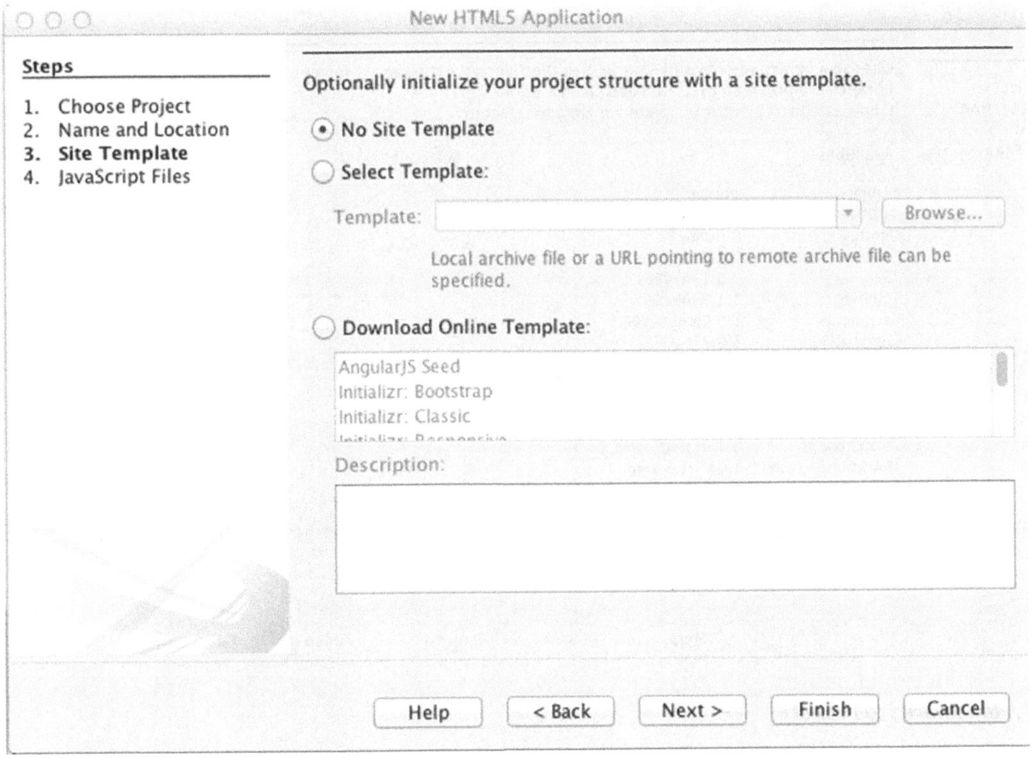

Figure 12-24. *Choose Site Template*

Lastly, choose any libraries that you wish to add to your HTML5 Project (Figure 12-25), then click "Finish".

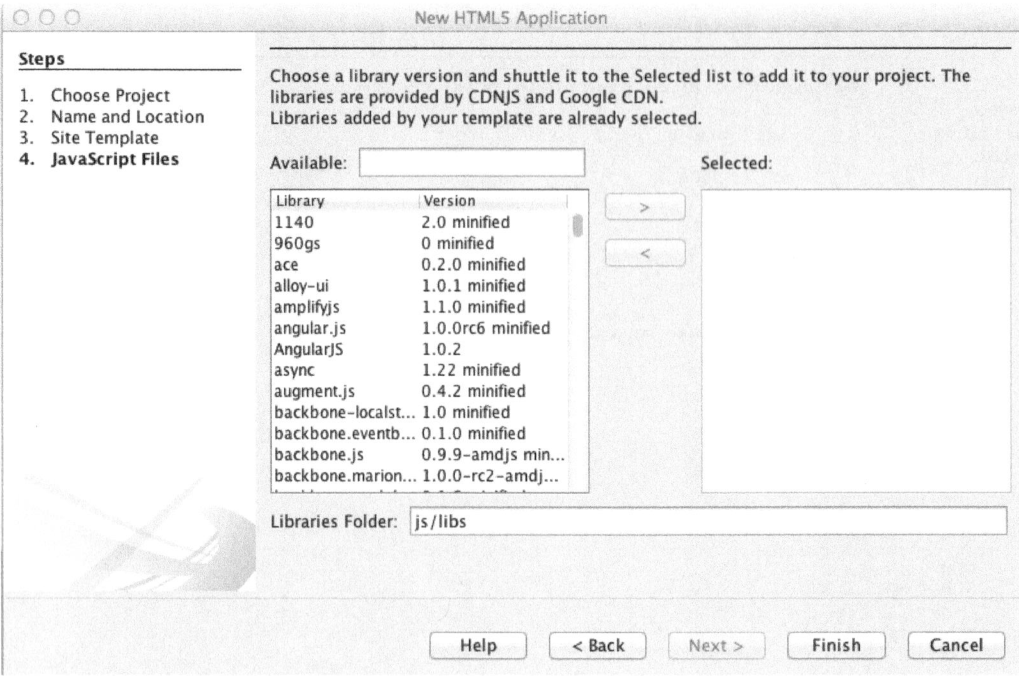

Figure 12-25. *Add Libraries to Project*

Once the project has been created, you can choose "Run" to have it opened up within Chrome, assuming that you have installed the Chrome plugin. If you have not yet installed the Chrome plugin, you will be prompted to do so.

Summary

The days of working in text files and your operating system file structure may be numbered. It is no doubt that utilization of feature-rich integrated development environments such as NetBeans can make application development much easier. Utilization of an IDE takes away worries such as the CLASSPATH, and makes it easier to develop by providing features such as syntax coloring, code completion, and wizards. The latest releases of NetBeans are no exception, as they provide full support for Java EE 7.

Index

A

B

C

D

E

F, G, H

I

J, K, L

M

N

O

P, Q

R

S, T, U

V

W, X, Y, Z

CPSIA information can be obtained at www.ICGtesting.com
Printed in the USA
LVOW01s0814191013

357677LV00007B/264/P